THE SPIRIT OF 1889

THE SPIRIT
OF 1889

RESTORING THE LOST PROMISE OF
THE HIGH PLAINS AND
NORTHERN ROCKIES

SAMUEL WESTERN

UNIVERSITY PRESS OF KANSAS

© 2024 by the University Press of Kansas

Sections of this book were previously published in "Finding Progressive Values in the Northern Rockies and Plains States' Constitutions," *Montana: The Magazine of Western History*, Summer 2021, 69–73, and in the Winter 2023 edition of *Western Confluence Magazine*.

Published by the University Press of Kansas (Lawrence, Kansas 66045), which was organized by the Kansas Board of Regents and is operated and funded by Emporia State University, Fort Hays State University, Kansas State University, Pittsburg State University, the University of Kansas, and Wichita State University.

Library of Congress Cataloging-in-Publication Data

Names: Western, Samuel, author.
Title: The spirit of 1889 : restoring the lost promise of the high plains and Northern Rockies / Samuel Western.
Other titles: Restoring the lost pragmatic vision of the high plains and Northern Rockies
Description: Lawrence, Kansas : University Press of Kansas, 2024. | Includes index.
Identifiers: LCCN 2023052261 (print) | LCCN 2023052262 (ebook)
 ISBN 9780700637041 (cloth)
 ISBN 9780700637065 (ebook)
Subjects: LCSH: Group identity—Great Plains. | Group identity—Dakota Territory. | Group identity—Idaho. | Dakota Territory—Politics and governement. | Great Plains—Politics and governement. | Political culture—Great Plains. | Political culture—Idaho. | Political culture—Dakota Territory. | Social values—Great Plains. | Social values—Idaho. | Social values—Great Plains.
Classification: LCC F591 .W467 2024 (print) | LCC F591 (ebook) | DDC 978—dc23/eng/20240227
LC record available at https://lccn.loc.gov/2023052261.
LC ebook record available at https://lccn.loc.gov/2023052262.

British Library Cataloguing-in-Publication Data is available.

I dedicate this book to every first adapter and risk-taker in commodity production, be they rancher, logger, farmer, or a combination of them all. I also dedicate this book to the community-minded citizens of the Great Plains and Northern Rockies, those who embrace the values of classical republicanism and pragmatism above the rusty and capricious sword of authoritarianism.

CONTENTS

ACKNOWLEDGMENTS

As with all projects years in the making, I don't know where to start giving thanks. The list is long. It must first include those who by the twists and unexpected turns of writing got left out. Parts of this book explore shifts in commodity production, largely in agriculture. Understanding these changes required getting a pulse on the status quo farming and ranching. The Peterson family of Wakonda, South Dakota, and the Molitor clan of Southwick, South Dakota, taught me much about agricultural markets, the vagaries of raising cattle, and the constant battle of debt. Yet this book explores where production agriculture and their surrounding communities are headed, not their current state. While these producers I interviewed might not be first adapters, they earned my unwavering respect. Despite razor-thin margins and rare stretches of profitability, they persevered, busting their asses to hold their families and communities together. These kind and generous people, lovers of black angus and good grass, took me into their homes, fed me, and shared stories about the perils of modern farming. I thank them. This book is hard enough on conventional agriculture. As for the Peterson and Molitor families, someone else can tell critical stories about their practices. I decline.

I owe a special thanks to Marshall Damgaard of Sioux Fall, South Dakota. His knowledge of South Dakota history and politics remains unparalleled. So is his generosity with time, observations—rafts of lyric and informative emails—and insistence on paying for meals.

Historian Phil Roberts got me going on this project. Friends like Lee Nellis, Laura Sands, and John Heyneman kept me honest. Mark Haggerty generously supplied me unique information and data. Editor Diana Di Stefano bravely printed an excerpt from this book in the summer 2021 issue of *Montana: The Magazine of Western History*. Thank you. Agricultural innovators such as Judy and Jeff Cornell, Ryan Pfiefle, Matthew Romsa (and family), and Ron Rabou entertained endless questions and offered plenty of wisdom. Ruby Marie Western gave excellent advice and counsel when it came to graphics.

I owe a debt to the queen of interlibrary loans at the Sheridan Fulmer Public Library, Christina Gonzalez. She searched facilities nationwide for arcane material. I'm also much obliged to the staff of the North Dakota State Historical Society and the South Dakota State Historical Society.

Finally, my gratitude to my wife, Jessica, for her unwavering support and endless readings of this manuscript.

PREFACE

I wrote this book during a unique epoch of American history. Residents of the South, Midwest, and rural West began acquiring new political power. Many gains were decades in the making, with conservative state legislatures moving, year after year, iteration by iteration, to shift the political landscape. Thus, it shouldn't have been a surprise when Donald Trump was elected president in 2016.

Yet this book was well into the idea stage by the time Mr. Trump reached the White House. In fact, since about 2008, I kept a folder on my desktop simply labeled: *Rocky Mountain Pluralism Project*. My main question: have the Great Plains and Northern Rockies changed so dramatically in the last 130 years? If so, what caused that change? These states (I call them 89ers, as they all wrote their constitutions in 1889) have long considered themselves "conservative." Yet, as we shall see, what constitutes a conservative value rests in the eye of the beholder.

It wasn't so much puzzlement about politics as it was about values. Historically, the Northern Rockies and Great Plains possessed a conservative streak, but one that strayed from orthodoxy. The region mixed libertarianism with central planning. The states displayed little appetite for what we call social conservatism, such as anti-abortion politics. The recent fever over Second Amendment issues, for example, is a bit of a mystery. Hell, in Wyoming everyone has a gun. On August 8, 2022, Tom Lubnau, Campbell County, former Republican speaker of the Wyoming House, wrote an editorial expressing his exasperation with the firearm issues that consume his fellow legislators. "No one from the Wyoming Legislature is coming to your house in the middle of the night to get your guns. The debate on the issues, especially this one, has driven itself to an absurd level. Soon, we'll see bills to have the State of Wyoming issue a Colt 1910 to every newborn."[1]

I've lived in Wyoming—with a three-year hiatus—since 1982. If there is a single 89er state that has abandoned wholesale the values found in its constitution, it's Wyoming. In 2016 and 2020, no state had a higher percentage of its voters pull the lever for Donald Trump. Mr. Trump, love him or hate him, represents the antithesis of commonwealth and republican values articulated in the founding documents of these 89er states. In 2022, Wyoming voters, by a whopping margin of 37 percent, tossed out Representative Liz Cheney, an old-guard Republican, in favor of Harriet Hageman, a Trump loyalist.

The irony is pretty thick. Wyoming was not only the first 89er state to grant an historic milestone in inclusivity—suffrage for women—it has a unique narrative involving it joining the Union as a territory.

The idea of Wyoming Territory sprang from the fertile and unorthodox mind of James Ashley, an Ohio Republican congressman. As *Harpweek*, a historical compilation of *Harper's Weekly*, describes him: "His support of school desegregation and voting rights for women and blacks distinguished him from most politicians of the period."[2]

Ashley was a major force in getting the Thirteenth Amendment (abolition of slavery) added to the Constitution through the House of Representatives.[3] That passed the House on January 31, 1865.

Three weeks earlier (January 5), Ashley had introduced a bill, House resolution 663, to establish Wyoming Territory. It forbade slavery in the proposed territory. It failed, dying in committee. As historian Jennifer Helton observed, "Ashley's bill represented an insurance policy of sorts. Had the Thirteenth Amendment failed to pass, Ashley reasoned that his Wyoming bill would still have prohibited slavery in a large section of the West and prevented Confederates from establishing a government there."[4]

Three years later, Illinois senator Richard Yates revived Ashley's bill in the form of the Wyoming Organic Act. It included an additional measure: it proclaimed something resembling universal male suffrage. "The legislative assembly shall not at any time abridge the right to suffrage, or to hold office, on account of the race, color, or previous condition of servitude of any resident of the territory."[5]

In other words, African Americans had the right to vote and hold office, although they struggled mightily just to maintain basic civil rights. In 1870, the Wyoming Territorial Legislature granted suffrage to women, the first state to do so.

In Wyoming, and the other 89er states, most alarming is the fading of the core rural West value of self-direction, which the psychologist Shalom H. Schwartz defined as independent thought combined with an action-oriented, creative, and exploratory mindset.[6] You've likely met the type of person who espouses these values: the independent-minded westerner.

Take the case of Badger Clark. Born in Iowa in 1883, his family moved to Dakota Territory so his Methodist preacher father could minister to the faithful. Clark tried college but quit and moved to Cuba. He contracted tuberculosis and headed to dry Arizona to assuage his ailment. There, Clark took a job as caretaker at an isolated ranch outside Tombstone. He began writing and publishing poetry. The tuberculosis faded. Clark moved back to South Dakota, settling in a cabin in Custer State Park. His literary career blossomed, albeit modestly; *Pacific Monthly* and *Scribners* accepted his poems. And the editorial page of the *Rapid City Journal* did not escape his attention. Clark's letters to the editor reveal him as a staunch individualist deeply suspicious of innovation and technology. He also despised bigotry and segregation. "We still owe the Negro for 250 years of unpaid labor, and we owe the Indian for some three million square miles of land," he wrote in one letter to the paper in 1954.[7] Replacing Clark's values are the darker elements of what Jonathan Haidt calls the moral foundations theory: loyalty, authority, purity, and authoritarianism.[8]

What? Maybe this could happen in the Deep South, which has a history of loyalty to lost causes and strongman populism, but not in states that had equality and the idea of the commonweal (common welfare) baked into their identity.

So began my exploration. I put thousands of miles on my various used cars, driving through shimmering Montana heat, frigid snow-blown highways in the Dakotas, and, in damp 2019, trying to navigate my way through regions riddled with flooded roads. I had two destinations: research rooms and living rooms. Each proved equally rewarding in their own way. In research rooms, I documented the region's history of commonweal values. A thorough reading of state constitutions—and the notes taken during the constitutional conventions of 1889—proved critical. Originally planned as a two-year project, the Covid-19 pandemic extended my research and writing process to five years.

My conversations with ranchers and farmers grounded my understanding of how rural communities work. These men and women were unbelievably generous with their time. They invited me into their homes, shared Sunday dinners, and let me ride around in their equipment while

I asked annoying questions. They were also transparent and honest. One farmer, Chuck Peterson of Wakonda, South Dakota, opened up his books for me, documenting the remarkable financial risks farmers take each year. Micheal Molitor, who ranches outside Hot Springs, South Dakota, told me that a producer has so little control over their future that they had to accept that this season—any season—might be their last year in the cattle business.

With these conversations came a shift in how I saw the values landscape. I originally relied on economic history as an explanatory lens. The political upheaval coming from the American heartland, the isolated West, and the South, I was convinced, was economic in nature. After all, rising economic disparity had hit rural America the hardest. Agriculture in particular endured years of hardship, interspersed by short-lived booms.

Yet, as I wrote and researched, I gained a new appreciation for the power of identity. These ranchers and farmers not only felt financial stress; they saw themselves as marginalized by society and deeply unappreciated. Much of this had to do with the march of technology, which has been hell on farm and ranch communities. It takes fewer people to farm. This equates to dropping student enrollment and, all too frequently, closing schools. And when a school shuts down, well, that's usually all she wrote for a community.

The nature of commodities (boom and bust) combined with the dependency on federal government policy also acted as a marginalizing agent. A farmer tending his/her own land is just as reliant on federal policies (as a result of various farm bills) as is an energy producer with a natural gas lease on federal land. Most farmers have no love for crop subsidies but feel too vulnerable without them. Taking crop subsidies sullies—deeply—their sense of independence. As my friend Lee Nellis observed, "If your stated philosophy is individualism and independence, then being dependent, and knowing full well that you are, is a horribly dissonant place to be." Out of this crucible, values got reprioritized. Yes, those in the commodity business cared about the bottom line. But they were also weary of being pawns of government policy and being pissed on by regions long done with commodities—to understand the latter issue, for example, tell someone in Silicon Valley or Boston that you're a coal miner from Montana and note their reaction.

All this leads to a toxic environment that blends identity with economics. Norwegian economist Martin Sandbu calls this the *economics of belonging*.[9] Economic grievances, says Sandbu, express themselves in cultural and value-driven behavior. A rising economic insecurity fuels a loss of personal control. People double down on group identity.[10]

This has created a civic and political nightmare, and the projection that there are no common values. "Distinctions between believable and unbelievable, true and false are not relevant for people who have found that taking up outrageous and disprovable ideas is instead an admission ticket to a community or an identity," wrote Rebecca Solnit.[11]

A pair of queries persisted as I wrote this book. First, is the 89er region any different from other parts of the country? Isn't it susceptible to the same political and economic shifts as anywhere else? Second, how did the region surrender so quickly its live-and-let-live approach to life in general? For example, how in the space of twenty years did Wyoming become, to quote Wyoming-born journalist and author Scott Farris, "Alabama with antelope?"[12]

The culture of the Northern Rockies and Great Plains states is not immune to national trends. This affirmation requires context, however. Let's first dispatch with the narrative of regional exceptionalism. In the American South, it's not uncommon to see ball caps inscribed with the credo: *American by Birth, Southern by the Grace of God*. You don't see many of these displays of exceptionalist regional pride in Montana or North Dakota.

In addition, from West Virginia hollows (or "hollers" in the local dialect) to the arroyos of New Mexico, Tip O'Neill's maxim, "all politics is local," has lost its sheen. More than ever, national political agendas play a direct role in state legislatures, including those in 89er country. Recall, also, that isolation is/was one the singular attributes of the Great Plains and Northern Rockies. Thousands of pioneer letters and diaries testify to the region's loneliness and solitude.

For a century, rural folks from mountain hamlets and tiny ranching towns on the high prairie counted on the radio, gossip sessions at the store, church services, and a weekly newspaper to keep informed. Then came television. The big three networks and public television kept the polarization narrative to a minimum, especially on a local level. Then, only a matter of years after the farm crisis of the 1980s—and when oil hit $9.30/barrel—came the internet and an explosion of talk radio. Fox and its analogue appeared shortly afterwards. Virtual communities replaced isolation. Those folks scraping by with two hundred head of cattle heard Rush Limbaugh—then Tucker Carlson—articulating their thoughts and dashing gasoline on the conflagration of their victim narrative. Many residents, especially older ones, never looked back.

Ergo, in the last two decades, the rural, aging, white American—particularly men—has executed a political right turn. This group feels excluded from power and prosperity. The result is what Nick Bowlin calls "default conservatism."[13]

This phrase succinctly describes the current political mode of 89er country.

However, I contend that the 89er region has a radically different political history than, again, the South, a reliable redoubt of conservative currents. In addition, with the exception of Boise (which still has a population of under five hundred thousand people), 89er country has no large cities.

These anomalies create a pair of singular dynamics. One creates political imbalance. In the most conservative regions, urban areas provide political parity, as Austin does for Texas. There is little of this in the Great Plains and Northern Rockies. What's notable is that until ten years ago, some of the states 89er country continued to put Democrats in the governor's seat or sent them to Washington. Montana still does. The Democrats' abandonment of rural America hit 89er country hard. The Democrats are now the party of urban American, a shortcoming in a land with no major city.

Second, as Richard Florida reports, urban America accounted for 97 percent of total job growth between 2001 and 2016, "with urban counties in large metros making up more than two-thirds of the gain. In contrast, rural counties accounted for less than 3 percent of job growth across this period."[14]

This segues into one of the book's central theses: the 89er culture and economic connection with commodities have created a values quagmire and political void. Yes, these shifts happened elsewhere, but they delivered a hammer blow to 89er country. Consolidation, technology, and advances in efficiency tore the heart out of the 89er commodity idyll. By the 1970s, sparsely populated places in the Great Plains and Northern Rockies were reeling. Most never recovered.

A threatened cultural identity invariably fosters the narrative of victimhood, a chronic theme in 89er county. "The outside world is doing *this* to *us*." As political theorist Corey Robins has noted, conservatism really does speak to and for people who have lost something.[15] A bone-deep crisis in cultural identity, closely linked with the failure of commodities to foster viable communities, created a political vacuum, which movement conservatism ably exploited.

Put plainly, the values of the Northern Rockies and Great Plains have been hijacked to a degree unequaled in any other region. The 89er system of government, which spliced libertarianism, egalitarianism, and central planning, is in retreat. In 1889, the states were nearly as "progressive" as New England and certainly more inclusive than the Deep South or Southwest. Now, the region is among the most conservative in the United States, espousing exclusive and authoritarian values.

Movement conservatism, with its hatred of the federal government, was perfectly positioned to fill the aforementioned political vacuum. Enmity towards Washington, always lurking below the surface, had been climbing in 89er country since the economic roller coaster of the 1980s, when commodities, especially agricultural commodities, were put through the wringer.

And yet, as the book demonstrates, commodity producers: ranchers, loggers, farmers and energy firms, are all inextricably connected with Washington, either by policy or federal land holdings. This leads to acute cognitive dissonance, which breeds odd political attachments.

As to the second question—how did the 89er region give up on its values with such speed?—the answers tend to be more allusive. Money and demographics are certainly part of the equation.

To a large extent—especially in Wyoming, Montana, and Idaho— wealthy non-native individuals have either bankrolled the movement conservative agenda or run for office themselves. This would include Montana governor Greg Gianforte, who came to the state in 1995. In Wyoming, Dan Brophy, a former commodities trader from Chicago who moved to Jackson in 2011, is one of the largest donors to movement conservative politicians. So is Susan Gore, an heiress to the Gore-Tex fortune, with her contributions through the Wyoming Liberty Group. Sometimes folks like Idaho Freedom Foundation chairman Wayne Hoffman, a Florida native, harness out-of-state money. Hoffman and his group believe there should be no funding for public education. Talk about a direct negation of the values of the 1889 constitutions, which were over the top about public education.

None of this happened without voter participation. This is where matters get murky. In 2022, *Montana Free Press* deputy editor Eric Dietrich went searching for data that validated the claim that partisan races for the Montana state legislature have accelerated due to new arrivals. His conclusion: not really.[16]

"The political composition of new arrivals looks a lot like the political composition of those who were born here," said Jeffery Lyons, associate professor of political science at Boise State University. "It is likely that there is some partisan sorting going on where Republicans who are dissatisfied and looking to move away from CA, OR and WA are more likely to come to Idaho than other places."[17]

This book contends the voter, wherever they were born, has been delivered a false promise, built on fabricated history. Thus, while the 89er region is part of the national fabric and participates in political changes, many of these shifts remain singular.

So then, how to understand and, with any luck, unwind this mess? We can start by not thinking in terms of Republicans or Democrats, but rather values. Specifically, are there values that hold universal appeal? Second question: Are there some parts of the country, due to their history and original state constitutions, that are equipped to put these values into action?

To both questions, a qualified yes. The states that made up the 1861 Dakota Territory (North Dakota, South Dakota, Wyoming, Montana, and Idaho) have these tools in their possession. Constitutions are part of a state's cultural DNA. The Great Plains and Northern Rockies historically favored live-and-let live credos. Their collective state constitutions, all written in 1889, set out the principles of egalitarianism, equality, reasonableness (for the era) voter inclusivity, and the idea that government had a role to play in society.

I do not paint an idyll. These states had bleak eras concerning Native Americans, African Americans, Mormons, and, in the late nineteenth century, Chinese. Women, while given suffrage earlier than most regions, continued to experience exclusion. Moreover, a dependency on commodities built precarious and often polarized communities—and communities, in their many forms, are what this book hopes to promote. By community, I mean a body or a place that endows a sense of belonging. Its power or influence is greater than the sum of its members. Values play a key role. "*The class of 1889*," as state constitutional expert Alan Tarr calls them, possessed a unique set of values. It's time to bring them back into circulation.[18]

INTRODUCTION

About a half dozen years ago, I had a conversation with historian Phil Roberts about the values and beliefs of nineteenth-century Wyoming. I was startled to hear Roberts say, "I've been studying the Wyoming constitution for years. Yet I'm starting to revise my opinion of it. It's actually more progressive than we think." I told Roberts to stop putting Jim Beam in his coffee. Nevertheless intrigued, I explored his premise. Not only did I end up agreeing with Roberts, but I discovered that, like Wyoming, four other states had written or rewritten their constitutions in August and September of 1889: North Dakota, South Dakota, Montana, and Idaho. These 89ers, as I call them, infused their founding documents with progressive ideas.

Their vision was both Republican in party and republican in philosophy—no mean feat in that era of clashing ideals and aspirations. The delegates were generally conservative: they respected tradition and free enterprise while recognizing that the Gilded Age had given too much to too few. As a result, egalitarianism and pragmatism were the bywords. The concept of liberty and the idea of the commonweal were not mutually exclusive. Despite the conservatism of the delegates, these constitutions were modestly populist, suspicious of corporations, wildly pro-agriculture, enthusiastic about republican virtues, and mostly pro-suffrage.

Pragmatism ruled the day, particularly the economic and demographic variety, but the definition of pragmatism can be slippery. Yet, in this case, pragmatism means practicality, not expediency. In 1889 the delegates of these constitutional conventions faced three problems: they were poor, their revenue stream was chained to the commodity index, and they badly needed to boost their populations. Fundamental matters, such as how they paid for state government and how to defend their farmers, came to the fore. Their need for more people rendered them pluralistic and pragmatic. While moral or ideological beliefs are part of human conditions, the 89er delegates thought these principles should pay their own freight or at least not interfere with the development of a fiscally solvent state with adequate population. Moreover, as we shall discuss, major economic and agricultural changes were afoot. This required a political nimbleness from these generally conservative men. They couldn't afford to be mired down in rigid ideals, a concept best expressed by the conservative Edmund Burke: "We must all obey the great law of change. It is the most powerful law of nature."

∽

If judged by modern standards, these constitutions seem painfully exclusive: they shoved aside Native Americans, African Americans, Chinese laborers, and—in Idaho—Mormons. Aside from being granted suffrage, women were only given minimal authority.

These five marginalized groups represented different threats (or promises) to the conventioneers. As historian Jeffrey Ostler observed, "Most European Americans took for granted that the world's peoples could be divided into 'races,' with the 'white race' above all others."[1]

The delegates dealt heinous cards to Native Americans. They wanted to forget tribes were even there, except when they had the chance to usurp their land, and they subscribed to the "disappearing or vanishing Indian" narrative. Conventioneers considered tribes wards of the federal government and, in practice, not worth their time.

This attitude toward Indigenous Americans changed little over the decades. In 1890, Frank Baum, author of *The Wizard of Oz*, was working as proprietor and editor of the Aberdeen (SD) *Saturday Pioneer*. After hearing of the Wounded Knee massacre, which killed over two hundred Lakota men, women, and children, Baum opined for the "total extermination" of the American Indians.[2]

The late twentieth-century acts of discrimination and atrocities (forced assimilation, Wounded Knee) are well known. Yet historians have overlooked other grim actions in 89ers country, including the Pick-Sloan Plan, which authorized the building of the Garrison dam in North Dakota. This

1947 project usurped 155,000 acres, the majority of them rich bottomland, from the MHA (Mandan, Hidatsa, and Arikara) Nation. These tribes had a reputation as being superior farmers and careful money managers. The default on federal loans to this tribal group was among the lowest in the nation. The government took their land at $35/acre. Vine Deloria Jr. did not mince words when evaluating this action, calling it, "without a doubt, the single most destructive act ever perpetrated on a tribe by the United States."[3]

African Americans were a touchier subject. Many conventioneers were sensitive and, in theory, sympathetic to the newly found freedom of Black Americans. In practice African Americans found prejudice from communities and government widespread in the West.

Conventioneers were also hostile to guest Chinese workers. But they had to be careful. The west, especially the railroad and mining communities, relied on Chinese labor. But unlike African Americans, who were citizens and had the protection (again more in theory than in practice) of the US government, Chinese workers were "aliens" and ultimately disposable. The Chinese Exclusion Act of 1882 suspended Chinese immigration for ten years, and it declared Chinese immigrants ineligible for naturalization. In 1870, the Chinese made up 28 percent of Idaho's population. By 1920, it was down to 0.5 percent.[4]

Women represented mostly promise to these conventioneers. In a 1900 *North American Review* article, suffragist Elizabeth Cady Stanton called women the greatest factor in civilization.[5] Convention notes show that ideas about suffrage and empowering women were all over the place. But the train of equality had already left the station. While there were many setbacks, well-organized and persistent women's groups (the National American Woman Suffrage Association, for example) made sure that any backsliding or prevaricating on behalf of politicians got prompt and negative attention.

While we cannot whitewash the constitutions delegates' actions, it's unrealistic to expect them to have written documents carrying twenty-first-century moral standards. These were generally tradition-bound men —and they were all men—who recognized the country was shifting. Change came in iterations, sometimes glacially.

Flawed as they were, when compared to other state constitutions of other western states, hoo-boy, the ideals found in the 89er founding documents were models of amplitude. Both California and Oregon banned, or tried to ban, all African Americans from the state. By contrast, the original Dakota Territory granted African American men the right to vote in 1868, as did Wyoming when it gained territory status.

New Mexico refused suffrage for women until the US Congress passed the Nineteenth Amendment in June 1919. Wyoming had women on grand juries as early as 1870, although the practice proved short lived.[6] In 1890, South Dakota voters refused to allow the state legislature to ban Native Americans at the ballot box. The action, however, had only nominal positive action on Native American voters. In fact, South Dakota used various devices to keep Native Americans from voting. Arizona and New Mexico only allowed American Indians to vote starting in 1948.

Instead, the 89er constitutions curtailed child labor and promoted affordable public education. They looked out for the working stiff and clamped down on railroads and irrigation companies to prevent monopolies. The secret ballot found favor shortly after statehood. Over the years, the 89ers accepted the odd duck and unconventional: Hutterites, Mennonites, syncretic New Age communes, white supremacists, doomsday cults, and Jewish colonies. The five constitutions enshrined an explicitly central-planning concept significant in arid states: state ownership of running water

Here's the paradox: the republicanism of the 89er constitutions bears little resemblance to present-day Republicanism, yet the two are often conflated. Derek Skees, a member of the Montana legislature, while attending the GOP state convention in Billings in July 2022, referred to Montana's constitution as "a socialist rag."[7]

In the last ten years, legislators from Boise to Bismarck to Cheyenne have: tried to keep Native Americans away from the voting booth (voter ID laws); criminalized protest during pipeline construction; banned crossover voting (voters must stay within the confines of their parties for both primary and general elections); attacked public universities; outlawed transgender operations; banned sanctuary cities; and curbed the initiative and referendum process.

Can you picture the constitutional conventioneers of any of these states curbing the rights of farmers of the era to protest? Imagine, if you will, the South Dakota 1898 legislature, who approved the nation's first initiative and referendum process (an idea they imported from Switzerland), trying to curb *any* part of the election process?[8] The GOP–dominated legislature in Pierre has been snipping away at the initiative and referendum direct process for years now.

This suggests that GOP fealty to "traditional values" is but window dressing. Ditto with the wisdom that conservative societies put great stock in the values of founding documents. In other words, the 89ers values have been usurped. The irony is that 89ers all began as part of the 1861 Dakota Territory; this new addition to the nation promoted small-r republican ideals, necessarily differentiated from the big-R Republican party. As historian Jon Lauck wrote in *Prairie Republic: The Political Culture of Dakota Territory, 1879–1889*, "The republicanism I find to be a powerful current in Dakota Territory relates the political ideology with roots in ancient Greece and Rome and early modern Italy and England." If you were unfamiliar with what republicanism meant in 1861, Lauck continued, "think of the general political principles of Thomas Jefferson, not the specific platform of Ronald Reagan."[9]

In short, the historical commonwealth values of these states' constitutions do not square with the values of the current political narrative. The term commonwealth is used here in the classical connotation, meaning a political community set up for the common good. It's an ancient concept that can even be found in the Bible, the English translation of the Greek πολιτείας (politeias), an ambiguous term meaning rights of citizens or form of government.

The idea of a commonwealth can be manipulated, however. If a powerful despot controls the narrative, commonwealths can take on the characteristics of a twisted iron-fisted covenant. Thomas Hobbes' Leviathan describes a "Common-wealth" that had several paths in preventing life from being "solitary, poore, nasty, brutish and short." Some variations evoked the idea that fear kept people in line. Oliver Cromwell, for example, ruled England with an iron fist under the guise of a commonwealth.

I'll talk more about this concept in the following chapter—and how it pertains to the 89ers—but I often interchange *commonwealth* with the idea of *republican values* mentioned by Lauck.

These two ideas are only roughly simpatico. Yet commonwealth and republican values share more similarities than differences. They are both social contracts focused on limiting tyranny, although classical liberty purists thought democracy (power of the majority) could be a form of oppression. Both concepts seek a society based on civic virtues, moral education, and the power of small communities. They also both believe that citizens should set aside personal interests to promote the common welfare.

The Midwest and southern Great Plains are also experiencing similar shifts in values and political narratives. In the past decades, historians and journalists have investigated political shifts in the flyover country. Perhaps notable among them is Thomas Frank's 2004 *What's the Matter with Kansas?* Frank attempts to explain why Kansans gave up their left-leaning populist roots. There was a time when the average Kansan had little patience for the machinations of big business. As Franks explains, "When business screwed the farmers and the workers—when it implemented monopoly strategies invasive beyond the Populists' furthest imaginings—when it ripped off shareholders and casually tossed thousands out of work—you could be damned sure about what would follow."[10]

Kansas eventually abandoned this stance. Maybe big business wasn't so bad; maybe it was out-of-state "elites" that were out to get them. This would include most every Democrat who subscribed to the Bill Clinton, Al Gore, Joe Lieberman, Terry McAuliffe creed of attending to the affluent, urban voter at the expense of rural America.

Ross Benes offers a similar explanation in his 2021 book, *Rural Rebellion: How Nebraska Became a Republican Stronghold.* Like Frank, Benes puts the blame for this shift squarely on the Democrats. Benes was reared to believe, as were most Nebraskans, that fiscal responsibility lay with Republicans and big government with Democrats. Benes interviewed Nebraska Democratic Party chair Jane Kleeb, who said "for too long, Democrats in Nebraska ignored rural areas and failed to consistently show up and make their case."[11]

Enter the works of Catherine McNicol Stock, a history professor at Connecticut College. Stock made a name for herself in Great Plains studies with her first two books, *Main Street in Crisis: The Great Depression and The Old Middle Class on the Northern Plains* (1992) and, in 1996, *Rural Radicals.* Stock posited that rural anger at elites is woven into our historical narrative—"almost a habit of the country," she writes, quoting historian Pauline Maier. Massachusetts farmers drove this historical discontent—Shay's Rebellion of 1786 was but one of many displays of discontent.[12] This tradition set the stage for later political upheaval among commodity-driven states, like the 89ers. In her third book on the topic of rural discontent, *Nuclear Country: The Origins of the Rural New Right* (2020), Stock gets more specific in cause and geography. She travels to North Dakota, exploring the history of missile silos. The installation and maintenance of Minuteman missiles, says Stock, inculcated a military mindset into agriculture families. With this type of conservatism came a movement away from a progressive agenda.[13]

Yet it was a bracingly original article that set the standard for digging deeper into core issues. Published in 2008, "Managing the Periphery in the Gilded Age: Writing Constitutions for the Western States" came out swinging—politely, but still swinging.[14] Author and political scientist Amy Bridges demonstrated that the delegates at western constitutional conventions had little interest in free markets. This wariness covered myriad areas of government, including holiest of the holies: irrigation. Taking to task historians such as Lewis Gould and William Lilley, Bridges showed that the west was not, as Lilley and Gould avow, a "prisoner of its belief that free enterprise alone should manage the work of irrigation."

Constitutional delegates, said Bridges, "did not design elegant, spare machines that would go of themselves, but complex governments with diverse institutions to address a broad range of tasks."[15] To the contrary, "although delegates were wary of state legislatures, and denied them many powers, at the Gilded Age conventions (this includes the 89ers), delegates affirmed and expanded the prerogatives and authority of state government. They created new institutions for managing their economies and wrote property law for settlement and growth. They also greatly expanded bills of rights, creating positive rights, which mandated activity by state government."[16]

Bridges' work drove home the point that while party affiliation remained important in 1889, a certain set of commonwealth *values* underwrote the planks of these state constitutions, ones beyond D or R. Yet why are these modern examinations of western states and Great Plains so focused on the *political* narrative?

Two reasons. Assumptions abound about the region's political history, mainly that the Great Plains and Northern Rockies have always been largely Republican (Montana excepted), pro-business, and "conservative." When I asked retired senator Alan Simpson, a Wyoming Republican, about this perceived GOP dominance, he balked. "Well, we can forget that notion. The longest-serving US senator in Wyoming history was a Democrat, Joseph O'Mahoney. He was in office for over twenty years. Look at Ed Herschler [another Democrat and the] only three-term governor we had. And he was just what we needed. We do not have a history of being a Republican-only state."[17]

Historian Marshall Damgaard possesses an encyclopedic knowledge of the Great Plains' political past, particularly his native South Dakota. He summed up the state's narrative this way: "Many people, even South Dakota residents, perceive that this state has, politically, always been a dependable (read: boring) conservative bastion. The historical record screams otherwise."[18]

Secondly, few bother to examine the complexity behind political labels. In 1889, *liberal* was a term of esteem, regardless of political affiliation. In the tradition of Edmund Burke, liberal was synonymous with generous and, up to a point, inclusive. Defending the idea of women's suffrage, at the Wyoming constitutional convention, John Hoyt asked for the support of a body of men "so intelligent, so high minded, so liberal as those who compose this convention."[19]

Conservative carried some of the same connotations as today's meaning. It meant cautious or prudent and encouraged following historical or judicial precedent. Henry B. Blackwell, co-founder of the national Republican Party and an advocate for women's suffrage, spoke to the Montana constitutional convention. He pitched a "very simple and conservative proposition."[20] Give women the vote. Why? Because it embraced the principles of equality found in the US Constitution. Conservative did not mean, however, anti-government, either federal or state. It did not mean exclusivity. Unlike liberal, conservative could infer negativity. Democrat James W. Reid told his fellow delegates at the Idaho convention that the press saw him as overly conservative and thus a mossback, or in other words, a stuck-up-to-the-hubs feudalist.[21]

Republicans took progressive stances on a range of issues debated at the 1889 conventions; they did not turn away from the progressive label—an umbrella term for anyone hoping to make economic or social progress.

Loyalty mattered. Party schisms notwithstanding, the GOP of the Great Plains and Northern Rockies had not drifted far from the party of Lincoln. They were Unionists, first and foremost; many of the 89er conventioneers had either served in the Union Army or had relatives who had. The GOP craved state autonomy and wanted to run their own affairs, but, given the memory of the Civil War, delegates were suspicious of extreme state sovereignty. This rejection of radical states' rights theory—which suggests that states can largely operate independent of the federal government—made them relatively progressive by modern standards.

The Republicans of the 89er era gave credence to security values, especially relating to safety and stability. They were attached to the business community and wanted minimal taxation but accepted taxes as necessary for proper governance. They subscribed to the gold standard and advocated for protective tariffs to safeguard domestic industry and investment. But they weren't so besotted with the bottom line as to ignore the darker sides of the Gilded Age's laissez-faire economic policies. Two years before, Congress passed the Interstate Commerce Act, subjecting railroads to federal regulation. In 1890, Congress further restricted monopolies with the Sherman Anti-Trust Act.

The GOP of most western territories had progressive opinions about labor, women's rights, and religion. They censured indentured servitude and child labor while protecting workers. In Montana, delegates expanded liability law in favor of injured workers. Women's suffrage sparked some of the most passionate debate. The delegates' attitudes were inconsistent when it came to other forms of inclusivity, especially concerning equal treatment for American Indians and religious freedom.

Their take on religion seems progressive but was in fact traditional. Chalk part of this up to Section Four of the Enabling Act of 1889, the federal legislation that made these states possible. It mandated that a "perfect toleration of religious sentiment shall be secured." Freedom of worship has deep roots in American history. While faiths besides Christianity were acceptable in the abstract, Christian sects proved problematic. South Dakota wrestled with anti-Catholic prejudice. The Idaho convention had a donnybrook over Mormonism.

If a core tenant of modern conservatism has been limited government, then these states face charges of ideological treason. Bridges' work underwrites the idea that the 1889 conventioneers did not subscribe to the adage that government is best when it governs least. They understood the potentials of state government and expanded its powers, passed laws that encouraged growth, and beefed up their bills of rights.

In 1889, a period of economic, demographic, and social upheaval, change wasn't about to be kept in a cage. Idaho Falls has had a city-owned electric utility since 1900. North Dakota has the only government-owned general service bank in the nation. The legislature in Bismarck established the Bank of North Dakota in 1919 to promote agriculture and commerce. If one definition of socialism is government control of the means of production, then the Bank of North Dakota is Exhibit A. In 1932, North Dakota passed an anti-corporation farm law that still stands.[22] In 1932, voters put Franklin D. Roosevelt in the White House. Out of 242 counties in the 89er states, only four voted against Roosevelt. North Dakota gave him a clean sweep. In 1980, South Dakota bought a failing railroad.

If the Northern Rockies and Plains have always been "conservative," explain this: from 1913 to 1989, Montana only elected one Republican to a seat in the US Senate for a single term. At the turn of the twentieth century, these states, particularly in the Great Plains, voted for Republicans, Democrats, Populists, Socialists, and Progressives. After World War II, the 89ers sent some of the most storied Democrats—all centrists—of the era to Washington: Mike Mansfield, Frank Church, and Gale McGee. In 1986, North Dakota sent Democrat Kent Conrad to Washington for a twenty-six-year stint as a US senator. A similar pattern applies to governorships. Between 1945 and 2010, a healthy twenty-six out of sixty-nine governors have been Democrats.

The most singular difference between these eras, roughly marked by the years 1900 and 2000, is how the 89er region dealt with change. Both these turn-of-the-century epochs, particularly the late Gilded Age, saw "wrenching transformations," as Robert Putnam called them.[23]

In the 1890s, merger mania swept through America, concentrating wealth and power into the hands of a few. Standard Oil, General Electric, DuPont, US Steel, and American Tobacco all grew through agglomeration. Between 2000 and 2010, over fifty American mergers took place, largely among financial and communication/internet firms. These latter companies garnered takeover and merger interest because technology represented the most promising financial future. Time-Warner, Vodaphone, Quest, and Viacom also revolutionized communication in America, just as the telegraph had in the later part of the twentieth century. Western Union built its first transcontinental telegraph line in 1861. By 1867, there were 5.8 million yearly messages. By 1900, it was 63.2 million.[24]

The revenues associated with communication technology are secondary to their social impact. They dethroned regionalism, ending the isolation of a thousand small towns. Suddenly, people had more information than they could possibly use, not to mention a surfeit of choices. Celebrity wealth arrived. By the 1890s, tycoons like E. H. Harriman, James Hill, Cyrus McCormack, Cornelius Vanderbilt, Gustavus Swift, Philip Armor, and John Rockefeller became household names, just as billionaires Bill Gates, Mark Zuckerberg, and Jeff Bezos entered the pantheon of familiar names by the early 2000s.

The phonograph and movies went from novelties to common, even in small towns. Ideas and norms from the outside world were no longer the provenance of big cities.

By 1900, catalog giants Montgomery Ward and Sears and Roebuck had put the fear of God into the small-town retail and dry goods store, as Walmart and Amazon did to local businesses one hundred years later.

Similar to figures in the post-2000 conservative movement, politicians and moralists demonized urban areas around the turn of the twentieth century. For example, Donald Trump called sanctuary cities incubators of crime; in 1889, nativist Josiah Strong declared that the "first city was built by the first murderer, and crime and vice and wretchedness have festered in it ever since."[25]

Wealth inequality burdened both epochs. "In 1896, social scientist Charles B. Spaur roughly calculated that one percent of the population owned more than half of all the national wealth, while 44 percent at the bottom owned only 7.2 percent."[26]

The Congressional Budget Office released a report in 2022 tracking shifts in American wealth from 1989 to 2019. They found a well-documented trend similar to the Gilded Age. "Families in the top 10 percent and in the top 1 percent of the distribution, in particular, saw their share of total wealth rise over the period. In 2019, families in the top 10 percent of the distribution held 72 percent of total wealth, and families in the top

1 percent of the distribution held more than one-third; families in the bottom half of the distribution held only 2 percent of total wealth."[27]

In both eras, immigration proved to be a hot-button issue. The 1900 census showed a total population of 76.2 million; 10.3 million, or 13.6 percent, were foreign-born, mostly from Germany, Ireland, Canada, Britain, Sweden, Italy, Russia, Poland, Norway, and Austria.[28] Alarmed nativists followed the words of US senator Chauncey M. Deprew to "stop the reservoir of European anarchy pouring into our country."[29]

To modern conservatives, immigrants are "invaders."[30] Under Donald Trump, White House Senior Advisor Stephen Miller promoted a zero-tolerance immigration policy: family separation, the Muslim ban, and ending the Deferred Action for Childhood Arrivals program.

What's singular, however, is how, in the space of a century, Northern Rockies and Great Plains society reacted to these shifts. The opposing reactions form the core difference between the twenty-first-century and nineteenth-century definitions of *conservatism*. Working off the foundation of their 1889 constitutions, the region set up a state structure, including governmental intervention that assured a degree of fairness and protection from predatory outside forces, like grain monopolies, for example, but attempted to be as socially inclusive as norms would allow, permitting all forms of pragmatism. By contrast, in 2000 ideological conservatism meant cutting—if not eliminating—governmental regulation on all levels, squashing attempts to promote egalitarianism, curbing immigration and voting, and stifling inclusivity.

So, how to make sense of this complicated and often confusing narrative? What about the accepted scholarly premise that core values may be reprioritized but rarely change?[31]

⸜⸝⸞⸟

I've divided this book into two sections: the first part explores the historical narrative; the second part is more journalistic in nature although history remains at the core. It carries the book's theme to the advocacy level, namely: that the commonwealth and egalitarian values found in these 1889 constitutions can be advanced into twenty-first century society; but only if we start tolerating—even liking—cities, particularly small cities, and consider a stewardship form of commodity development.

Contradictions abound in forming early state narratives. The first section of *The Spirit of 1889* lays out possible reasons, beginning with the constitutional conventions themselves. These states faced an irreconcilable split in values from the beginning: one cultural, the other economic. The 89er delegates used *tradition* (church, respect for hard work, acceptance of customs) and *conformity* (respecting social norms and delayed gratification) to gain *security* (harmony and societal/economic stability). These values, essential to any functioning society, also have a dark side. Those who embraced them have little use for change. Yet in 1889, change wasn't about to be kept in a cage. Progressivism breathed down the delegates' necks, bringing with it the value of *self-transcendence*: social justice, fairness, and equality.

The 89ers transitioned from territory status to statehood on the wings of commodity optimism and hope. Sure, there had been busts and flash-in-the-pan gold mines but, for the long term, what could possibly go wrong? Although technology was already roaring down the two-track and the demise of the Jeffersonian agriculture ideal well underway, the delegates thought the balm of progressive legislation would solve foreseeable problems. It did not.

Yet even before these constitutional conventions, the faro dealers in Washington dealt the 89ers bad hands. The second chapter, "The Poison Seed," demonstrates that since territorial times the federal government promulgated divisive decisions, from appointing corrupt governors to contradictory land policy. Even as territories, the 89er economy lived by the commodity index, hardly a source of stability. Over the next century, boom and bust ruled the economic roost. Finally, a wild and often devastating financial ride in the 1980s, marked by grain embargos, inflation, an oil spike (then collapse), and agricultural chaos, ginned up a lasting anger at the federal government. It has never gone away. Hardened loyalty to identity overtook pragmatic values.

But What of the Future?

The third chapter of this book is titled: "Yield and Pounds Do Not a Community Make: The Case for Stewardship Agriculture." The timeline starts in 1886 with Charles Ingalls, father of writer Laura Ingalls Wilder, selling his farm in De Smet, South Dakota. The narrative moves quickly, however, into twenty-first-century agriculture. The chapter assumes a critical role in this book due to the enormous cultural and economic identity the 89er region put on agriculture.

At the turn of the nineteenth century, the Great Plains and Northern Rockies, and production agriculture and the idea of rural community, were inseparable. When agriculture prospered, so did the town. The values meshed. Now declining populations and economic stasis in regions dependent on commodity agriculture means a struggle to honor those historic values. You can't have schools without children, for example, and the assessed valuation to support them. It's now reached the point where a working community is no longer important to production agriculture. If the school closes, the rancher or farmer will seek employees not from the local labor source, but through the H-2 visa program. I suggest that a hybrid form of production, which I simply call stewardship agriculture, is challenging the dying town narrative. We will meet four farmers and ranchers determined to make a change.

Not only did the constitutional delegates embrace an overly optimistic projection about agriculture, but they also acted on their Jeffersonian mistrust of cities—not an uncommon attitude for the day. Horace Greeley did not say, for example, go to western *cities*, young man. Constitutional delegates limited the power of municipalities, mostly by restricting their power to levy taxes. The Great Plains and Northern Rockies remain the only region of the country without a major city, although Boise will soon be in the running.

In chapter 4, "Cities of the Plains: The Cost of Demonizing Anything Urban," I explore how this suspicion created chronic economic and cultural challenges, including those associated with gender. Cities have long been revenue and job creation machines. Seeing cities as secondary, the 89ers handicapped themselves with economic monoculture, one focused almost solely on commodities. Boom and bust became a part of life. Missing was the economic and cultural diversity brought about by urban areas. Increasingly, this lack of vital urban areas, both large and small, has created hardships for women. The majority of jobs, circa 2023, pursued by women are found in cities and towns. Thus, I suggest that any sort of sustained revitalization of rural areas needs to include its urban places.

At first blush, all these issues appear to be wrapped up in economics. Yet, the cultural connection—the sense of identity—with these industries carries more clout than the paycheck. Mining, ranching, and logging create strong tribal identities. Even though some states like Idaho have, to some degree, weaned themselves off commodities, the cultural identity remains. In my final chapter, "Dismantling the Cult of Commodity Prosperity: Breaking the Cycle of Victimhood and Resentment," I suggest these hidebound attitudes inhibit societal shifts and, as the nation grows more urban, foster a greater sense of isolation, powerlessness, polarization, and cultural humiliation.

The Spirit of 1889 champions a fundamentally conservative ideal: if people want economically viable, small to medium-sized communities, if they want stability and a societal model that permits the inclusion of responsible citizens of all stripes—the values embodied in all these state constitutions—then extractive industries must be seen as the icing on the cake, not the cake itself. When commodity extraction is perpetuated through political means as critical to the community's existence, an economic roller coaster with social consequences, like rural population loss, is inevitable.

The 89er states remain unable to reconcile their cultural identity, a rural exceptionalism linked to commodity production, with the pluralistic society of our future. This book seeks to explore how the 89ers can amend that narrative.

A RECKONING IN AUGUST

1

On August 5, 1889, Major John Wesley Powell stood before the state constitutional convention in Bismarck, the capital of Dakota Territory. He had arrived on a special train carrying the members of the newly formed Select Committee on Irrigation and Reclamation of Arid Lands. No known record of the speech in his handwriting exists. Twenty-seven years after having his right arm amputated at the Battle of Shiloh, writing with his left hand remained slow and ponderous. Powell most likely spoke from notes or ad hoc.

The speech was short: 1,423 words.[1] The brevity may have had to do with Powell's dislike of political theater. In fact, he told the audience he had never made a political speech in his life. This wasn't actually true. As director of the US Geological Survey (USGS), Powell had appeared before countless committees and departments in Washington, defending the funding for the USGS and his beloved Bureau of American Ethnology. Still, he confessed, "it seems to me I am almost out of place here."

He admitted to knowing something about water and irrigation. Powell focused his attention on the drier parts of the Dakota territory—those lands west of the Missouri River— saying its prosperity relied on running streams.

The 1890 federal census would show roughly 2.5 million acres under irrigation in the Great Plains and Northern Rockies.[2] But Powell wasn't there to discuss the advances in irrigation. He was on a political crusade: privately owned water was evil. "Fix it in your constitution that no corporation—no body of men—no capital can get possession and right of your waters," he said. "Hold the waters in the hands of the people."

Such an approach, said Powell, if inscribed in the state constitution "will prevent your great agricultural sources from falling into the hands of the few." He framed the problem in personal terms: "Think of a condition of affairs in which *your* agriculture—which *you* will have to depend on largely—depending on irrigation, is at the mercy of twenty companies, who own all the water. They would laugh at ownership of land. What is ownership of land when the value is in the water?"

Powell spoke the delegates' language, tapping into their dreams and ambitions. He was one of them: born on a farm, son of pious Methodists, a self-made man who wouldn't let his loss of an arm slow him down. A man of ambition, Powell had made two trips down the Grand Canyon and became one of America's foremost naturalists.

But he was not one of those preachy preservationists like John Muir. He was a political pragmatist and believed in harnessing nature for the betterment of society. When Denver businessman John M. Brown and engineer John B. Stanton proposed building a railroad along the Colorado River to bring Utah and Colorado coal to ocean ports, Powell thought it "a most desirable thing to accomplish."[3]

Powell was one of agriculture's chief evangelists. In his lifetime, Powell made countless references to his devotion to small-time farming. The older he got, the more dedicated he became to the concept of the family farm. Before this audience, that mattered. No occupation was mentioned with more reverence at the constitutional convention in Bismarck than agriculture. "The great agricultural state of North Dakota," as delegate Reuben Stevens effusively described his adopted home.[4]

The possibilities were limitless. In 1889, ex-officio territorial statistician Frank Hagerty calculated that the two combined Dakotas had a total land mass of 96 million acres. Out of that, Hagerty figured that 80 million acres were fit for agriculture.[5] "The foundation of the wealth and prosperity of the Dakotas is in their agricultural products," he said.

One of Powell's biographers called his words "probably his most famous speech."[6] It was also one of his most prophetic. His prescience wasn't so much about water ownership; it was a subliminal mixed message that burdens the state to this day. Powell was asking North Dakota to codify a form of political and economic schizophrenia.

In essence, Powell was telling the delegation that their constitution must embrace a form of commonwealth governance. The term commonwealth is used here in the classical connotation, meaning a political community set up for the common good. More to the point, Powell is avowing they must not be seduced by the *commercial republic* model of government. This was a big ask. A commercial republic looks after the concerns of commerce and a legal structure to protect their interests. It also provides capital and jobs.

Morton County delegate Albert S. Parsons, an employee of the Northern Pacific, spelled out the heart of the conundrum: "We are largely dependent on corporations. Corporations in North Dakota will always have a stronger influence than they have elsewhere. With all due justice to them—we wish to encourage them—we wish to help them—but we must beware the day when they will shackle us and control our people."[7]

The Commonwealth vs. Commerce

Powell was sowing seeds on fertile ground. In the Dakotas, the press had been after delegates for years to create a "self-governing Dakota commonwealth."[8]

North Dakota's quandary was not theirs alone. As described in the introduction, North Dakota, South Dakota, Montana, and Idaho all finished their constitutions in the hot August of 1889. Wyoming wrote their state constitution in September of that year. All struggled with balancing the commonwealth versus the commercial republic models of government.

The commonwealth model had roots in Dakota Territory. In fact, the original 1861 Dakota Territory incorporated all 89er states. The capital was Yankton. When the territorial delegates met there in 1862, they set an example for their predecessors. It was a vision of commonwealth exceptionalism. "In treating the makeup of the Dakota Assembly, it is important to remember that its members were very conscious of the fact they were laying down the foundations of representative government in a new area in the Northwest. They likened themselves to the pilgrims at Plymouth or the founding fathers at Philadelphia," wrote Howard Lamar in Dakota *Territory 1861–1889*.[9]

This political vision described by Lamar differs profoundly when describing early forms of governments in the South, Southwest, or even California. In these regions, versions of the commercial republic model prevailed. Ideas of the common good applied to the wealthy and large land holdings. In the early Dakotas, landholders, by contrast, were relatively small and in abundance.[10]

In the South, Europeans set the foundations for a slavery, plantation, and sharecropper economy. Large portions of the coastal south had strong historical and commercial connections to Spain, Britain, and France. Tobacco, rice, indigo, and cotton drove an export-oriented economy. The small individual landholder, Black or white, struggled. As historian Douglas F. Dowd said of the Antebellum South, "There was no place to go for most whites but down, or out."[11]

The Spanish had long been in the Southwest before the advent of English-speaking newcomers. Land grants—some exceeding 1.7 million acres—from the Spanish crown informed generations on rules concerning land ownership, irrigation, the makeup of communities, and the basic economy.[12] The Catholic Church played a significant role in society. By contrast, the delegates of the 89er conventions wrote documents that were scrupulously non-sectarian.

This did not go unnoticed by Congress. When New Mexico was being considered for statehood in 1882, the *New York Times* opined in an article titled "Greasers as Citizens":

> The Mexican men are very much under the influence of the priests. A sort of superstitious fear governs them, and if it were to the interest of the priesthood to play upon that fear it would be made an important factor in politics. I think it nor fear wrong to say that about two-thirds of the population of the Territory is of mongrel breed known as Mexicans—a mixture of their blood of Apache, Negro, Navajo, white horse-thiefs [*sic*], Pueblo Indian and old-time frontiersman.[13]

Similar elements played out in early California colonization.[14] The church and state controlled land distribution. For example, "In 1773 the Viceroy of New Spain authorized the commanders of the San Diego and Monterey presidios to distribute land to colonists and Indians, as long as they did not move away from the boundaries of the presidio or mission on which they were already living."[15]

In many respects, these 89er conventions were ordinary, both in aspirations and results. They were not the loci of original political ideas. None wrote constitutions from scratch. Instead, they lifted key passages from other states, an old tradition. Delegates from the 1776 North Carolina convention, for example, studied the constitutions of Virginia and Maryland.[16] The 89er conventioneers borrowed from the founding documents of Colorado, Minnesota, Indiana, Iowa, Illinois, Pennsylvania, New York, and California.

Out of the roughly 344 delegates of the five 89ers conventions, not one of them was born in the territory in which they lived. They came from the Midwest, New England, Canada, and Europe, regions and nations familiar with the commonwealth ideal. The delegates probably made up a fair representation of the populace. "The people of Montana are mainly from the Middle and Western States, and are energetic, enterprising, and intelligent, law-abiding, liberal, and patriotic, and are of the right kind of material to found the leading commonwealth of the great New Northwest," said territorial governor B. F. Potts in his 1878 address to the legislature.[17]

Adjusting to a Proper Fit

In the seventeenth century, states in New England, as well as Virginia, Pennsylvania, and Kentucky, imported forms of the commonwealth principles. Yet, the sheer size and population differences between the Great Plains and Northern Rockies suggested that, say, a New England commonwealth model might be impractical. In 1889, the five New England states had a landmass just shy of 72,000 square miles inhabited by 7.1 million people. By contrast, the 89ers combined covered 475,500 square miles inhabited by roughly 835,000 souls.

Political agendas and priorities had shifted since the formation of the original states. New Hampshire's 923-word 1776 constitution concerned itself with getting rid of the British monarch. Vermont's constitution expressed a similar demand as well, as they were worried about being usurped—God forbid—by the state of New York. Puritan religious language infused Massachusetts's 1780 constitution, much of which late-nineteenth century citizens would find overbearing. It also had monetary and property requirements to run for public office.

The economics were also a mismatch. New England's access to the Atlantic made international trade its chief source of revenue. Never much of an agricultural powerhouse, the Northeast states quickly moved beyond raw commodities into manufacturing. "By 1750 American ironmasters [all located in the Northeast] became major suppliers of iron to British manufactures and by 1775 they were the third-largest producers of iron in the world," wrote historian Brian Albright.[18] By 1820, Massachusetts alone had 96 textile mills.[19]

The closest model the 89ers could possibly emulate were the states that made up the Northwest Ordinance of 1787: Ohio, Indiana, Illinois, Michigan, Wisconsin, and Minnesota. That analogue wasn't a good fit, either. By 1880, Illinois had over three million people. With their access to the Mississippi River and Great Lakes, these states quickly developed revenue streams that paid for the government. The entrepreneurial Bezaleel Wells, for example, built a woolen mill in Steubenville, Ohio, in 1815. In Illinois, Cyrus McCormick opened an automatic reaper plant in 1847, fifteen years before any of the 89ers were even a territory.

The Blueprint for an Extractive Colony

Instead, in the territorial years, the Great Plains and Northern Rockies were stuck with a type of commercial model: railroads that ran as near-monopolies, grain cartels, limited access to markets via the water transport, pastoral grazing economies plagued by booms and busts (and controlled by out-of-state or foreign syndicates), little manufacturing, and no major cities.[20] The rare hard rock mine that didn't play out in a few years, such as the Homestake Mine in South Dakota or Anaconda Copper in Butte, provided a scarce but steady source of income and revenue.

Some found this corporate hegemony untenable. In 1885, when South Dakota tried—unsuccessfully—to write a constitution that satisfied Congress, fiery Hugh Campbell, the US Attorney for Dakota Territory, asked his fellow delegates: "Gentlemen, how do corporations and an individual get along? Peaceably, like a lion and a lamb. They could get along peaceably because the lamb is eaten up."[21]

Yet, these budding states did not have the luxury of entirely rejecting the commercial republic model—even a version dependent on commodities.

North Dakota best exemplifies this push and pull between the two ideas of government. The constitutional conventioneers in Bismarck edited a document created by James Bradley Thayer. A Harvard law professor and the author of the influential legal article "The Origin and Scope of the American Doctrine of Constitutional Law," Thayer was a progressive and leading advocate for the concept of judicial restraint.[22] Unlike Powell, his brand of progressivism didn't have much patience with grassroots democracy. Yet like Powell, Thayer thought ill of government legal oversight. His form of progressivism, said legal scholar Steven Calebresi, "disliked courts, judicial review, originalism, and bills of rights, which they saw as tools of the rich."[23]

Thayer had written the constitution at the bidding (and payment) of Henry Villard, finance officer for both the Populists and the agrarians' chief enemy, the Northern Pacific Railroad. Talk about conflicting values. At the time, Northern Pacific owned one-quarter of all the land in North Dakota—most of it in federal land grants—and 120 town sites. Research undertaken a century later by North Dakota lawyers Herbert L. Meschke and Lawrence D. Spears revealed the degree of influence that Northern Pacific Railroad had on the North Dakota constitution.[24]

Progressivism Won't Go Away

Another quandary of the era: when the states of the Northwest Ordinance entered the union (Minnesota, the last, joined in 1858), the authors of those constitutions did not have the winds of progressivism—other than the abolition of slavery—blowing through their convention halls. By 1890, the term "progressive" carried a lot of different freight. Fairness represented the central value, something both parties of the era saw as important. Progressives promoted a government not controlled by political machines. Suffrage—especially for women—mattered. The idea of the family farm that could count on fair prices, not monopoly control, was a progressive icon. As a result, many "conservative" 89er delegates, particularly those connected with agriculture, embraced a considered progressivism.

Historians generally peg the 1890s as the beginning of the Progressive

Era. But for 89ers change was already afoot. The agricultural advocacy group The National Grange, founded in 1867, had moved into southeast Dakota Territory by 1873.[25] And for good reason. South Dakota historian Doane Robinson called the 1883 grain market so bad as to be "unspeakable."[26] The Dakota Farmers Alliance wanted, first and foremost, direct government intervention against an unfettered agricultural market.

Delegates reined in railroads, the "perennial despoiler of nineteenth-century fortunes," as Caroline Fraser observed.[27] The owners of the rails were, in fact, the progressives' whipping boy. "By the eighties they [railroads] had alienated a remarkable range of Americans," wrote historian Robert H. Weibe. "The farmer saw them as the arrogant manipulator of his profit, the small-town entrepreneur as the destroyer of his dreams, the city businessman as the sinister ally of his competitors, the labor leader as a model of the callous, distant employer, and the principled gentleman as the source of unscrupulous wealth and political corruption."[28]

All the 89er constitutions made railroads and telegraph lines common carriers. Railroads did not have the final word on freight and passenger rates, either. These "stupendous corporations," as Idaho delegate A. E. Mayhew, soon to be a district court judge, called them, had to open their books to the public.[29]

Yet progressives dealt with more than just regulating markets. They demanded good government (transparency and the end of political machines), suffrage, and Prohibition. They sought, with populist conviction, better working conditions. In Montana, delegates rendered "absolutely null and void" contracts that stipulated that a corporation shall have no liability if a worker was injured on the job. The conventioneers in Helena "abrogated what was known as the 'fellow-servant' rule, a legal doctrine that prevented workers from collecting for work-related injuries."[30]

It's difficult to exaggerate the emphasis delegates put on education. It started with literacy. "We have only two percent of the people in this territory who cannot read and write," H. E. Teschmacher told his fellow delegates in Wyoming. "I want the 1890 census to show that it has fallen to one percent."[31] Literacy, said John Hoyt, delegate and future president of the University of Wyoming, "will ensure the prosperity and success of the commonwealth."[32]

All the 89ers made education compulsory as territories, with Wyoming leading the way, passing the statute in 1876.[33] All five state constitutions created permanent public school endowment funds. "We in this constitution will publish to the world that we are in favor of public schools, that we are in favor of education and the dissemination of knowledge and of the arts and sciences," said Idaho's J. W. Poe, a delegate from Nez Perce County.[34]

Current educational movements in some 89er states demonstrate how far removed they have become from values found in their constitution. South Dakota ranks roughly fortieth for per pupil spending but ranks first in federal funding per student.[35] Total educational expenditures demand 2.96 percent of taxpayer income—the lowest in the nation. Even states with a history of neglecting education, like Mississippi, require more of their taxpayers for funding schools.

Idaho has also not been extravagant in funding public education. In 2021, the legislature in Boise sliced $2.5 million from state colleges and universities despite a surplus. A libertarian group, the Idaho Freedom Foundation, wants further cuts.[36]

In 1991, Idaho historian Carlos Schwantes noted that, "Although public funding at all levels of education has been meager throughout Idaho's history, education still accounted for a whopping three-quarters of the state's general budget in the mid-1980s. In addition, Idaho's literacy rate remains one of the highest in the nation."[37]

Parts of this legacy remain. "Idaho continues to dedicate a significant part of its general fund expenditures on K-12 education," said Matthew May, an education policy specialist at Boise State University. "In addition, our annual state survey shows that up to 75% of Idaho residents prioritize spending public revenues on education." Still, in 2022, Idaho ranked twenty-fifth in literacy.[38] This mixed message is typical of 89ers' public education values. South Dakota may have low per-pupil expenditures, but it has one of the highest literacy rates in the nation.

Rights for Women and Separation of Church and State

Even as a territory, the legislature in Cheyenne approved suffrage for women. "The woman suffrage movement rippled across the Northern

Great Plains at a continuous but irregular pace," wrote Lori Ann Lahlum and Molly P. Rozum.[39]

Women gained full suffrage courtesy of just one 89er state constitution: Wyoming. In 1870, Esther Morris of South Pass City was appointed justice of the peace. The following year, two women served on juries in Laramie. Delegate Anthony C. Campbell, a Democrat from Cheyenne, tried to keep suffrage for women out of the constitution on the basis that the public deserved to vote on the issue. The idea received a polite but firm and passionate rejection from his peers.

Idaho followed Wyoming's example shortly after statehood, in 1896. All 89ers states, however, granted suffrage to women before the passage of the Nineteenth Amendment to the US Constitution in 1920.

In North Dakota and Idaho, the delegates set in writing that women could own property. They also protected children from labor exploitation. No child, the delegates in Bismarck wrote, under the age of twelve could work in a mine or factory. In Idaho, the age minimum for such work was fourteen. South Dakota, North Dakota, and Montana constitutions permitted foreign-born men who had begun the naturalization process to vote.

The delegates were particular about separation of church and state, especially concerning education. The Enabling Act of 1889 was partially responsible. It mandated that the state was exclusively responsible for education, "free of all sectarian control." Idaho, burdened with fiery partisanship concerning Mormonism, very nearly banned the reading of the Bible in the classroom. Instead, the delegates declared "no books, papers, tracts or documents of a political, sectarian, or denominational character shall be used or introduced in any schools."[40]

As mentioned, however laudable their efforts to educate all and create a more inclusive society, the delegates excluded many people. Besides suffrage for women, delegates made only nominal efforts toward inclusivity when it came to race or gender. African Americans and especially the Chinese immigrants got short shrift. In Idaho, Mormons were denied the vote. Native Americans, marginalized since territorial time, got no attention at all, other than to exclude them from voting.

How the states dealt with water provides the most demonstrable act regarding the commonweal. Powell went on to speak at the constitutional conventions of Montana and Wyoming. No matter that he skipped the South Dakota and Idaho conventions; delegates on all five 89ers conventions gave ownership of running water to the state.

Wyoming led the way, thanks to Elwood Mead. A former engineering professor at Colorado Agricultural College (now Colorado State University), the thirty year old had been hired as Wyoming's territorial water engineer in 1888. While he stayed in the background during the convention, two of Mead's ideas ended up in the constitution: state-owned water distributed courtesy of a state-issued permit. He also advocated for a state board of control to establish rights and settle water disputes. On this key issue, the state did not trust the free market.

A Pox on the Territorial System

The delegates acted out of experience. Left without any government oversight, corporations had had their way with territorial legislatures. Citizens had witnessed patronage and corruption everywhere: judges, jury systems, railroads, sales of state land, cities, corporations, tribal affairs, distribution of federal land, and bankers. "They had been helpless witnesses to the misdeeds of territorial legislatures who squandered the people's money and otherwise demonstrated their unfitness to govern," wrote John Hicks in his seminal observation *The Constitutions of Northwest States*.[41]

Faced with this "corrupt, inefficient, and archaic political system," Hicks continues, the delegates were also "confronted by the immediate expansion of state activities to meet new and unprecedented conditions."

Reform weighed on the conventioneers' shoulders. The convention, said North Dakota delegate William E. Purcell, had a duty to create a document of which they would be proud. Straying from the path, Purcell said, is an invitation to chicanery. "We not only bring on ourselves the disrespect of our constituents, but the disrespect of every citizen of the United States, because, sir, we have had it hurled in our teeth for 10 years at least, that the territory of Dakota was composed of more schemers than all the rest of the union combined."[42]

Convention delegates simply saw government as a source of certainty. They witnessed how miners in western Washington Territory (now Idaho and parts of Montana) became increasingly exasperated by lackadaisical interest from the territorial capital in Olympia, eight hundred miles away. These men were desperate for local government oversight that validated property rights and ran functioning courts. In fact, the miners were in the thick of it when Congress created Idaho Territory and Montana Territory. In 1863, President Lincoln sent Sidney Edgerton to present-day Montana, which at the time was part of the Idaho territory, to become chief justice. Edgerton quickly recognized the value of the gold being produced in the Bannack area and the need for this region to have its own territorial government. In 1864, Edgerton returned to Washington to advocate for this idea.[43]

It would be a mistake to call any of these delegates proponents of big government or paternalism. They didn't see state intervention in those terms. They merely sought to protect their new state from the excesses of the Gilded Age. This required a three-pronged approach: curb the power of the legislature, bolster the role of the state, and build institutions. In that era, that's what progressive conservatives—those who sought to embrace change by iteration—did.

Putting the Breaks on Lawmakers

When it came to legislatures, territorial profligacy caused the greatest concern.[44] State convention delegates micromanaged when it came to debt. All five constitutions required balanced budgets and limited borrowing. Idaho's constitution stingily prevented any borrowing that exceeded 1.5 percent of the state's total assessed valuation (Article 8). The delegates of most states also limited political subdivisions (counties, cities, and towns) from raising the local mill levy much beyond five mills. Delegates in all five states forbade counties, cities, and towns to build debt obligations beyond 3 to 5 percent of their assessed valuation.

Of the South Dakota constitution, historian Doane Robertson wrote:

> The limitations upon the legislation were exacting. Laws of merely local application were prohibited. No aid could be granted to any person or corporation: no obligation to the state might be compromised. It was the first American Constitution to largely legislate within itself. Rigorous economy was enjoyed by it. Salaries were fixed at the minimum.

The limitations upon taxation for State purposes made it exceedingly difficult to finance the necessary operations of this young state.[45]

As admirable as they may seem, Robinson continued, "the original constitution nearly financially hogtied the state when it came to basic expenditures. . . . The state, as such, could not build a mile of highway or make an internal improvement of any sort."

Hybrid Progressives

Considered collectively, these constitutions balanced progress with tradition. The commercial republic model did not fade. A stout thread of traditional conservatism, particularly in regard to low taxes, and deference to established legal precedent (including protection for corporations) ran through these conventions. Yet delegates embraced a type of hybrid liberalism not found in other state constitutions. Idaho's constitution did not strictly follow conservative lines, for example. As historian Ronald Limbaugh observed when reviewing Dennis Colson's *Idaho Constitution: The Tie That Binds*, in "limiting religious liberty (restrictions on Mormonism), restricting trial by jury, and curtailing private property rights through the use of condemnation power, Idaho's constitution went farther than any previous charter to enhance the power of state government at the expense of the individual."[46]

Delegates were also chary of conservative interpretations of constitutional phrasing. For example, close to the end of the Wyoming constitutional convention, a telling exchange occurred between Republicans Henry G. Hay, an indefatigable entrepreneur, banker, and cattleman, and George C. Smith. On the final reading of a bill, Hay wanted this language inserted: "The provisions of this clause are mandatory unless by express words they are qualified or declared to be otherwise."[47]

In other words, Hays wanted a literalist interpretation of the language. Not so fast, said Hays' fellow conventioneers. Convention president Melvin C. Brown, another Republican, thought it "would be a very dangerous matter to incorporate" the amendment.[48]

Smith was more blunt: "It would demand a strict construction of these matters instead of liberal as intended."[49] Hay withdrew his amendment.

State constitutional scholar Gordon Morris Bakken chose this exchange to point out that "a liberal construction and complete enumeration of rights were prevalent features of the Rocky Mountain bills of rights."[50]

After the Closing Ceremonies

The first half of the 1890s brought hard times. Companies continued to manhandle state legislatures. In 1890, not only did the Northern Pacific own a quarter of North Dakota, but they also paid no income or property taxes.[51] The Dakota wheat boom had died. In fact, from 1890 to 1900, North Dakota only had four good wheat crops.[52]

The Depression of 1893 severely curbed the nation's appetite for commodities. The prices of all major crops tumbled. The largest ranch in Wyoming, the Warren Land and Livestock Company, went into receivership.[53] The Union Pacific and Northern Pacific, the central arteries of commerce for the Great Plains and Northern Rockies, filed for bankruptcy.

Toward the end of the 1890s, things began looking up, however. The Golden Age of Agriculture (1897–1919) would prove the delegates right, at least temporarily, that their heavy bets on commodities would pay off. Sheep ranching boomed and cattle ranching recovered. From 1910–1914, farmers enjoyed a short-lived epoch of parity: equilibrium presided over supply and demand. Grain and cattle prices allowed the producer to purchase necessities without excess borrowing. State legislatures pressed forward with progressive agendas. In 1898, South Dakota, the state that wrote the most conservative constitution of all the 89ers, passed the initiative and referendum process. This allowed citizens to circumvent the legislature when they felt their representatives were not acting in the public interest. Montana followed in South Dakota's footsteps in 1903. Socialists came to minor power in Montana, culminating with the election of a socialist city government in Butte in 1911. Socialist Hall still stands at 1957 Harrison Ave.

Montana granted suffrage to women in 1914. The 1916 Montana legislature welcomed Maggie Smith Hathaway from the Bitterroot and Emma Ingalls of the Flathead as the first two women members.

For twenty years, 89ers, especially the Great Plains states, led the nation with political and economic reform. Few men crusaded for stricter food and product safety than North Dakota Agricultural Experiment station chemist Edwin F. Ladd. He shocked the state with his revelations of toxins and adulterations of food stuffs and household goods sold in North Dakota.[54]

In 1906, North Dakota progressives began tearing down the empire of Alexander McKenzie, the state's seemingly bulletproof Republican kingmaker.[55] Never a man overburdened by scruples, McKenzie was the *capo dei capi* of North Dakota. He had a finger in many financial pies, including banks, real estate, and the Northern Pacific Railroad. Countless politicians counted him as a friend, including the president of the United States, McKinley, who pardoned McKenzie for his role in an Alaskan mining fraud conviction. McKenzie spent three months in jail before the pardon.

The mining fiasco marked the beginning of the end for McKenzie. In 1906, Progressives came into power with Democrat John Burke as governor, rearranging the political landscape and depriving McKenzie of his base. By 1908, McKenzie had to relinquish his position as North Dakota Republican committee chairman. In 1910, Republicans regained power, but McKenzie had to make concessions. In 1915, the Nonpartisan League came to the political fore in North Dakota, further weakening the power of the McKenzie Machine.

After McKenzie died in 1922, the public discovered he had remarried after divorcing his first wife. He kept this second marriage secret. That fact that she and their children lived in New York City helped him maintain this clandestine status.[56]

South Dakota not only continued to curb the power of corporations, but it established a food and drug commission and a telephone commission. The state became known for its liberal divorce laws.[57] In 1917, the South Dakota legislature passed a rural credits law. This permitted farmers to borrow money from the state at below-market rates. Two years later, the legislature created a state-owned coal mine and cement plant.

Then, alas, came 1919. A scorching drought—the worst in Montana's history, according to Michael Malone—followed by severe post-war deflation.[58] The next winter brought no respite. The March 1920 blizzard cost thirty-four North Dakotans their lives.

Powell's commonwealth vision wobbled, mostly due to economics. No legislative action, progressive or conservative, could pull the Great Plains and Northern Rockies out of their holes. The 89er delegates now paid the price for putting their economic eggs in one basket. It would take twenty years and a war to get the region back on its feet. And after WWII, things weren't the same, especially for farming. Those great agricultural resources that Powell warned must never "fall into the hands of the few," did just that.[59]

Powell's vision—so Jeffersonian—faded. "The laborer in the field should be the owner of the field," Powell said. He was speaking of those "who cultivate the soil with their own hands," not "farming corporations and water corporations of the west."[60] Moreover, Powell's minimalist ideal of government intervention disappeared almost completely. He did not want Washington managing forests and watersheds. "I say to the Government: Hands off! Furnish the people with institutions of justice, and let them do the work for themselves."[61]

Instead, the government continued to weave itself into every aspect of agriculture and commodity production, an action that, as we shall see in chapter 2, did not endear itself to the regions' residents.

2

James Beard Smith Todd resists easy description—he's a bit of an enigma. Todd left behind almost nothing for the historian.[1] These papers primarily pertain to army or government business. Notes on personal affairs and opinion are conspicuously absent, including any mention of his wife and six children. Yet his life warrants detailed exploration due to 1) his ability to anticipate a rapidly changing western frontier; 2) his direct participation in that change; and 3) his faith in the democratic electoral process and confidence in the federal government as the arbiter of public good.

Todd had traversed the heart of the rough-hewn West and had all the characteristics of a Manifest Destiny hero. He had survived American Indian battles, lived through combat with the Mexican army, and fought sand fleas at Veracruz. The cholera and dysentery that so often felled the members of the frontier military failed to stop him. Todd had endured frigid nights at Fort Pierre, a fortification located near what is now the center of South Dakota.

Todd was, first and foremost, a federalist. He rejected southern secession. A Lexington-born War Democrat who supported Lincoln and the Union army, he graduated from West Point Military Academy as a captain, thirty-ninth out of a class of fifty. His career followed a path common to a commissioned officer of the era: fighting in the Second Seminole War in Florida; duty in what was then called Indian County (now located in modern-day Oklahoma), and

Figure 2.1. James Beard Smith Todd, photo probably taken between 1866 and 1870. Courtesy of the Library of Congress.

participating in the Mexican-American War of 1846–1848. He had trav-
eled tens of thousands of miles, much of it on horseback, throughout the
continental United States.

He was no ordinary Democrat, however. His cousin, Mary Todd, was
married to the Republicans' rising star and presidential aspirant, Abraham
Lincoln. If Lincoln ascended to the White House, Todd knew he would
have political clout.

Todd was also no rustic. He was in a different social category than the
illiterate Kit Carson or Jim Bridger, the heroes of the western romantic
narrative. Todd reportedly had the first Durham bull and gamecock in
Dakota Territory. The man possessed something close to panache. One
historian said Todd was

> easily at home in all Washington social and political circles. Straight
> back and dignified, with an impressive beard, he combined many of
> the qualities of a Kentucky gentleman with those of a professional West
> Pointer. But carrying his silver headed cane and wearing elegant pale
> gloves, he hardly seemed the type who would choose to settle in the
> bare Dakotas.[2]

Todd foresaw a new era of settlement. In this epoch, there was no such
thing as a land policy free of Washington's control. Such a creature never
existed, of course. Yet the earliest white settlers fancied themselves free
of federal oversight, a fiction that exists to this day. The Jacksonian era
(1825–1855) promoted land acquisition with minimal restrictions, such
as the 1841 Preemption Act. This legislation, which Thomas Donaldson
called "the hope of the land grabber and the land swindler's darling,"
would be eclipsed by the Homestead Act of 1862.[3]

The fur trade was on its last legs, at least in most of the Missouri River
drainage; its demise created a new type of settler. Gone were the trappers
and mountain men. In their stead came speculators and families, all searching for land. The power of the tribes was vanishing, or greatly diminishing.
These tribes not only contributed to the fur trade but their lands were
being, for all practical purposes, stolen.

Todd, anticipating these shifts, became an entrepreneur. His central
business partner? The federal government. On September 16, 1856, while

serving at Ft. Pierre, Todd resigned his army commission. The strategically minded recognized that tribes were an asset beyond a source for buffalo robes and furs. Services took precedence over commodities. Supplying the food and provisions obligated by Congressional treaties was a lucrative undertaking. A single boat churning up the Missouri could carry as much as $30,000 of American Indian annuity goods.[4] More than that, Todd saw the economic potential of Indian land.

Todd joined with fellow West Pointer Daniel Frost of St. Louis (also a Democrat) in a mercantile enterprise. Frost, Todd and Company became the official sutler of the newly created Ft. Randall, located in what is now Gregory County, South Dakota. In addition, they built a headquarters/general store/warehouse in Sioux City, Iowa, a growing trading center. Next came outposts along the James River and within lands owned by the Sioux. The settlers called it the Yankton Triangle.

Left to conjecture is how Todd perceived the collapsing world of the Sioux. No document, either written by him or about him, indicates any particular enmity toward Indigenous people. Perhaps, as Richard Slotkin observed of Kit Carson's largely fictitious genteel projection, Todd had "civilized man's sympathy for the Indians."[5]

Todd had a Calvinist streak laced with moral ambiguity. While he had a reputation for business acumen, gentility and probity, evidence suggests these qualities were reserved for white settlers. He most likely saw the tribes as paternally exploitable. Their world was doomed. He might as well benefit, in a conventional and acceptable way, from their demise.

We can only guess how Todd met the powerful Yankton Sioux chief, The-Man-That-Was-Struck-By-the-Ree, otherwise known as Strikes-the-Ree. The origin of the name remains obscure, although it likely pertains to a battle the Sioux had with a member of the Arikara tribe, who are also known as the *Ree*. The meeting may have happened when Todd was hunkered down at Ft. Pierre during the frigid winter of 1855–1856. The Interior Department, possibly aware of this relationship between Todd and Strikes-the-Ree, approached Todd. They requested his assistance in rekindling Sioux interest in signing a treaty relinquishing title to the Yankton Triangle.

Recognizing the opportunity of a lifetime, Todd agreed. Before

Christmas of 1857, Todd, French-Canadian translators Theophile Bru-
guiere and Charles E. Piccotte ("Shaggy Face," as the Indians called
Piccotte), and a delegation of Sioux travelled nearly 1,300 miles to Washington. They made the first part of their trip—Yankton to Iowa City, the
nearest railroad point—in three lumber wagons. It took a week just for
that leg.[6]

Once they arrived in Washington, negotiations lagged. Weeks turned
into months. Todd used the time to ply his powers of persuasion. He got a
clause inserted into the proposed treaty that gave Frost, Todd and Company the right to purchase 160 acres within this new land at every place
the firm had a trading post.

Todd acquainted himself with Washington political power brokers,
preparing for an even greater prize. The opening of fifteen million acres
of tribal land would increase the chances of Congress granting Dakota
territory status. This meant rafts of federal dollars annually coming into
any new territorial capital. Todd aimed to have Yankton crowned as the
new territory's center.

The Old Versus the New

Todd excelled at capitalizing on these changes—and a good thing, too.
He had competition. His chief rival was the Jacksonian Democrat Samuel
Medary, the last governor of the Minnesota Territory. When in Wash-
ington, Todd had to undo the work of Medary, who had been there five
months earlier, schmoozing with congressmen, importuning them to grant
Dakota territory status with Sioux Falls—not Yankton—as the capital.

Todd worked around the tricky business of looming secession. With it
would come the defection of many Democrats to the Confederate states. In
addition, Andrew Jackson's legacy now haunted every Democrat. Political patronage, a timeless institution, had been elevated to new glories by
Jackson. The Republicans were not immune from the philosophy that to
the victor go the spoils. The logic went that if a Republican was elected
president, he would send his party faithful westward to govern new territories and states. A Democrat, even one as loyal as Todd, wouldn't be
granted a political spoil the size of a speck of sand.

Meanwhile, Strikes-the-Ree returned home depressed. He told his tribe:

> The white men are coming in like maggots. It is useless to resist them. They are many more than we are. We could not hope to stop them. Many of our brave warriors would be killed, our women and children left in sorrow, and still we would not stop them. We must accept it, get the best terms we can get and try to adopt their ways.[7]

⌀

With the mindset that Washington was the benefactor, not the enemy, Todd concentrated on a trio of objectives: acquire official territory status for the unorganized land mass known as Dakota Territory. Secondly, secure Yankton as the capital of that territory; thirdly, get himself elected to represent this new territory in Congress.

The first two goals were intimately linked. For Dakota to acquire territory status yet not have Yankton as the capital would deal Todd a serious financial blow. Moreover, his competition from Minnesota was on the move. As territorial governor, Medary had given his blessing in May 1857 to a charter organized by the St. Paul–based and resolutely Democratic Dakota Land Company, or DLC. They had financial clout and wide-sweeping power "to secure title and sell land east of the Missouri River."[8]

As a counteroffensive, Frost, Todd, and others formed the Upper Missouri Land Company. The firm moved strategically, outmaneuvering their competition. The Dakota Land Company suffered from a pair of handicaps: they were Democrats in an era of ascending Republican power. They also had credibility problems, especially when it came to establishing new political subdivisions. The squatter era or creation of extralegal territory was coming to a close, at least on the Great Plains. The Democrats in general and the DLC specifically appeared blind to this change.

In early 1857, speculators, many connected to the Dakota Land Company, pushed the legislature in St. Paul to recognize "paper cities" in southwestern Minnesota. Once these municipalities had been acknowledged—although not officially incorporated—there were opportunities for land speculators to hawk their wares to gullible immigrants. DLC agents sold lots in gossamer towns like Lake Shetek, Oasis, and Cornwall City.[9]

Then, an incident far removed from pitching patches of prairie soil tore the DLC's plan asunder. In September, the SS Central America, carrying thirty thousand pounds of California gold, sank off the coast of the Carolinas. New York banks, counting on the shipment of gold, wobbled. The public smelled trouble and a run on the banks commenced. The Panic of 1857 was on.

The paper cities of the southeast Minnesota plains fell as quickly as they rose.[10] Bowed but not broken, the Dakota Land Company moved to set up shop along the Big Sioux River, which lay just miles beyond the westward boundary of the Minnesota Territory. If DLC wanted to be the epicenter of all things Dakota, they had to act while Buchanan still had the presidency.

They sent hotelier Alpheus G. Fuller and his companion Byron Smith on a boat down the Big Sioux to claim land for the DLC at Sioux Falls City. They were disheartened to find that the Western Town Lot Company of Dubuque had arrived first.[11]

No matter. Fuller and Smith were apparently confident that they could maneuver the Western Town Company to get what they wanted. They even shared an office. Just to cover their bases, Fuller and Smith established another paper city, Emanija, downstream from Sioux Falls City. In late 1857, the DLC successfully got the Minnesota legislature to create paper or extralegal counties around the city of Sioux Falls: Big Sioux, Midway, and Rock Counties. Only Rock County exists today, and it was not formally organized until 1870. The DLC then held elections in these counties, showing their candidate, Fuller, had been duly elected by the people of Dakota to represent their interests in Congress. In May 1858, the DLC sent Fuller to Washington, asking that he be seated as a delegate from Dakota.[12]

Fuller foundered. Throughout the humid summer of 1858, he plied Congress to no avail. It denied Fuller a delegate's seat; in addition, his mission to get Dakota recognized as a territory—the DLC's real reason for sending him to Washington—collapsed.

His rival from Yankton had sabotaged his plans. First, Todd proved to the Congressional Committee on Elections that the "election" that gave Fuller the plurality of the vote was a sham. Moreover, they had been held in Midway County; not only was this in Minnesota, but it had "paper" written all over it. Midway and its county seat, Medary, ceased to exist during the winter of 1859.

Todd again anticipated changes. He grasped that Republicans like Galusha Grow, a member of the House Committee on the Territories, would likely increase their power.[13] Grow, a tall, no-nonsense partisan from Pittsburgh who had fisticuffs with southern Democrats over slavery, had little patience for extralegal political settlements.

Legitimizing squatter government, Grow declared, "is the most chimerical idea ever heard of, that any number of people may go outside our territories and build up a government outside of the jurisdiction of the United States, and without its authority."[14]

Grow was elected Speaker of the House in 1861.

Why were people like Todd and the DLC so fixated on cities and government? It was more than speculation and being in control of capital spoils, although these factors undoubtedly acted as the driving forces. Todd and his competitors of the era grasped a concept that soon faded from the memory of the residents of the Great Plains and Northern Rockies, who were so focused on commodities and extractives: towns and government were important.

As historian Howard Lamar pointed out, the Dakota Land Company "used the institution of government to *create* property and wealth—an aspect of frontier government of which Todd and Frost were also conscious." Lamar continues, writing that the Dakota Land Company "saw governments as an instrument which could be used to *protect* the individual and his property but control them as well" (Lamar's emphasis).[15]

The DLC, however, continued to stick to old ways. In the fall of 1858, they held another election asking for people's support in gaining territory status. Again, they counted votes from four counties, all of them extraterritorial or unorganized. Fuller returned to Washington, asking for admittance as a delegate. He was thwarted again. This time, however, Fuller did not go home. Instead, he marshaled the muscle of Henry Rice, a Moccasin (a reference to his connection with the fur trade) Democrat and the first person elected US Senator from the newly declared state of Minnesota.

Rice was powerful, but lacked sufficient influence to push legislation that promoted a Democratically controlled Dakota Territory. In February 1859, the then chairman of the Senate Territorial Committee, James

S. Green of Missouri, reported adversely on Rice's bill.[16] The question of slavery was reportedly the problem. However, Green was close friends with Daniel Frost, Todd's partner in crime.

Finally, seeing opportunity slipping away, the DLC changed tactics. They sidelined Fuller and in 1859 sent St. Paul resident Judge Jefferson P. Kidder in his place to Washington.[17] Kidder, a former lieutenant governor of Vermont, supposedly had the right kind of connections in Washington. The Dakotans deferentially called him Governor Kidder. Moreover, because he had been a lawyer and a Democrat in thoroughly Republican Vermont, the DLC might be forgiven for thinking Kidder might be skilled at outmaneuvering the enemy.

He was not. On April 12, 1860, Congress rebuffed Kidder as a candidate for a delegate's seat. He persisted. This time he aped Todd's strategies and latched onto a member of the Committee on Public Lands: Representative Eli Thayer of Massachusetts, an eccentric Republican progressive.

Thayer embraced a romantic self-government notion of squatter establishments. He thought ad hoc towns superior to any government organized under territorial auspices. "What would they do with our protection? And if they do want it, what protection would they get except a government of broken-down politicians, which is what the President of the United States would send them."[18]

This was exactly the kind of attitude appreciated by the DLC. Yet the sand had slipped through the hourglass. Kidder's and Thayer's ambitions came to naught. Lincoln would win the 1860 presidency.

The primary reason for Kidder's defeat, wrote George Washington Kingsbury, was "the persistent opposition of Gen. J.B.S. Todd of the Missouri slope and General Frost of St. Louis, who had large interests at Yankton, and were fearful that if Kidder should be admitted as delegate, the capital would go the Sioux Valley instead of the Missouri."[19]

⁓

On Friday, February 14, 1861, Senator Green reported a bill "to provide a temporary government for the territory of Dakota and to create the office of survey general therein."[20]

What motivated Green, who had formerly rejected the idea of a Dakota Territory, especially one controlled by Republicans, to change his mind remains a conundrum. However puzzling, it paled in comparison to what came next. The question of slavery, which so inflamed discussions on new territories and states, became a merely minor point of debate. The Territory of Dakota, along with Nevada and Colorado, came into existence free of acrimony over the subject of popular sovereignty. The action stunned abolition advocates. James G. Blaine of Maine called it "one of the singular contradictions in the political history of this country."[21]

In other words, for the first time ever, equality between the races was taken for granted, at least in theory.

After the bill reached the Senate floor, it passed on February 26. It passed the House on March 1 and received the approval of President Buchanan on March 2, less than forty-eight hours before his term as president expired. It took eleven days for the news to reach the new Dakotas.

Todd had done it. He had outlasted and outfoxed all to get a new territory, regardless of their political affiliation. Then he peaked. While he continued to be in politics, Todd's influence waned, but not before getting Yankton named territorial capital. He also got to represent the territory in Congress, but only after once again proving voting fraud. However, he lost more elections than he won. Moreover, after fits and starts, land fever began to infect the Dakota Territory. Todd showed little interest. No documents suggest that Todd invested or speculated in farmland outside of holdings surrounding Yankton.

Territory status granted, the shape and size of Dakota Territory began morphing. In 1863, Idaho Territory expanded, claiming nearly all of Wyoming and Montana as part of a region larger than Texas. It was a short-lived hegemony—fourteen months. In the interim, territorial politicians had to deal with gold-crazed miners, furious Indigenous Americans (Bannock and Nez Perce) who used martial means to defend their homelands, and vigilantism. Tragically, 1863 was also the year when the Nez Perce tribe, realizing they were outnumbered, conceded to a drastic reduction of their reservation from 7.5 million acres to 750,000 acres.[22]

Congress granted Montana its own territory status in 1864 but also gave what constitutes most of Wyoming back to Dakota. Then in 1868, Congress granted Wyoming territory status. The Dakota Territorial legislature, without a dissenting vote, said, in essence: *you can have it*. As Wyoming historian T.A. Larson said, "Rarely in history has a government given up control over so large an area [nearly 98,000 square miles] with such unanimous approval."[23]

Seeds of Conflict

A new type of leader replaced Todd. He—and the leaders were always men—was equally ambitious, but willing to see the government as not only a business partner but worthy of manipulation. This shift may seem banal, a standard trope of frontier fiction or 1940s Western movies about the greedy land baron. But, in fact, the advent of the government-appointed miscreant with an appetite for graft created permanent ill will between Washington and the West.

There is little evidence to suggest that there was a widespread belief that active federal government was evil. White settlers sought government assistance. The idea was in circulation, however. The credo that the government is best when it governs least, commonly attributed to Henry Thoreau, actually came from the vitriolic pen of John O'Sullivan. In the first edition of the *United States Magazine and Democratic Review*, published in 1837, O'Sullivan declared: "A strong and active democratic government, in the common sense of the term, is an evil, differing only in degree and mode of operation, and not in nature, from a strong despotism."[24]

Moreover, three historic acts—all signed in 1862—benefitted the westward movement: The Homestead Act, The Morrill Land-Grants Act (established land grant universities), and the first Pacific Railroad Act. The latter mostly profited the railroads; but without these laws, settlement of the Great Plains and Northern Rockies would have developed much differently.

These were monumental pieces of legislation for the 89ers; all gifts, as it were, from the federal government. They acted as critical economic engines, giving away millions of acres of land to settlers and speculators—not to mention setting aside land (eleven million acres) to support new universities.[25] Yet natural resources development, from oil drilling to mining to grazing, made up the majority of rents from these lands. This made them vulnerable to boom-and-bust cycles.

Lastly, the residents of Dakota Territory in 1861 were fervid Unionists. Thus, despite misgivings about Washington, too much blood had (and was continuing to be) spilled in preventing secession for Dakota residents to harbor deep-seated enmity toward the federal government. When petitioning to join the Union, territories bent over backwards to be accepted. They acknowledged the support of the federal government as critical. They would do the same some twenty-eight years later when they petitioned for statehood status.

Two developments created conflict. One involved the government attitude toward land. The federal government eventually granted millions of acres in homesteads (270 million acres total) but simultaneously began regulating and limiting access to natural resources.[26] This inconsistency spawned anxiety. The Mining Law of 1866, for example, was a measure of singular generosity. It declared lands, both surveyed and unsurveyed, were free and open to exploration and occupation by all US citizens. Yet, as legal scholar John Lacy noted, there were those who felt any federal mining law "was an infringement upon established rights."[27]

Patronage spawned the second thorny issue. Under the terms of their organic acts, the sitting US president chose a territory's governor, secretary, head of the Indian Office, chief justices, associate judges, US attorney, and US marshal. But there was a galaxy of more picayune positions: postmaster, treasury department collectors and assessors, surveyor general, mine inspectors, and land office staff.

Problems immediately arose with the Indian Office, the precursor to the Bureau of Indian Affairs. The office turned out to be the ideal position for graft. Lucrative for the individual—and those connected to him—but bad for a working relationship with the federal government. In fact, the combination of corruption and patronage at the Indian Office created a no-win situation for Washington.

The Indian trade did not enjoy a wholesome reputation. Indian agents "stole themselves rich" was the common saying. General George Crook declared that Indian agents caused "ninety-nine-hundredths" of all tribal woes. [28]

"There is no more malodorous chapter in the history of the frontier than that of dealings involving supplies for Indian Agencies," wrote Mark Brown. "Even honest men were harassed and subjected to libelous statements and in the end the Indian was the loser."[29]

It's difficult to declare what patronage recipient was guilty of the greatest venality, but Walter Burleigh didn't do too badly for himself. Burleigh was the ultimate hustler, peripatetic speculator, and government contract opportunist. Known for his charm, he was both a physician and attorney. Burleigh used his lawyerly skills, assets, and insider political knowledge to his advantage during—and after he left—the Indian agency.

Appointed by President Lincoln as Indian agent in Yankton, Dakota Territory, in 1861, Burleigh began lining his pockets immediately. The 1866 Report of the Commissioner of Indian Affairs spells out, in detail, the degree of Burleigh's venality.[30] He put his father-in-law, Andrew J. Faulk, on the payroll at the Yankton Sioux agency. Burleigh signed a voucher for building a schoolhouse, paying carpenters $1.75 per day. Inspectors could find no school house. Burleigh paid and billed the government for a grain mill that barely functioned, if at all. He put his son, Timothy B. Burleigh, on the payroll at $40.00 per month as a laborer. Timothy was 13 years old.

Burleigh made employers and contractors sign blank vouchers so Burleigh could pad the expenses. For example, he bought corn and potatoes at $.25/bushel, then billed the government $1 dollar per bushel. He stole logs and lumber, bringing them to his own farm.

In short, Burleigh looked after himself and family, not the tribes. The *Yankton Press* estimated that in nine years as Indian agent, Burleigh fleeced the government of $200,000.[31] Investigated by numerous powers, including then governor Newton Edmunds, Burleigh evaded charges. When Lincoln died, Burleigh convinced his old friend Andrew Johnson, who just happened to be the new president, to give Newton the boot as governor and replace him with—naturally—Burleigh's father-in-law. Edmunds was eventually dismissed on corruption charges.

In what was described as possibly the largest real estate transaction of the time, Burleigh sold 2,500 acres of land in Bon Homme County to Hutterites in 1874.[32]

After he left the agency, he beat JBS Todd in an election for territorial representative. He did so by buying the controlling interest in the region's largest newspaper, the *Dakotian,* thus assuring favorable coverage. After defeating Todd, he served two terms in Washington and then lost when he ran for a third term.

For a spell he freighted supplies for the Dakota Southern and Northern Pacific Railroad on his steamboat, the Miner. Burleigh acquired the contract to grade fifty miles of new Northern Pacific railroad bed east of Bismarck. Then, using his knowledge of where the railroad would cross the river, he set up a town: Burleighton. The Northern Pacific changed the site of the bridge, costing Burleigh plenty.

Congress again beckoned in 1874, but Burleigh—running as a Democrat, no less, withdrew after voting improprieties came to light. Burleigh moved to Iowa to farm but quit and moved to Bismarck. Dissatisfied with his opportunities, he shuttled west to Miles City, Montana, to practice law. He tried politics but with little success. However, he was elected to the Montana constitutional convention of 1889. He moved back to South Dakota to serve a term in the state senate. He died in 1896.

Curiously, for all his entrepreneurial skills and ability to enrich himself, Burleigh didn't leave much of a legacy, except for the North Dakota county that serves as his namesake. None of his three children made much of an impression on the new state of South Dakota. Only one child, Andrew Faulk Burleigh, lived to middle age. He is buried in Pennsylvania.

In some ways, Burleigh was small beer when it came to Indian Office contracts. Pennsylvanian J. W. Bosler—namesake of the unincorporated town of Bosler, Wyoming—carried out various contracts supplying goods and services to the territories. He specialized in cattle. In 1870, he entered into a contract for $756,700 to deliver live cattle to various territorial Indian agents. But he testified to Congress that he subcontracted the job, skimming roughly $117,510 (about $2.5 million today) off the top.[33]

Consider the economic plight of the average working man in the Dakotas, circa 1870. Nobody had any cash. Many paid for goods by trading grain and eggs. In 1870, a skilled farmhand was making about $25/month.[34] Many settlers saw having an Indian agent unafraid to dole out cash, contracts, and hush money as not only advantageous but worthy of protection.

Juries refused to convict corrupt agents. The federal government became a prying and unwanted element. Alexander Johnson, a federal agent inspecting territorial Indian agencies—including Burleigh's—failed to find anyone who would speak ill of the Yankton Sioux Indian representative. The one Johnson did find, Jacob Rufner, "refused to be sworn, unless I first explained to him what I desired. 'I want to what know what you want,' he said. Because if it's any slur on Dr. Burleigh, I ain't going to have anything to do with it. If I do he will fix it so I'll never get anything in the world and he will drive me out of the country."[35]

On a fundamental level the literature of the American West documents, beyond all doubt, the hostility whites felt toward tribes. In an 1868 column in the biweekly Wyoming territorial newspaper *The Sweetwater Mines*, the author (probably either one of the two publishers, J. Edward Warren or C. J. Hazard) wrote:

> Kill off the Indians. In order to do this let every military man be sent east of the Mississippi river; let the Indian agents—every one of them—be sent east of the Ohio river; let the government offer $50 in gold for every red skin scalp between the Mississippi River and the Pacific, and then wait one year and see how many Indian troubles the future develops.[36]

Ten years later, little had changed. Army Brigadier General John Pope, in an article published in the 1878 *Army and Navy Journal,* wrote that the "rough-and-ready settlers usually look upon redskins as vermin that ought to be exterminated." Pope, who tangled with both the Apache and Sioux, evinced anguish for the treatment of tribes, "the disgusting story of Indian gents, traders, gamblers, whiskey sellers, with their rings within rings, for abusing, cheating, and robbing both the Government and the Indians."[37]

The companies and individuals with federal supply contracts, therefore, were delivering goods and services to a people they held in contempt. This dynamic alone doomed any hope of good relations with Washington, never mind the tribes.

In addition, perception grew of a federal government standing in the way of wealth creation. Settlers bitterly opposed plans to preserve Indian lands. General T. Sherman forbade gold exploration in the Black Hills, citing the fact that it was official Indian territory. Miners went anyway. Pioneers didn't like that the army had shut down the Bozeman Trail after losing Red Cloud's War. Eventually, the army gave up and in 1876 permitted travelers.

The ultimate irony of this belief was the federal government's willingness to abrogate Indian land treaties in favor of the new settlers. From the 1809 Treaty of Fort Wayne to the 1868 Treaty of Fort Laramie, the US government unilaterally annexed native land theoretically protected by treaty.

The patronage problem wasn't only relegated to the Indian Office, however. Despite the remuneration some appointees doled out to loyalists, the territories eventually saw patronage appointments—especially governors—with the same disdain as southerners saw with judges appointed under federal Reconstruction.

Underpayment may partially explain appointees' less-than-stellar behavior. Governors' salaries of the era rarely exceeded $2,500 per annum, which was half of what congressmen of the time were earning. Prompt payment for their services proved the exception. In 1864, Governor Sidney Edgerton paid the expenses of Montana's territorial government using his personal funds for more than a year. "The first mistake I made was in accepting the position . . . and I am left pecuniarily in a very embarrassing condition," wrote Dakota governor John Pennington to President Rutherford B. Hayes in 1878.[38]

Federally appointed territorial judges were another sore spot. In addition to their duties on the supreme court, the justices also presided over one territorial judicial district. This meant that a defendant or plaintiff, expecting their case to be heard by a new judge for the first time, could not appeal a lower court ruling before a territorial supreme court; one of those men behind the bench had already heard the case at a district court level and had affirmed or denied the decision.

One can hear indignation as John A. Riner, a Laramie county delegate to the Wyoming constitutional convention, goes after this system:

> One of the greatest evils of a territorial government, and it is considered by men who take the opposite view, that one of the great evils, is that our people are denied of their right of appeal. They are deprived of a right which they are entitled to have so as to have their property rights protected, to have their rights retried by three impartial men in an independent Supreme Court.[39]

Not all judges were cads. Historian Kermit Hall said that despite partisan considerations and occasional corruption or ineptitude, most territorial judges could, at worst, be guilty of mediocrity. Besides, most stayed four years or less.[40]

But bad appointments made up for all those with rectitude. Of the ten territorial Dakota governors appointed by various presidents, half were dismissed due to some impropriety or, worse, a perceived act of disloyalty toward the sitting president.

Some appointees were out-and-out thieves. In Idaho, territorial secretary Horace C. Gilson embezzled $41,000—the entire territorial treasury—and decamped to Hong Kong. Idaho governor Caleb Lyon embezzled $46,418 of federal money that was dedicated to Nez Perce.[41]

The authorities never apprehended Gilson; Lyon was never charged for his theft. After Lyon served his term as governor, he returned to his home on Staten Island. There, he purchased a ducal home referred to as Ross Castle, constructed to replicate Windsor Castle. Considering that Lyon had liberated the modern equivalent of about $1 million from the US government, it's not hard to imagine where he found the funds to buy the home.

Animosity against federally appointed governors reached a new high with the reign (1880–1884) of Nehemiah G. Ordway of Dakota Territory. Ordway moved the capital from Yankton to Pierre. He also fought statehood, declaring that Washington knew better than the residents of the territory when to cut the cord. In 1884, a grand jury indicted Ordway for corrupt practices in office. President Chester A. Arthur removed him from office.

Grievances Over Land

The pioneer relied on railroads and then, realizing the power and monopoly the federal government granted rail-owning corporations, developed a love/hate relationship with the silver rails. In 1871, the federal government granted the last railroad grant, a short eleven years after they had first been issued. Attempts at land reform weren't far behind.

The following year, President Ulysses S. Grant created Yellowstone Park, taking 2.2 million acres out of the public domain. In fact, when Grant toured the west in 1875, he observed "that existing laws regulating the disposition of public lands, timber . . . and probably the mining laws themselves are very defective and should be carefully amended and at an early date." [42] Many on the land had little interest in reform, unless it benefited them.

Congress couldn't seem to pass workable and prudent legislation that encouraged legal settlement. "The present system of laws seems to invite fraud. You cannot turn to a single state paper or public document . . . but what statements of fraud in connection with the disposition of the public lands are found," said Thomas Donaldson, in his epic tome on the history of public land.

Congress kept promoting land acquisition on the cheap, encouraging an extraction economy: the 1873 Timber Culture Act gave homesteads an additional 160 acres if they planted part of the land with trees. The Desert Land Act of 1877 granted individuals 640 acres if they reclaimed and irrigated semiarid public land. The Timber and Stone Act of 1878 permitted sale of western timberlands.

We think of these deals as giveaways of the past—not so. You can still file for land under the Desert Land Act, although the acreage has been decreased to 320 acres. In the 1950s, a curious agricultural economist with the United States Department of Agriculture (USDA) began looking into the Desert Land Act. Karl Landstrom discovered that in 1954, the Bureau of Land Management (BLM) had 4,192 applications pending decisions. The price: $.25/acre; add a dollar per acre when the applicant fulfills the obligations for the patent.[43] Idaho had, at the time, nearly 80,000 acres classified as suitable for disposition.

According to the BLM, as of 2022, it has thirty-five applications under the Desert Land Act of 1877.[44]

In the later part of the nineteenth century, however, there was a problem. Lands were falling into the wrong hands; that is, speculators, not homesteaders. Speculators had cash. Homesteaders, who brought land largely on payments, had little. Cash won. "Cash sales are now more than three-fourths of the revenue received from the sales or disputation of public lands," wrote Donaldson, who called cash sales "a vicious disposition." "It is the highest national importance that not another acre of public lands shall be sold outright for cash, warrants, or scrip," Donaldson declared.[45]

Swindle plagued legislation. One inspector estimated that 90 percent of all entries under the Timber Culture Act "are made purely and simply for speculation."[46] In fact, such blatant fraud accompanied these acts that they were dismantled or substantially reformed in the early 1890s.

Congress amended these laws at a glacial pace. American West historian Harold Dunham observed in *Government Handout*, "One of the most astonishing facts in public land history arises from the fact that instead of endeavoring to meet these problems the government persistently neglected them. It would be difficult to over emphasize the significance of the government's ignorance of its treasures even while it was disposing of them."[47]

The government didn't totally ignore their responsibilities. In the 1880s, it stepped up its oversight. In 1882, Secretary of Interior Henry M. Teller sued—and won—a Wyoming rancher, Alexander H. Swan, for illegally fencing public land. More suits followed. In 1884, Thomas W. Jaycox, a special agent for the Interior Department in Dakota Territory who would later go on to be chief water engineer for the state of Colorado, wrote, "In my opinion, not more than 30 percent of the land in this district entered under the provisions of the preemption and homestead laws is occupied by actual settlers."[48]

In 1885, the Land Office, a branch of the Department of the Interior, announced that it had recovered 31,824,481 acres of land gained under fraudulent auspices. Roughly three-quarters of these acres came from railroad companies that had failed to complete sections of track as promised.[49]

Also in 1885, William Andrew Jackson Sparks, Commissioner of the General Land Office, closed all public land entry—except standard homestead entries—as well as entries made under the Timber Culture Act and the Desert Land Act. [50]This meant you couldn't buy a homestead entry with cash outright or rely on the 1841 Preemption Act. You had to purchase the entry in yearly payments then prove up.

Western representatives fought restrictions. A *New York Times* article declared: "There are men in Congress who sympathize with those who have defied the laws. Whenever the land office becomes a subject of debate he (the Land Commissioner) is roundly denounced by western legislators who have themselves acquired large tracts of public lands or have powerful constituents engaged in the land business."[51]

Government Becomes the Official Whipping Boy

Partisan politics hardened views toward Washington. The federal government gained enmity from the hinterlands; not only had Washington fought 89er territory status but statehood as well. If, in 1880, one could dial back time and interview a Dakota settler and ask him or her their primary concern, they'd likely say, "Them damned bureaucrats in Washington and them damned Democrats in particular."

"Congress blocked statehood for territories of the far northwest because the Democrats, who at various times control either the Senate or the House, did not want to admit states that appeared likely to vote Republican," wrote Idaho historian Carlos Schwantes.[52]

Ironically, it was a combined effort of two presidents, one Democrat, one Republican, that enabled the transitions from territory to state. Grover Cleveland, the outgoing Democratic president, signed the Omnibus Enabling Act on February 22, 1889. This got the ball rolling for the Dakotas to split into two separate states. It also laid out the welcome mat for Washington Territory and Montana to enter statehood. Wyoming and Idaho, seeing their neighboring states close to grasping the golden ring, quickly convened constitutional conventions. They rode into statehood on the coattails of their neighbors. Republican president Benjamin Harrison admitted all five into the Union as states.

Newly minted constitutions in hand, these states had expectations of at least modest prosperity. But they had walked into a trap—they continued to put all their economic eggs in one basket: commodities. This made them susceptible not only to market volatility but to government policies affecting supply and demand. The 1893 Depression wreaked havoc on commodities. The federal government—the Democrats—were, of course, to blame.

Statehood for the Northern Rockies and Great Plains states dovetailed with a new era in conservation. Two pieces of federal legislation: the Omnibus Land Reform Bill of 1891 (or the Land Revision Act) and the Organic Act of 1897, both seminal bills in public land history, curbed the power of the land speculator.

The Land Revision Act repealed the Timber Culture Act of 1873 and (finally) the Preemption Act of 1841; it tightened up requirements for the Desert Land Act of 1877. It also gave a president the power to set aside unclaimed parcels of forest still in the public domain.

The Organic Act of 1897 included much of the same language of an earlier failed piece of legislation: the McRae Bill of 1893. Introduced by Congressman Thomas C. McRae, a Democrat from Arkansas, it focused on halting timber pilferage from the Forest Reserves.

Delegates for western states ripped into the bill, predicting dire consequences and portraying it not as a conservation measure, but one that promoted the destruction and monopolization of timber resources. Their spin was that it would strip the lowly homesteader and ma-and-pa sawmill

Figure 2.2. The Depression of 1893, caused by commodity speculators and a bubble in railroad stocks, was blamed on the Democratic Party. Courtesy of the HathiTrust Digital Library.

of timber. What they were objecting to, really, was that timber was no longer free. Logging now required a permit from the federal government.

Former US representative and Sheridan resident Asa Coffeen of Wyoming fulminated that "the bill, while it purports to protect timber, is calculated in every provision from title to terminus to destroy our timber through the operations of corporations and mill owners who are authorized to buy the timber under the provisions of the bill."[53]

In an action that would be repeated by 89ers politicians for the next hundred years (strike conservation regulations and restrict the agencies that enforce them), Coffeen went as far as to offer an amendment abolishing all reserves. The irony is that Sheridan now houses the headquarters to the 1.1-million-acre Bighorn National Forest, a body of land central to Sheridan's cultural and economic identity. In 2016, a study showed that the Bighorn National Forest created over $27 million in annual income for the surrounding towns.[54]

Charles S. Hartman, Democratic representative from Montana, pronounced the McRae bill "infamous in the extreme." "It means," he said, "that thousands of miners all over our western country will be precluded from obtaining the timber necessary for the shafts in mines which they are working. It means too that settlers engaged in agriculture, in stock raising, and in various other industries pursued in the West will be compelled either to violate the laws of the United States and become timber thieves or else freeze to death."[55]

Not to be outdone in summarizing catastrophe, *The Deadwood Pioneer Times* on February 25, 1897, wrote: *"It means, briefly interrupted and summed up, a death blow to our country."*[56]

The curbs on federal land exploitation continued. In 1906, Teddy Roosevelt doubled the size of the Forest Reserve and transferred it from the Department of the Interior to the Department of Agriculture. He canned the name Forest Reserve. In its stead rose the US Forest Service. Sheep operations found themselves having to pay five to eight cents per sheep to graze on federal land. Cattlemen, twenty to thirty-five cents per head.[57] Neither type of stockman had any love for this new imposition.[58]

The same year, President Theodore Roosevelt withdrew more than sixty-four million acres of land from coal entry. Roosevelt had no hesitation using the Antiquities Act, also enacted in 1906. Under the Antiquities Act, Roosevelt issued his first proclamation to protect Devil's Tower in Wyoming.

Here's the irony: despite these withdrawals and regulations, the Great Plains and Northern Rockies thrived from 1897 to 1919. The prosperity came about courtesy of weather, war, and the whims of Washington. Often called the golden age of American agriculture, this twenty-two-year epoch of amplitude included the Great Plains and Northern Rockies. By 1910, agriculture surpassed mining as Montana's leading source of revenue.[59] The parity—the purchasing power of the farmer—of this era has never been exceeded.

This economic equality would have flopped without support from the federal government. The sagging sheep business received a godsend in the form of a seemingly innocuous piece of legislation called the Dingley Tariff, named after Representative Nelson Dingley Jr. of Maine. The legislation, which doubled the tariff on wool, had the support of Senator Francis Warren of Wyoming, a senator known as the greatest shepherd since Abraham. The Dingley Act of 1897 kicked off a second boom in sheep. In 1890, there were 712,500 sheep in Wyoming. By 1900, the number of sheep in Wyoming exceeded five million.

The other form of federal support came in the form of reclamation projects. These began even before the Golden Age of Agriculture. The Carey Act of 1894 (also known as the Federal Desert Land Act) permitted companies to build irrigation systems in the western states, including the Dakotas, Wyoming, Montana, and Idaho. Idaho and Wyoming most notably benefited from this legislation. By 1903, new land entries in Montana, filed under the Carey Act, had reached 2,300.

The feds had already opened the floodgates. On June 17, 1902, Roosevelt signed into law the National Reclamation Act—or Newlands Reclamation Act. North Dakota senator Henry Hansborough and Nevada representative Francis R. Newland convinced Congress to designate reclamation projects to sixteen states, including Idaho, Montana, North Dakota, South Dakota, and Wyoming. No farm larger than 160 acres could receive irrigation water under this legislation.

Congress originally gave farmers obtaining water under the Newlands Act ten years to repay the federal government for construction costs. It proved unworkable. So, Congress extended the loan to twenty years, then forty years. Then "ability to pay" became the standard. Today, only 10 percent of the revenue that streams into the Reclamation Fund comes from the water users themselves. More than three-quarters of the money comes from revenues from offshore drilling on public waters. Reclamation stands as one of Washington's greatest gifts to the western farmer. Congressional Research Office historian Charles Stern reported that "reclamation estimated that the total replacement value of its water resource facilities was $99 billion as of 2015."[60]

From 1909 onward, the federal government continued to pump money into the rural west. The Enlarged Homestead Act passed in 1909, doubling the allotted acreage from 160 to 320 acres. The national Stock-Raising Homestead Act passed in 1916 and granted an additional 640 acres for ranching purposes. The number of farms in North Dakota peaked during this period.[61]

The government got into the banking business. The 1916 Federal Farm Loan Act addressed the demand for credit for land and farm machinery loans on reasonable terms. The legislation created the Cooperative Farm Credit System of twelve banks, which were run as cooperatives owned by their borrowers. The Farm Credit System now has seventy banks, dedicated to serving rural communities. The legislation of the era also included: the Warehouse Act of 1916, the Smith Lever Act of 1914, the Grain Standards Act 1916, the Rural Roads Act 1916, and the Smith Hughes Act of 1917, the last of which advocated for vocational education in agricultural and industrial trades.

All this effort had a single purpose: to encourage commodity production. World War I boosted the income of anyone working in natural resources. Commodity indices rose, particularly grains and wool, two products favored by the Great Plains and Northern Rockies.

The Killer Twenty Years: The Government Giveth but What's the Use?

The golden age turned to lead. The year 1920 was arguably the most deflationary year in US economic history. Matters did not improve much as the years passed. The 89er states, dependent on commodities, felt the trend most acutely. In 1924, Wisconsin governor Robert LaFollette, quoting the USDA, stated that 62 percent of the farmers in Montana were bankrupt. In Wyoming it was 50 percent. In North and South Dakota, roughly 40 percent of the farmers faced bankruptcy.[62]

The depression lifted momentarily and then deepened after the stock market crash of 1929. "In 1933, the low year, the per capita personal income in the United States was $375, but in North Dakota it was only $145," wrote historian Elwyn Robinson.[63] A 900-pound low-grade (canner) cow could be had for $9.00. A 350-pound hog went for $2.00. Farmers sold eggs at $.04/dozen.[64]

These prices, of course, led to farmer bankruptcy and evictions. The Farmers' Holiday Association did not take farm repossession lightly.

Wyoming lost one-third of its population in the 1930s.[65] It took decades for the state to recover. WWII offered a brief economic respite but then the state stagnated, especially during the 1960s.

For example, during an interview in 2000 with former governor Stanley Hathaway, he said that one day in 1968, the state treasurer came to him saying there were only eighty dollars in Wyoming's general fund.[66] In 1969, the *Wall Street Journal* ran an article titled, "The Lonesome Land: Wyoming is Emptier and Its Economy Lags as People Move Away."[67] Wyoming's representatives in Washington protested the article, commenting in the Congressional Record that Wyoming was "the land of opportunity."[68]

Wyoming has historically had an adversarial relationship with Washington. But in 1932, all of Wyoming's 23 counties, save one—Big Horn County, ironically dependent on agriculture—voted for Franklin D. Roosevelt. In fact, out of 242 counties in the five states of the former 1861 Dakota Territory, only four failed to vote for Roosevelt. North Dakota gave him a clean sweep.

With Roosevelt's election came another raft of federal aid, dwarfing the money distributed by legislation not twenty years prior. Laws providing aid included the Agricultural Adjustment Act of 1933 (first farm bill); the Farm Credit Act of 1933, which created the Farm Credit Administration; $1 billion dollars in loans from the Farm Credit Administration, which refinanced more than 20 percent of all farm mortgages and helped millions of rural Americans fight off foreclosure; the Emergency Farm Mortgage

Figure 2.3. Farmers' Holiday Association, based out of Iowa, preventing an eviction in Cass County, North Dakota, 1934. Courtesy of the State Historical Society of North Dakota.

Act of 1933; the Commodity Credit Corporation; the Farm Security Administration; and the Rural Electrification Act, which brought power to farms and rural areas.

Some farmers remained unimpressed. Ann Marie Low's *Dust Bowl Diary* provides testimony of her family's exasperation with Washington. Low expressed particular anger at the federal government's manipulation of farmers in an attempt to have them sell land for Arrowwood Wildlife Refuge, located in Pingree, North Dakota. She left the farm but kept in touch with former neighbors, including one she simply calls Grover. "Many years later Grover spoke to me about the years he had lost when the government took, at a fraction of its value, everything he had spent his youth working for."[69]

"Government" increasingly carried negative connotations: begrudging gratitude (nobody likes taking relief) at best and outright resentment at worst. This umbrage was not solely directed at the bureaucrats on the federal payroll. After all, it was "experts" including some in state government that told them that rain follows the plow. The Dust Bowl was largely preventable. Homesteaders plowed up millions of acres of virgin prairie, often in low-moisture areas, on the advice of Samuel Aughey, a geologist at the University of Nebraska, and his huckster-in-chief, journalist and amateur scientist Charles Dana Wilber. The latter, a privileged educated easterner, was a spokesman for the idea that *rain follows the plow.*

A particularly disturbing chapter of government arrogance took place in Wyoming.[70] Beginning in 1927, staff working for John D. Rockefeller Jr.—in collusion with Yellowstone National Park superintendent Horace Albright—sweet-talked and lowballed dozens of ranchers to sell their holdings to the Snake River Land Company, a secretive shell company controlled by Rockefeller. According to environmental historian Laurie Hinck, in 1927, Rockefeller's political fixer Kenneth Chorley "went directly to the Secretary of Agriculture to explain the entire project and ask for their cooperation."[71]

The goal was to move Jackson Hole away from its marginal ranching roots and replace it with high-end tourism and recreation. Snake River Land Company bought 35,000 acres, a significant amount in a county that contains only 3 percent privately owned land. The holdings eventually became an addition to Grand Teton National Park.

The Second World War and a Deepening Animosity

The Second World War cemented the relationship between commodity producers and Washington. It also set the stage for a new, vitriolic anti-government stance that would explode in the late 1970s.

From 1941 to 1945, the government viewed the Great Plains and Northern Rockies solely through the lens of extracting its natural resources, a renewed policy of internal economic colonialism. After the war commodities generally prospered, especially agricultural commodities. The Marshall Plan encouraged crop export. Total net farm income—after production expenses were taken out—rose from $3.5 billion in 1940 to $15.4 billion in 1947. The Korean War then boosted commodity prices. In 1954, Congress created a Food for Peace program that exported US farm goods to needy countries.[72]

Yet from 1950 to 1970, half the farms in the United States vanished.[73] The number of people involved in agriculture also halved, from twenty million to ten million. By 1968, South Dakota was losing one thousand farms per year.[74] The federal government was not a passive bystander in this development. Neither were think tanks that aimed to influence federal policy. A 1962 report from the Committee of Economic Development (CED), a nonpartisan group made up of two hundred corporate executives and economists, recommended reducing the farm population. They suggested cutting it by one-third in five years.[75]

Under President Richard Nixon, a contrarian, Earl Butz, took the helm at the Department of Agriculture. Butz suppressed efforts to raise price supports. Instead, under the Agriculture and Consumer Protection Act of 1973, the free market largely took over.[76]

Fortuitously, this coincided with a world food shortage. Exports soared. From 1972 to 1974, wheat prices nearly trebled, according to USDA statistics.[77] Butz offered his famous words of encouragement: "plant fence row to fence row" and "get big or get out."

Ironically, it was Butz who ultimately poisoned the relationship between agriculture and the federal government. Larger farms, especially those with minimal debt, benefitted from the policies of the Butz administration. Smaller operations did not. By the late 1970s, thousands of farmers were financially in trouble. They put the onus squarely on Washington. In 1978 and 1979, they drove tractors to Washington, exasperating commuters and doing $1 million worth of damage to the National Mall. Roughly three thousand producers participated in the 1979 Tractorcade event.

Economic matters did not improve, chiefly courtesy of the Federal Reserve, which in 1979 declared war on inflation. Interest rates of 21 percent, surplus grain production (encouraged by various farm bills), and $120/barrel oil added to the anger against Washington. In December 1979, President Jimmy Carter imposed an embargo on US grain sales to the Soviet Union in retaliation for their invasion of Afghanistan. In four years, wheat, corn, and soybean exports fell from twenty-six million to sixteen million metric tons.[78]

Farmers continued to borrow heavily. It ended up burying them. In 1962, the total farm debt was $60 billion; by 1983, it was $216 billion. In 1985, the Federal Farm Credit System recorded a $2.7 billion loss, at the time the largest one-year loss of any US financial institution.[79]

"Losing a farm was not a minor embarrassment. It was a deeply personal loss, enmeshed with meaning. It was also a very public humiliation," wrote Pamela Riney-Kehrberg in her 2022 book on the Iowa farm crisis of the 1980s. "Shame is not a brief, passing emotion."[80]

Riney-Kehrberg also documents, in heartbreaking detail, the farmers' collective belief that the federal government had a duty to rectify the situation. One farm wife from Story County, Iowa, upon hearing that Governor Terry Branstad was going to Washington, pleaded to have him take a copy of the *Des Moines Register* on his trip. The newspaper had covered—and photographed—the bankruptcy and subsequent sale of the woman's farm. "Can you please take these pictures to President Reagan?" she asked.[81]

Yet three months after the sale of her farm, Reagan, speaking on March 25, 1985, to the Gridiron Club, commented on his recent veto of emergency farm credit legislation. "I think we should keep the grain and export the farmers," he said. He refused to apologize for his remark.

The 1980s farm crisis reignited a hostility still lingering from the Depression. Many of the fundamentals were the same: overproduction, low prices, unbearable debt, and a government slow to respond to farmer's needs. Yet by the 1980s producers were fed up with the growing cadre of agricultural authorities telling them what to do. As Catherine Stock phrased it, the "intellectual imperialism of academics and other 'experts' who think they know better than farmers what is best for the land and the communities of the northern plains."[82]

Stock offered the example of the Buffalo Commons: a theory that a portion of the Northern Great Plains was unfit for agriculture; as such, it needed to be turned into a wild game preserve, largely for the benefit of bison. This concept came from Frank and Deborah Popper, two academics then at Rutgers University. The Poppers have been accused of ignoring the input of those who actually live on the land.

This is not necessarily true. According to Amanda Rees, a professor of geography at Columbus State University, between 1988 and 1994, the couple made sixty-three presentations in the Great Plains. She quoted Frank Popper, who said, "I don't think we've turned down an invitation to the Plains yet. I don't think we've turned down an invitation, period, subject to scheduling constraints."[83]

Still, residents of the northern Great Plains responded with outrage to the Poppers' proposal, feeling that the initiative rubbed salt in old wounds.

Energy Collapse

Other commodities suffered a similar fate in the 1980s: a boom, then a bust. In 1973, the Organization of Petroleum Exporting Countries (OPEC) imposed an embargo against the United States for its support of Israel. The ensuing oil shortage sent the economies of Wyoming, North Dakota, and Montana through the roof. Wyoming in particular experienced a gold rush in carbon-based fuels. It wasn't exclusive to oil, either. As the state with the greatest deposits of exploitable coal, cheaply extracted through strip mines, billions of dollars came rushing into Wyoming. The federal government had a direct hand in this hot market for coal. In 1970, the Clean Air Act mandated that new coal-fired power plants curb their sulfur dioxide emissions. This meant unprecedented demand for Powder River Basin low-sulfur coal. In 1969, Wyoming produced 4.6 million tons of coal. By 1990, it was 180 million tons. By 2000, it was 340 million tons.[84]

Federal regulation and demand for cheap energy combined to give the coal industry a hall pass in the 1980s energy bust. The oil and gas industries weren't so lucky. The near collapse sent the price of West Texas crude reeling, plunging from $103.95 in April 1980 to $9.25 in July 1985. Natural gas prices dropped 40 percent.[85]

Environmentalism and Regulation

It started benignly enough. In 1924, Aldo Leopold convinced Congress to put 500,000 acres of New Mexico's Gila National Forest into wilderness. Beginning in 1964, Congress embraced a new enthusiasm for creating wild places, passing the Wilderness Act. It then pertained to 1.9 million acres. After that, hardly a year passed without new acres being added to the wilderness system. In 1970, twenty-three new wilderness areas came into being. In 1980, 60.7 million new acres were given to wilderness designation, much of it in Alaska.

Today the National Wilderness Preservation System consists of 803 wilderness areas covering 111,368,221 acres. In Montana, Wyoming, and Idaho, they exceed 11 million acres.

For advocates of more environmental policies, the 1970s were heady times. In 1970, Richard Nixon signed both the National Environmental

Policy Act (NEPA) and the Clean Air Act. Six years later, President Gerald Ford signed the Federal Environmental Policy Act, which pertains to lands administered by the Bureau of Land Management. Ford also signed the National Forest Management Act.

Then came the backlash.

The new regulations created resentment. In 1976, a young Wyoming Republican named Malcolm Wallop upset incumbent Democratic senator Gale McGee for a seat in the US Senate. At one point, the polls gave Wallop gambler's odds: McGee led 72 to 18 percent. Wallop turned it around. The key message: Washington has gotten out of control with regulations. The most memorable campaign ad pictured a cowboy towing a pack horse with a port-a-potty strapped on its back. The voice over announced that "if you don't bring a portable facility to you on a round-up, you can't go. We need someone to tell the federal government about Wyoming. Malcolm Wallop will."[86]

The voices of protest and indignation grew beyond regulations. During the 1980s, one could see bumper stickers (not to mention a billboard on Interstate 25) in Casper that read: *Mindless Marxist Ecologists Working for Russia*; the logic being that it was environmental groups who blocked logging, mining, and drilling and grazing, particularly on federal land. This mindset might have made sense during a boom. Wyoming, for example, successfully used oil, gas, and coal development as a ticket out of subsistence living. The last thing the state wanted were roadblocks. Then came the bust. I was living in Casper when oil bottomed at $9.25. It was a window into heartache. From 1980 to 1990, Natrona County (Casper) lost ten thousand people. Environmentalism became a code word for anti-business and anti-jobs.

In 1980, Reagan chose two Wyoming natives to serve in his cabinet: James Watt to run the Department of the Interior and Anne M. Gorsuch (mother of Supreme Court Associate Justice Neal Gorsuch) as the first female administrator of the Environmental Protection Agency. Both were hostile to environmental regulation, particularly on public land. Reagan made hating the government respectable. Even though Gorsuch and Watt served for under two years, they fostered the hope in the commodity West that private interests could prevail.

This era gave birth to the Sagebrush Rebellion, an anti-federal group with hotspots in New Mexico, Utah, and Nevada. The end of the 1980s saw the creation of the pro-extractive Wise Use movement. Their message influenced any western state with significant acreage of federal land. At a 1988 Wise-Use conference in Reno, Nevada, writer Ronald Arnold sketched out twenty-five goals. At the top of the agenda was a *Wise Use Public Education Project*, which would be run by the US Forest Service. Key message? "The federal debt can be managed through prudent development of federal lands." Out of twenty-five goals proposed by the Wise Use movement, twenty-two had to do with federal land policy.[87]

The edgy '80s set the stage for growth for *movement conservatives*. This form of Republicanism was staunchly anti-communist, anti–big government—anti-government everything, really—anti-abortion, and held no affection for affirmative action. Movement conservatism had its roots in the 1930s, led by Republicans upset by the New Deal. The Great Society policies of the Johnson administration gave the idea a boost. Now evangelicals and Second Amendment boosters joined.

Movement conservatism largely eluded the Great Plains and Northern Rockies. Democrats continued to be included in the political lineup. Yet anti-government groups began to coalesce in Montana and particularly Idaho. They espoused myriad ideologies: survivalism; radical patriotism; Christian or white supremacy; sovereignty. All had one ideology in common: contempt for the federal government.

Originally, some members of these groups, such as the Montana Militia or Freeman, who felt they were above government and taxation, were from one of the 89er states. Freeman Rodney O. Skurdal was born in Broadview, Montana. LeRoy M. Schweitzer was another Montana native who formed "Justice Township." The federal government convicted Schweitzer and Skurdal on a long list of charges, including conspiracy, bank fraud, mail fraud, and wire fraud. Skurdal was sentenced to twelve years in prison. Schweitzer died in the maximum-security Florence (Colorado) Federal Correctional Complex.

These men proved to be the exception; most other founders of these groups came from somewhere else. Richard Butler, founder of the Idaho-based Aryan Nations, was born in Colorado but raised in Los Angeles.

Randy Weaver of Ruby Ridge fame was born and raised in Iowa. Eric Parker, founder of the Real 3%ers of Idaho, grew up in Phoenix. Stewart Rhodes of the Oath Keepers lives in Big Arm, Montana, but was born in California. Jeff Stankiewicz of the Idaho Lightfoot Militia claims Connecticut as his state of birth.

After the Southern Poverty Law Center squashed Ku Klux Klan leader Louis Ray Beam for his harassment of Vietnamese refugee fisherman in Galveston Bay, Texas, he decided to move. Destination: Butler's Aryan Nation compound in Hayden Lake, Idaho.

All that is to say, these movements did not grow from long-time disgruntled Idaho or Montana residents. As we shall explore in chapter 4, Idaho does indeed have a veritable racist history. Yet a history of tolerating racism cannot fully explain why these transplants move to sparsely populated sections of mountain and prairie; they exploit and promote a projected, largely imagined form of old West freedom. But freedom, whatever form it takes, is secondary to their central modus operandi: fear. Fear of government tyranny (especially martial law); fear of a dissolution of property rights; some dread of a coming race war; fear of gun confiscation; fear of a New World Order. Many groups declare their aversions to any federal law. Accordingly, their world revolves around concepts of defense and protection.

North Dakota historian Clay Jenkinson got so weary of the anti-federal cant in circulation that he penned a biting editorial in an August 16, 2015 issue of the *Bismarck Tribune*.

> The settlement of North Dakota was made possible by the federal government. We have been propped up by the federal government. We have been rescued in times of great stress by the federal government. We have been protected from real and perceived threats by the federal government. Our natural and human resources have been developed by way of federal subsidies. And we continue to be subsidized by the federal government in countless ways. In spite of these unmistakable facts, we North Dakotans love to pretend that it is our gumption that has brought us to this great moment in our history, and we love to rail against federal intrusion into the sovereignty of North Dakota.[88]

The Long Road to the Bottom

J. B. S. Todd's vision of the federal government as a business partner and arbiter of the common good died along with him in 1872. Yet something else was born, an idea—a mythology—that the West was "settled" by those toiling under their own initiative. Without a doubt, white settlers suffered sometimes extreme deprivation and hardship. They were no strangers to sweat equity. Yet they were sold land at the rock bottom price of $1.25 per acre—in installment payments, no less. Todd would likely be skeptical of the self-made narrative. He was formed in the crucible of West Point; even though he resigned his commission in 1856, he never really surrendered his attachment to the federal government. Without Washington, Todd could not have executed any of his plans that favored new immigrants—colonizers, really—of European ancestry.

Yet exploiting available resources does not an independent man or woman make. As Jenkinson points out, it takes only a short foray into the history of the American West to realize how dependent white settlers were on the federal government. Yet they were also dependent on corporations (especially the fur trade) and each other. As to this last point, this need for cooperation likely contributed to the commonwealth values—those favoring the common good—that found their way into the 1889 constitutions.

Still, under the surface, the narrative of the self-made man morphed into a creation myth. Such inventions have proven immune to reinterpretation. The concept of *risk* plays an essential role in this Rock of Gibraltar immovability. Indeed, many white settlers took breathtaking risks. Yet somehow the risk/reward ratio got skewed; because they took such chances filled with peril, the credit for their efforts should go to them and them alone. Over the years, the keepers of the creation myth eliminated the role of the federal government from scripture.

It remains snuffed due to the all-too-human feature of selective memory. This self-made mythology has no use for heretical information. It only focuses on the federal government's mistakes, of which there were many. The billions Washington—other taxpayers' money, really—transferred to 89er country in the form of infrastructure, land, and outright appropriations since territorial times has conveniently been forgotten. These farmers and ranchers subscribe to being "pro-subsidy but still anti-government," as Nate Schweber wrote.[89]

Farmers in 89ers country elect those who promote this self-made narrative, even to their detriment. In the 1980 presidential election, production agriculture in the Great Plains and Northern Rockies saw former peanut farmer Jimmy Carter as unfriendly to their needs. They chose instead individualist icon Ronald Reagan. In return, Reagan handed producers a calling card from reality. He picked John "Auction" Block as Secretary of Agriculture and David Stockman to direct the Office of Management and Budget. Stockman thought ill of modern agriculture, saying those producers who used FDR–era programs enjoyed a "way of life based on organized larceny."[90]

This projected view harnesses another human fallibility: to see the world in terms of *us* versus *them*. As propagandists have known forever, this tribalist mindset is among the most powerful of political tools. Except for brief interludes—perhaps between 1940 to 1970—the relationship between the 89ers and Washington has steadily declined. Washington is now the enemy.

The connection with commodities, again, plays a major factor. The feds own 62 percent of Idaho, 48 percent of Wyoming, and 30 percent of Montana. It's not the surface acreage alone. Western states contend with the split estate: the surface and the subsurface can have two owners. The serious money—usually—lies hidden in the subsurface. If the federal government is the owner of the subsurface, the states have a stake in developing it. A portion of the revenues from exploiting the subsurface, usually from extracting coal, oil, or gas, comes back to the state of origin. Roughly 75 percent of the coal and gas reserves in Wyoming belong to the federal mineral estate. Various federal agencies may only own four percent of the surface of North Dakota, but the Bureau of Land Management controls 5.6 million acres of subsurface acres in the state. In Montana, they have title to 37.8 million subsurface acres. In 2021, Wyoming received $1.1 billion, North Dakota received $83.9 million, and Montana received $19 million from these mineral leases.[91] Yet when it comes to natural resources and agriculture, what's critical are regulations and appropriations. You don't have to have a federal grazing or mineral lease permittee to feel the federal government's grip. A farmer in South Dakota operating entirely on private land is equally susceptible to changes in federal policy, such as if the Energy Department changes support for ethanol, for example.

The cultural connection—the sense of identity—with these industries carries more clout than the paycheck. Mining, ranching, and logging create strong tribal identities. Even though some states like Montana and Idaho have, to some degree, weaned themselves off commodities, the cultural identity remains. People ordinarily don't welcome change that threatens identity. Limiting timber cuts on National Forests, protecting species, such as eagles, salmon, wolves, and the northern Spotted Owl, are seen by rural Americans as ultimatums to their very existence. The natural reaction is a defensive stance, fostering a greater sense of isolation, powerlessness, polarization, and cultural humiliation.

In the next chapter, we will explore ways to expand that identity without threatening core values. It pertains to the most central 89er identity of all: agriculture.

YIELD AND POUNDS DO NOT A COMMUNITY MAKE

The Case for Stewardship Agriculture

3

In 1887, when Dakota was but a single territory and not yet broken into two states, Charles Phillips Ingalls, father of Laura Ingalls Wilder, moved off his 157-acre farm outside De Smet, located one hundred miles northwest of modern-day Sioux Falls. He took a job in town.[1] He eventually sold the homestead in 1892, clearing only $700.[2] His timing was good. It was at the end of the Great Dakota Boom and the beginning of fifteen years of depressed prices and drought. In 1881, a bushel of wheat brought a Dakota farmer $1.19. By 1894, it earned him only $.49.[3]

Ingalls had promised his long-suffering wife, Caroline, that they would finally settle down. Town was where you could make a steady, or at least steadier, living than farming. Family history may have influenced Ingalls' decision to move. Ingalls was no stranger to having his land repossessed or sold off for failure to pay taxes. In 1862, Ingalls and his father saw their Wisconsin farm auctioned off.

The collective experiences of father and son dispel any sentimental notions of an epoch of easy agriculture. It's always been a precarious occupation.

It remains so today. About 360 miles north of De Smet, two brothers from St. Thomas, North Dakota found out the hard way. In 2016 Ron and Larry McMartin, having expanded their operation from 160 acres to nearly 50,000, folded their cards, owing over $50 million. Their corporation,

McM, cratered for many reasons, including a collapse in commodities and the rising cost of their leveraged rented land.[4]

In the McMartin brothers' lifetimes, St. Thomas lost nearly half of its population. McM's fall came quickly; the shrinkage of St. Thomas took a little longer. Both are products of modern agricultural policy. The McMartin brothers may have been extravagant in their ambition, yet banks and the USDA encouraged such blind drive. BMO Harris Bank, N.A, a Chicago-based subsidiary of the Bank of Montreal, kept increasing their line of credit. The brothers, and their various corporations, received over $5 million in USDA crop insurance and disaster subsidies over the years.[5]

In other words, the McMartin brothers were just following government and banking incentives. Speculation, a focus on yield, mind-boggling government subsidies, and a disregard for the concept of sustainable agricultural communities induced this behavior. The creators of the 1889 North Dakota constitution would likely find such ambitious operations unsettling if not distasteful. These delegates were not saints; they liked making money. Yet they enshrined agriculture, both as an economic engine and the pillar of their cultural identity. In doing so, the delegates planted the seeds of trouble. Specifically, they promoted agriculture using a single metric of success: yield. Or, for cattlemen, pounds. It worked for a short time (1897–1919), then faltered. Over 130 years later, it comes down to this: Where do you want to hitch your agricultural wagon—high yields or self-determining economies of the rural West? You can't have both. Stewardship agriculture offers an alternative.

A Singular Place for Agriculture: Why 89er Country Is Different

A caveat: in the interest of economic history, I have covered 89er agricultural issues for over thirty years. This does not make me an expert on agricultural finance and ranch management. However, one does not need an advanced degree in any agricultural or economic discipline to see gaping holes in its prosperity narrative. Mainly, regions that depend on agriculture are in deep demographic and economic trouble. They have been since World War II. I find this remarkable given the billions the USDA has allocated to rural America. As a result, in this chapter I advocate for systemic change.

The 89er region has approximately 120,000 farms/ranches. They average 1,600 acres, with Idaho having the smallest average operation (468) and Wyoming the largest (2,430). The number of farms in the region peaked around 1935, an era in which 280,000 farms dotted the Great Plains and North Plains. Farm numbers continue to decline but at a significantly slower rate than from 1935 to 1980.[6]

When white farmers/ranchers arrived in the Great Plains and Northern Rockies, they anticipated prosperity. It arrived in fits and starts—mostly fits. It was not only drought, grasshoppers, prairie fire, and apoplectic Indigenous Americans; the price of wheat slowly decreased over the years. Number two spring wheat had peaked in 1867 at $143/bushel.[7] "By 1890 the plains farmer was an angry man," wrote historian Lynwood E. Oyos. "He was not the happy and self-sufficient yeoman and master of his fate envisioned by the Jeffersonian idealists. The independent farmer was an illusion. The history of farmers on the northern plains since the 1880s has been one of dependency."[8]

As John W. Powell predicted for the region, water—except for the eastern Dakotas—became an issue. A place that receives eighteen to twenty inches of rain per year, like Whitefish, Montana, is considered luxuriant. Most landscapes, like Boise, Idaho, Casper, Wyoming, and Dickinson, North Dakota get by on ten to fifteen inches of rain. The United States averages thirty-eight inches of rain per year.

Over the decades, the region has walloped farmers with meteorological extremes, from 70 below zero at Rogers Pass, Montana in 1954 to 120 degrees in Usta, South Dakota, recorded in 2006. The year 1889 was a tough one: "This was another dry year," wrote North Dakota meteorologist Frank Bavendick. "Small streams dried up and only a few of the lakes remained full. Crops were poor."[9]

As Canadian writer Candace Savage noted, the normal precipitation values on the Great Plains are "truly abnormal."[10]

Enter climate change. "Over the past several decades, temperatures in the Northern Great Plains have increased more than any other region in the U.S., with an average warming of 1.7°F," says a National Oceanic and Atmospheric report.[11]

Even less rain falls upon land that traditionally receives little. Or, when it does rain, it arrives in biblical proportions. In 2019, South Dakota had its wettest summer since 1895, over twelve inches above the average. In 2021, North Dakota experienced a historic drought. Since 1900, the growing season in North Dakota has been extended by thirty days. Not much better conditions exist for their immediate western neighbor. As of September 2022, most of Montana suffered severe or extreme drought.[12]

This paucity of precipitation obviously limits agriculture. Second, persistent drought threatens the flow of rivers and groundwater supplies in 89er country, both essential for irrigation.

Pragmatism dictates an emphasis on low-moisture crops. What the American agricultural market values most—corn and soybeans—is either limited to the eastern section of North and South Dakota or grown with the aid of irrigation. The latter puts farmers at a competitive disadvantage. Irrigation boosts input costs: water, labor, power, and particularly equipment are expensive. States favoring natural rainfall outstrip the 89ers in corn and soybeans. In 2021, Iowa, for example, produced twice as much corn annually as North Dakota and South Dakota combined.[13]

Crops that prosper under dry land agriculture tend to be of secondary value. For example, in 2021, the combined value of all corn and soybeans harvested in the United States exceeded $130 billion. This dwarfs the $12 billion total value for wheat the same year and the $604 million for all barley production.[14]

Yet it's just these types of crops that grow best in the Great Plains and Northern Rockies. North Dakota and Montana are among the top wheat-producing states in the nation. When it comes to 89er barley production, Idaho tops the charts. Yet 80 percent of Idaho's barley came from irrigated production in 2021.[15] Other drylands or irrigated crops favored by 89er's agriculture include lentils and oats. Montana ranks at number one for lentils; South Dakota is number one for oats.

Little has changed. In 1900, North Dakota and South Dakota led the country in wheat production and were close to the top in barley production.[16] They were middling when it came to rye production and harvested very little corn. Wyoming produced so little grain that the census only occasionally included the state in graphs.

Drought remains the primary reason producers sell their stock—an old pattern. A story written in 2012 by the agricultural magazine *Farm and Dairy* is just as relevant to one hundred years ago as it is today. "Drought has been particularly cruel to the beef cattle industry," said Purdue Extension scientist Chris Hurt. "Brood cows remain the last major livestock industry that is land–extensive. So when dryness causes wide stretches of land to be unable to support cow grazing, producers have to buy feed or send cows to town."[17]

Jim Magagna, head of the Wyoming Stock Growers Association and never one to mince words, put it this way: "There's no real profitability in the livestock business today as it is . . . These people are dedicated to their lifestyle and their industry."[18]

Bad Math . . . Then and Now

The revenue situation hasn't changed much either. The 1900 census of agriculture also shows that while the 89er states were among the top of average (gross) value of farm products per farm, they were at the bottom when it came to average value of net farm products per acre. Farmers and ranchers in 89er county—except Idaho—were clearing less than $4.00/acre.

Net farm income has never been a popular subject in agricultural media. When reading commercial farm reports, the net gain per acre, or net overall revenue, rarely makes an appearance. If it does, it's buried deep in the text. Instead reports focus on yield, prices, and the state of price supports.

Operations that rely on volume are constantly under financial stress and, usually, a heavy debt load. Net profit vacillates wildly from year to year. For example, in 2018, the North Dakota State University Extension Service noted, "Previously, average net farm income dropped to $133,466 in 2013, $76,404 in 2014 and $28,600 in 2015 as North Dakota marketing year average cash prices from 2012 to 2015 plummeted from $14 to $8.49 for soybeans, $6.46 to $3.28 for corn and $8.19 to $4.59 for spring wheat."[19]

Let's look at some examples from the agricultural press the last few years. In 2021, writer Mikkel Pates of *Agweek* spelled out the sorry situation for North Dakota producers. "The 2020 net profit was $33 per cow, and that's after including $113 per head in accumulated federal payments to compensate for marketing impacts of trade retaliation, livestock forage programs related to drought and COVID-19 compensation. If not for those payments, producers would have lost $80 per head on average."[20]

Even when trying to look at the big picture (that is, not just cattle), the math is discouraging. In an article titled "ND Producers' Net Farm Income Up in 2020," a *Dakota Farmer* reporter admitted, "In 2020, the average operating expense ratio was 69.4%, and the average interest expense ratio was 4.3%. This means that for every dollar the producer earned, he or she spent 69 cents on operating expenses and 4 cents on interest. Of that dollar, a producer also spent about 8 cents in depreciation and was left with about $.18 cents of that dollar in profit."[21]

Even as the Covid-19 pandemic caused commodity prices to soar, producers in 89er country suffered. "It's tougher than it's ever been," said Sage Askins, owner of a ranch outside Lusk, Wyoming.[22]

All this portends a troubled future for the conventional 89er farmer or rancher and the community in which they reside.[23] In sum, we are left with these questions: What has been the cost of agricultural socio-economic calculus from the era of 1889 to 2023, a 134-year stretch? Has the quality of life in rural 89er communities improved? If so, where? And is this improvement connected in any way to farming or ranching? In most places, stores and services have disappeared, not to mention schools. Decade after decade, people barely hang on. Since 1920, declining populations and economic stasis in communities dependent on commodity agriculture have caused a struggle to honor historic values found in 89er constitutions, such as public education. You can't have schools without children and the assessed valuation to support them.

Yet in this massive area—475,000 square miles, five times the size of the United Kingdom—agriculture and the idea of rural community were once inseparable. When agriculture prospered, so did the local area. Classical republican values meshed. Yes, individual freedom and tradition mattered, but so did concepts of egalitarianism and relative inclusivity.

The Road Ahead

Commodity agriculture has endured many changes but few so important as the one it faces now: How do we get away from yield and pounds and start focusing on stewardship agriculture?

We will get to what that is in a minute. First, a couple of shibboleths that beg to be challenged. We surrender the idea that agriculture is a hidebound occupation and therefore incapable of change. Yes, agriculture has a conservative streak, but we can divide practitioners roughly into three categories: innovators/first adapters, partial adapters, and non-adapters, or, as the agricultural academic press calls them, *laggards*.

The first category is self-explanatory; innovators/first adapters are the risk takers. The Climate, Food, and Agriculture Dialogue group, run by the Meridian Group consultancy, is pretty blunt about their numbers: "We do not have a comprehensive assessment of how many early innovators exist."[24]

We can assume they are in short supply, yet they can and do drive shifts in agriculture. They embrace change, be it organic or regenerative or even something relatively small, like shifting to no-till. They also likely have three additional attributes: they're customer-centric, focused on soil quality, and interested in how their operations connect to the community at large. We'll meet four of them in this chapter.

Second, we acknowledge the reality that community is no longer important to production agriculture. If the school closes, so what? The rancher or farmer will seek out employees to run autonomous tractors or drones not from the local labor source but through the H-2A visa program. If we want to change that narrative, then we need to change the way we farm or ranch.

Third, we can't disconnect the farmer or rancher from the system. Producers are under tremendous pressure to adapt: lower inputs, reduce chemicals, protect soil, capture carbon, use less water, and so on. The farmer/rancher can only change so much on his or her own. Society, from banks to food processors to government, must be stakeholders in accommodating those changes.

Finally, the toughest hurdle: we, as a society, need to push back against the narrative that the American farmer must feed the world. Throughout the history of American agriculture, it's had one constant problem: overproduction. The title of one of the most notable books in the American agricultural canon doesn't beat around the bush: *The Curse of American Agricultural Abundance*, by Willard Cochrane.[25]

That we produce too much is not the message conventional agriculture—in any part of the world—wants to hear. It's no accident that after predicting famine and extremely high food prices due to the 2022 Russian invasion of Ukraine, the opposite occurred. After March 2022, world food prices fell for ten consecutive months, according to the United Nations food agency.[26]

If you have to feed the world, then yield must be the critical metric. It's all based on the scarcity narrative. It's another version of Thomas Malthus's dire warning in 1798 that we'll run out of food as populations rise. Within this dramatic view of world food supply lies a subtle and powerful message: the ends justify the means—that is, let's use all the tools at our disposal to boost yield, no matter the environmental consequences. If you want to read a scathing observation about this "feed the world" narrative, see Dr. David Montegomery's article from *Scientific American*, titled *3 Myths About Modern Agriculture*.[27]

The problem begins with an obvious—and exhaustively documented—phenomenon. The millions of acres of corn and soybeans planted each year in the United States don't go to feed humans; they're fed to animals. Livestock consumes roughly 45 percent of all corn grown in the United States. Another 40 percent is used in making ethanol. Humans consume approximately only 10 percent of American-grown corn and one-third of that is in the form of corn syrup.[28] And it's been that way for over one hundred years.[29]

According to Iowa State University researchers, "Roughly 60 percent of US soybean exports (or put another way, 25 percent of the total US soybean crop) finds its way to China."[30]

And when they arrive in China, they're fed to livestock. The majority of soybeans are crushed into oil and soybean meal, and approximately 75 percent of the soybean meal that is produced in the world is fed not to humans but to pigs or poultry, according to scientists at the University of Illinois.[31]

The other hole in the feed-the-world narrative is waste. Research in 2021 shows the percent of food produced in the United States that goes to waste has risen from 33 to 40 percent.[32]

Stewardship Agriculture

These problems have been with us since at least WWII. There have also been countless attempts to resolve them. The fallout from the 1980s farm crisis forced many in agriculture to reconsider the current system.[33] The

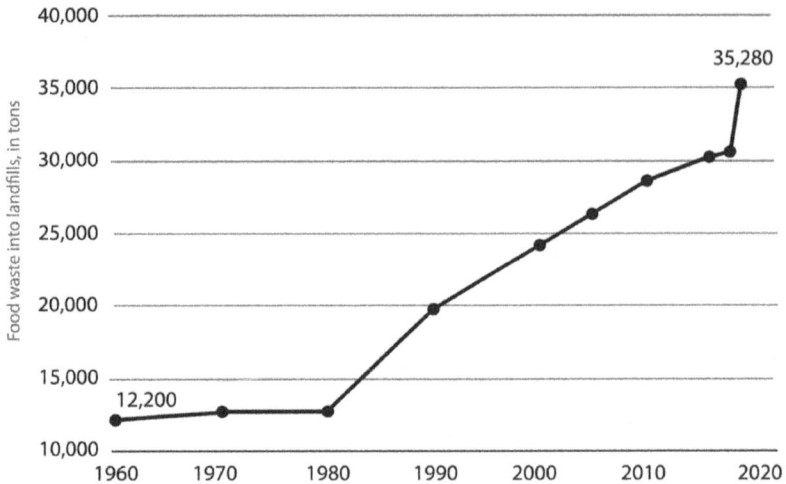

Figure 3.1. Increasing food waste in landfills. Courtesy of the Pew Research Center.

concept of stewardship agriculture might be called the next step. In doing so, this means moving away from the traditional definition of stewardship, which is synonymous with guardianship; that is, guardians of the land. The modified definition of stewardship is more inclusive: it expands from not just taking care of the land, but the community.

Most farmers and ranchers become indignant at the suggestion they don't qualify as stewards. Undoubtedly many do—probably most do in some form. However, core metrics suggest a narrative in need of clarification. Let's define the traditional approach to stewardship. As noted, conventional agriculture, with its focus on efficiency, is a community killer. The goal is maximum yield using the fewest people possible. Under this calculus lie the thousands of crumbling or abandoned towns.

Producers haven't been particularly good stewards of their most precious asset: soil. While there have been improvements (soil erosion rates on cropland decreased 35 percent between 1982 and 2017), we're still losing nearly two tons per acre per year of soil.[34] Montgomery, a geomorphologist at the University of Washington, calls this "skinning our planet."[35]

No one really knows how much soil has been lost nationwide. Montgomery said, "Soil erosion is a complex process."[36] Agronomists Richard Cruse and Dennis Keeney put it succinctly when discussing government

Figure 3.2. Exhibit at a rest area on Interstate 80 near Adair, Iowa, indicating soil loss. Courtesy of RDG Planning & Design and Doug Heatherington.

soil policy: "Seldom has such an important policy been based on such a dearth of defendable data."[37]

Still, we're losing a lot. "It takes centuries to build an inch of topsoil and conventional ag is losing that much in decades," said Montgomery.[38] A 2021 study by the Environmental Defense Fund, The Nature Conservancy, and the marketing research firm Beck Ag showed that out of one hundred Iowa agricultural operators, only 35 percent of farmers discussed soil health with their lenders.[39]

And then there's the water issue. According to the USDA, as of 2017, "55 percent of assessed rivers and streams; 71 percent of lakes; and 84 percent of bays and estuaries nationally have impaired water quality. Agriculture is the largest source of impairments in rivers and streams and the second-largest source in lakes and ponds."[40]

Finally, nitrogen from runoff continues to plague farm and ranch communities. A 2022 Rice University study found total annual damages from various nitrogen fertilizers were nearly $100 billion. Those from "ammonia were much larger overall—at $72 billion—than those from nitrogen oxides ($12 billion) and nitrous oxide ($13 billion)."[41]

What makes stewardship farmers and ranchers different? They have ten common attributes:

1. They believe in diversified markets, an alternative to the open commodity market. This means shying away from contracting to large packing houses or grain elevators.[42] If they do sell to substantial operators, they do so as part of a cooperative that can command premium pricing.
2. They carry minimum debt and avoid operating loans when possible. They strive for a reduced reliance on government support or direct payments. That's because stewardship agriculture is a bottom-up, not top-down, movement. Many still count on the availability of government credit, however. This often involves diversifying revenue streams.
3. They have low input costs, which usually means few chemical amendments, herbicides, and irrigation obligations.
4. Cooperation and collaboration are key, including with state and federal government–based conservation programs. They are generous with their knowledge and practice open-source agriculture, particularly in sharing technology.
5. They take risks—some measured, some major—and gravitate toward experimentation, like using organic or regenerative methods, or a combination of the two. Soil health is paramount. "Taking risks while being grounded in tradition," as one rancher said. "Our history isn't perfect, but it literally got us here."
6. They invest in their communities, including areas outside agriculture.
7. They take care of their employees and encourage their entrepreneurial bent. "Skilled labor is not just a cost," said Cole Mannix, who runs Old Salt Coop in Montana, "but also the primary asset in managing complex biological systems. Observation, experimentation, monitoring, iteration, repeat!"
8. Tend to focus on profits/markets, not yields.
9. Go to bed at night thinking about how they can a) create another value-added product or b) how can they do more for their soil?
10. They seek a balance between work and time with their families.

Three features stand out: care of the land (particularly the soil), care of the people who tend the soil, and care of the communities in which these people live. Ranchers in Winnett, Montana (we'll meet one of them shortly), for example, are just as concerned with the condition of the county courthouse and elementary school as they are with their wheat and cattle production.

An Ancient Practice

Stewardship agriculture is not new. The intercropping Iroquois of the northeast subscribed to basic stewardship principles. The nineteenth-century founders of farm and ranch communities around the West would probably have expressed similar aspirations. But over the decades, the quest for yield gradually erased these dreams.

The revival of stewardship agriculture began at least forty years ago. The movement has numerous parents, including: J. I. Rodale, founder of the Rodale Institute organic research facility; Wes Jackson of Kansas's Land Institute; Bill Mollinson, co-founder of permaculture; Masanobu Fukuoka, author *The One Straw Revolution*; and Alan Savory, father of modern rest and rotation theory for cattle. All cared passionately about the soil, a core principle of regenerative agriculture. As for the type of farming one does, there's no one formula for being a stewardship producer. You can be organic, regenerative, biodynamic, or even—up to a point—a conventional producer.

Stewardship agriculture pays it forward: getting young people involved in agriculture or its attendant industries. Often, but not always, these individuals have little education or training in agriculture. Production agriculture has a problem: drafting young farmers. The reasons are myriad: too much work, assuming staggering debt, and cost of entry.[43] Instead, the new agricultural recruits focus on niche markets around larger cities. The 2017 Census of Agriculture showed an increase in young agriculturalists, most of them farming less than nine acres.[44]

Economic analysis of stewardship agriculture remains scarce. Sustainable agriculture, rather, has gained attention, particularly with the publication of such books as *Planting the Future: Developing an Agriculture That Sustains Land and Community*.[45] Yet most observers of agricultural trends acknowledge that the term "sustainable" has been employed to pack water for every conceivable type of production.

For example, in February 2022, JBS, the world's largest beef producer, sponsored a report published in Politico magazine. Called *Feeding the Future*, it quoted JBS USA CEO Tim Schellpepper as saying, "Sustainability is about more than achieving net-zero (greenhouse gasses); it also demands investing in people, in communities and in future generations."[46]

This may sound a bit hollow, as the same month, JBS agreed to pay $52.5 million to settle litigation alleging that the company and other packing giants colluded to drive up beef prices.[47]

As the report title suggests, Schellpepper also employed the "feed the world" rhetoric. "Failure to act (on climate change) means that, one day, there may not be enough food for everyone."

Bob Quinn

Our exploration of stewardship agriculture starts with a farmer in the heart of 89er country: Bob Quinn of Big Sandy, Montana. He's a crusader who changed the face of American agriculture—especially in 89er country.[48] He pioneered the idea that you can dry farm organic grains on a commercial scale and do it hundreds—if not thousands—of miles away from organic hot spots.

A *hot spot* is the agriculture shorthand for regions rife with both organic producers and paying customers. Typically, they are clustered around large cities. Not surprisingly, California leads the nations with organic hot spots in forty-three out of its fifty-three counties. Producers focus on organic dairy, fruits, and vegetables.

According to the Organic Trade Association, there are zero organic hot spots in the Great Plains and Northern Rockies.[49] Quinn wasn't going to let that slow him down. In the 1980s, he showed there was money in organic grains, even if you do have to truck it thousands of miles. The demand has only grown.

I find Bob Quinn in his orchard picking sour cherries with his wife, children, and grandchildren.[50] Bob and wife, Ann, live outside Big Sandy, a town located about eighty miles northeast of Great Falls. It's ninety-five degrees in northern Montana. In the heat, Quinn moves around like he's forty-five, not seventy-four years old, his age at this interview. It's not exactly a hustle but deliberate movements with a conservation of energy. Dressed in a light plaid shirt, Dickey's, and a straw hat, he roams the orchard to find me a bucket to use for a seat as I take notes. He finds one, but then the timer on his cell phone goes off. He's also watering apple trees and every twenty minutes needs to change the hose.

Quinn is just one of the US farmers who contributes to the 20 million bushels of organic wheat annually. Yet the United States produced a total of 1.65 billion bushels of wheat in 2021, meaning organic production remains statistically insignificant. People like Quinn have altered that narrative, iteration by iteration. Increasingly, so are other farmers and ranchers in the region. In fact, two 89er states (Montana and Wyoming) lead the nation in organic grain production.[51]

In the last three decades, we've seen growth in not only organic production, but regenerative (focuses on soil health) mixed crop-livestock grazing, perennial grains (no replanting needed), agroforestry (mixing of trees and crops), all forms of conservation farming, and biodynamic (emphasizes on-farm fertility) agriculture.

Quinn created stewardship agriculture through his value-added ventures. Over the years, he has sold most of his enterprises. This includes Montana Flour and Grain, a milling company in Ft. Benton that trademarked and successfully marketed (including to Europe) an ancient Khorasan wheat called Kamut; Big Sandy Organics, which creates snacks out of organic grains and lentils; and the Oil Barn, a processing facility for safflower oil. Quinn helped found the Montana Chapter of the Organic Crop Improvement Association.

Quinn now leases most of his land—about four thousand acres—to former employees, Seth Goodman and Chad Fasteson. He walks me down to his test vegetable plot, all grown without any chemicals and no irrigation; among flitting grasshoppers, he comes to his chief aspiration. "We farm 4,000 acres and here's how I look at it: In the pioneer days, 4,000 acres would support about 12 farms. So what I've tried to do is have my 4,000 acres support 12 decent paying jobs."

Quinn feels that if more people quit what he calls "industrial agriculture," with its emphasis—above all—on yield, places like Big Sandy have a chance. "It's got to be quality over quantity. Farmers must differentiate their product and create value added in order to be viable," he said.

Quinn isn't giving up on experimentation: "I intend to turn my attention to the creation of a regenerative organic research, education and health institute on 700 acres that I will take out of the middle of my farm," he said.[52]

Furthermore, it's worth exploring what happened to one of his original enterprises. In November 2020, Quinn sold Big Sandy Organics to an employee, Thomas Dilworth, and his wife, Heather.

Founded in 1887 with the arrival of the St. Paul, Minneapolis & Manitoba Railway, Big Sandy is a classic 89er ranch and farm town. It's maintaining, although its population peaked in 1980. Institutions such as their senior center struggle to stay open. Still, school enrollment is slowly climbing, as is the county's assessed valuation. Most impressive is the drop in the median age. In 2017, Big Sandy's median age was 51.2 years. By 2021, it had dropped to 42.3 years.

That's likely because people like the Dilworths arrived. Thomas originally came from Idaho, Heather from Colorado, but they met in Utah. First they lived in nearby Ft. Benton, but they eventually moved to Big Sandy.[53]

The purchase of Big Sandy Organics wasn't without risk. The business wasn't profitable, said Heather. "Bob was getting ready to retire. It took about a year to negotiate the sale, which included a loan from the SBA, which went through a local bank."

At first, it was just the two of them, working out of a little facility in town. "My husband and I did everything, from the cooking of the grains, cleaning, and packaging the snacks, which was mostly Kracklin' Kamut. It was just him and me the first year."

Then, a game changer: Big Sandy Organics landed a contract with Caroo, then called Snack Nation. Among other services, Caroo sends out boxes, via subscription, that "include all sorts of goodies," says Heather. "They asked us if we would be willing to have a package of Kracklin Kamut be in one of their subscription boxes."

The Dilworths agreed only to find that Caroo wanted three hundred thousand units. "That required 20,000 pounds of Kamut. Compare that to the 18,000 pounds of Kamut we used the entire previous year," she said. "It really tested the limits of what we could do."

Another large order came along, this one from the Salt Lake–based Young Living, which centers on selling essential oils. Young Living had a problem. They rotated their lavender crop with a heritage wheat called Einkorn. They had tons of the grain sitting around in bins. "They said, 'we've tried your Kracklin Kamut and it's delicious. We love it. We were wondering, if you would be willing to try and experiment with our Einkorn in the same way you have your Kracklin Kamut or maybe try different oils or salt?'"

The Dilworths rolled up their sleeves, experimenting with different cooking time, oils, and flavorings. It paid off. "Ultimately," says Heather, "they placed a massive order: five semi-trucks full of product. The most we'd ever done was one full semi-truck load." Young Living has made Big Sandy Organics their exclusive producer for this snack. "Young Living is an international company. They sell all over the world, so that gives us great exposure," she said. Along with the larger contracts, Big Sandy Organics has also added a number of small contracts cooking lentils, barley, and other snack products for companies like Patagonia. Rapid growth required expansion. The Dilworths converted their modest modular home into an office and staffed it with a full-time office manager. Their production facility got two expansions. When the Dilworths bought the company, they employed three full-time workers and three part-timers. In the past three years, their number of full-time employees has varied from two to eleven.

Heather repeatedly expressed her and her husband's intent to participate in the tenets of stewardship agriculture: supporting community and encouraging community growth. Adding jobs and bringing more commerce into their town have been prominent in their discussions: "I really like Big Sandy, and I really love Montana. My husband's vision was: We need to keep jobs here. We need to keep people employed. We need to be able to keep our grocery store. I mean, he wants to see the community thrive. Our goal is to support our community however we can." She also expressed gratitude for the government's help throughout the pandemic. "The federal grants have been such a blessing to us. I don't know where we'd be without them. Because we live in rural America, we qualify for these kinds of grants. We all rise together, if we all work together. We're more than a company, we're a community. If we do well and nobody else in Big Sandy does well, that's not going to work." Part of that government money includes an American Rescue Plan Act or ARPA grant of $400,000. The Dilworths want to use it to build a new facility.

Heather and I got into her car and drove around Big Sandy, looking at places where they were considering setting up their new shop. At the time they had made no offers, although subsequently several parcels became available. Waiting until their cash flow improves, Big Sandy Organics has put off construction until 2024. When they do build, they aim to include a daycare and small recreation center with a basketball court.

Twenty-five years ago, the idea of a local food processor—who buys from local farmers—putting in a daycare and a recreation center would have been the stuff of fantasy. What's different about the Dilworths and Big Sandy Organics?

First, they accept that they need a financial relationship with the federal government. Most involved in agriculture have contempt for Washington. They take the money but hold their noses. The Dilworths, both Mormon and politically conservative, understand that they are handicapped without federal assistance. In the last two years, they have applied for and received over $600,000 in grants from the state and federal government. Whatever their politics, the Dilworths are inclusive, big picture, and aspire to run a big tent kind of business.

Second, they relentlessly harness technology, including in marketing. "That's really changed," says Heather.

> Going to big food shows used to be obligatory. Now it's secondary. Repeatedly we went to the nation's leading natural food show, Expo West. It's an ordeal to get there, you know? Packing up all your products, driving all the way to Anaheim. Setting up your booth, which cost $10,000. We met a lot of interesting people and great contacts but never got a sale. Social media and technology have changed all of that. We've cut out advertising and TV and radio.

Big Sandy, in other words, is benefiting from stewardship agriculture. Think of this situation as an earthbound version of an extended slack tide. Commodities grown by small producers and their supporting infrastructure have been moving away from places like Big Sandy for decades.

Grain elevators sit empty. But the tide in Big Sandy is slowly coming back in.

Just Cows

If you're young and interested in regenerative ranching, you could do worse than work for Bill and Dana Milton. Through their arrangement with the Quivira Coalition they have apprenticeship positions open from time to time.[54]

Here's what the Miltons seek from a candidate: honesty, a good work ethic, a collaborative nature, adaptiveness, openness to new experiences, flexibility, patience, imagination/creativity, curiosity. Just your ordinary ranch hand.

Maybe not. Bill and his wife Dana have a different aspiration than most cattle operations: "We practice regeneration on the ground and we practice regeneration with people," they advise applicants. "The ranch itself applies a fairly aggressive approach to time controlled and high stock density grazing practice involving frequent moves to optimize plant rest and soil cover impact."[55]

At seventy-three, Milton is tall-ish and thin, endowed with the kind of frame found on a center of a small, midwestern basketball team. He's well-read on myriad subjects, contemplative, relentlessly curious, relaxed, and philosophical—not surprising, as he's a Soto Zen priest, ordained in 2014.[56] He's also devoted to regenerative agriculture, cattle, collaboration, and community.

The Miltons run 350–500 (depending on the moisture) head of cattle on 15,000 acres north of Roundup, Montana. Their ranch is part of one of the largest intact grasslands in the world. The Miltons have gained a reputation for innovative grazing and bringing disparate groups together to resolve thorny issues.

Ideas on grazing had been shifting for some time, Milton said. Range science has long been working on rotational grazing. "In the 1920s, grass scientists in Nebraska were looking at grasses and root systems and developing the idea that if you take care of something, it will arrive at a steady, static state. Those ideas have been evolving and continue to evolve," he said.

Milton's formal initiation into regenerative ranching came from attending a Holistic Resource Management workshop with the Zimbabwean-born ecologist Alan Savory in 1984. Milton praises Savory for his "shot across the bow" in challenging grazing orthodoxy. "He introduced the critical element to the concept of rotational grazing."

Savory also encouraged people to stop focusing on yield. Milton says,

> Alan kept trying to tell people not to concentrate on how to run more animals on your place. That's the production hat we all wear. That centers on how heavy your calf is or this or that. You should be asking yourself: why are you running this business? What's important in your life? What sort of production system would support that? How would you manage the grass to support your production system? And that becomes a more thoughtful inquiry for a family.

Along with a holistic approach, Milton says cooperation is key to successful ranching. "No matter how successful and resilient a ranch, it's still dependent on its neighbors. There's the idea that you could just run your own place and market your animals and just focus on your own business plan. You can't do that. I can have the best damned place in the world; it's totally vulnerable if everything else around you is cratering, particularly if it's wildlife or weeds or whatever."

If you avoid that isolationist lens, says Milton, you'll become attuned to what he calls "community resiliency." In other words, rethinking how rural communities can thrive. "You start to see that resiliency comes with people collaborating within the community around the health of the entire landscape. They're more transparent and willing to work cooperatively because they can leverage resources."

As an example of community resiliency, Milton offers the Winnett-based group known as ACES, an acronym for Agricultural Community Enhancement and Sustainability. Winnett lies north of Roundup. It is the county seat for Petroleum County, one of the most rural and least populated counties in the country (as of 2021, 412 people). A tour of Winnett suggests a town with its back to the wall: there are a lot of empty buildings but, at the same time, it seems determined to hold on to what it has. Winnett is relatively well-tended, and endowed with critical amenities:

a hotel, a feed store, a grocery store, a municipal building, and two bars.

To keep from being another grim statistic, locals decided to try a different approach than just conventional agriculture, according to Laura Nowlin, who ranches with her husband and two children north of Winnett.[57] In 2016, she got together with a group of Petroleum County residents.

"Our initial reason for gathering was to manage wildlife from the ground up. We had BLM, land managers, ranchers and producers in the room. There were twelve of us. But we ended up talking about more than just wildlife," said Nowlin. "The biggest issue was: where is the community going? We talked about absentee ownership. It affects this community in so many different ways; when a property sells (to someone who values it for recreation) that means less of us. That impacts all of us."

Soon, however, this conversation morphed into the possibility of creating a grazing association (a form of grazing cooperative). "At that first meeting, we said: let's see what we can do. Well, the US Fish and Wildlife Foundation offered a grant to start a grass bank. Some of us didn't know what that was," said Nowlin.

A grass bank works as a common grazing area shared by a group of ranchers. ACES hired a consultant to write a feasibility study. "Bill (Milton) invited a guy from the Nature Conservancy to a meeting. Nobody else knew he was coming. We're all too polite to ask him to leave. So we listened to what he had to say. The people of ACES are conservative, but they are also open-minded and willing to find solutions," she said.

"That opened up a whole new world," said Nowlin. "All these partnerships opened up a whole new world we didn't know was out there. Nobody five years ago would believe that we're having lunch with the Nature Conservancy and enjoying it."

At the initial meeting, Milton said he went around the room, asking about the benefit of working collaboratively or collectively on these complicated deals with groups like the Nature Conservancy, or with groups outside their traditional partnerships. "We had people from the '30s to '50s in the room. This is Petroleum County; they've developed this sort of informal type of leadership. So many parts of their community has to be covered. They're a conservative bunch."

They weren't easily convinced. "After the first round of conversation, a lot of people said it wasn't possible to move beyond the perception that people just don't like us. We need to accept that," they said. "People don't get it. I'm tired of fighting these people."

Not everyone agreed with that assessment. "Then there were these young people who said, 'well, I don't know. I'd like to get beef in the schools. I'd like to buy a ranch.' Some of them had parents who had been working on cooperative endeavors. But as the talks went on, by the third round, people were saying, 'yeah, let's do this.'"

Nowlin said the second development among the group centered around the fate of the town of Winnett. The town has new and restored structures, one quite imposing at almost twelve thousand square feet. Indeed, one cannot help but notice the activity, the roar of equipment and echoing of hammers, as workers erect the Petroleum County Community Center. Once completed, it will serve as a gathering place for community events: weddings, adult education classes, and receptions.

One might reasonably ask: What's going on? How can a county with a $1.8 million total assessed valuation be building a $5 million community center? The answer is that extractive-based money funded most (county residents chipped in, too) of this structure. Native son Larry Carrel, a petroleum engineer, made his money in oil and gas. He gave back to a place with disappearing oil and gas reserves. The community center officially opens in April 2023.

Oil isn't the only commodity paying it forward. Just up the block from the construction activity sits a well-worn, boarded-up structure. The Odd Fellows Hall—built in 1914—rests upon a new foundation. It took 245 hours of volunteers to dig, shoot grades, haul dirt, set footings, and pour the concrete. The building, with much celebration, was moved from its original site on February 7, 2022.

The ACES holds the title to the Odd Fellow's Hall. This non-profit 501c(3) has renovation in the works, including a major interior remodel. They're putting in an addition with public restrooms and showers. There's discussion of a retail and coffee shop on the first floor and apartments on the second. And there's more. The ACES actually owns four lots on Main Street. They plan to keep one lot open as community space but then develop another lot with tents for bicyclists and perhaps even a hostel.

Down the street, ACES is rehabilitating the upstairs of the county courthouse, a structure built in the last years of the First World War. The National Register of Historic Places identifies the architecture of this worn, well-used, and well-loved structure as Early Commercial. The renovated space will house five small offices and four apartments. All the offices and one of the apartments have commitments of occupancy. Nowlin said the fundraising for the $1.7 million remodel is progressing according to plan, "but we still have some work to do. We're looking for an architect right now and hope to have the project complete by this time next year (February 2023)."

When it comes to attending to local agricultural affairs, the ACES has a full-time employee focused primarily on soil health education for landowners. They've also taken to heart the problem of ranch succession. In partnership with the Malta-based Ranchers Stewardship Alliance, ACES has started a Perennial Roots program dedicated to keeping young producers in ranching.

This takes an almost unimaginable amount of work, optimism, and persistence. The community is especially interested in—the toughest of tasks—preserving their K–12 school. According to Karl Stauber, now retired but who spent years in Washington serving in the higher echelons of the US Department of Agriculture, including as deputy under secretary for rural development, "We are at a strange point in our history. The economic reality of agriculture has displaced the cultural reality of community."[58]

Stauber continued:

Education, broad-based education, is no longer necessary for the farmer to prosper. If a community loses its champion high school, how does that relate to the farmer/rancher? What do farmers need to prosper? That's different from what communities need to prosper. I think more farmers and communities haven't realized this yet. As a producer, my problems with getting work force doesn't have to do with the schools, it has to do (with the availability of) H2 visas.

Milton said there's probably data that supports the vision that schools have no relationship to community. "But we have a competing vision. We believe that these self-governing, self-organizing circles can support that vision. We have that capacity. And it includes more than agriculture."

"We (agriculture) can't be disconnected from the town. There is an urban-rural divide in Winnett," Nowlin said, somewhat mirthfully. "How do we fix that? We're an agricultural community but we can't survive without those who live in town."

Milton said despite the challenges connected to these changes, it didn't take long for residents to acknowledge that the ideas had possibility.

"Even the older generation?" I ask.

Oh, yes. Everyone's super onboard. They can't believe that they're getting stuff done. Someone called me the other day and said, "This is a lot of fun." They're no longer spending 90 percent of their time at stock growers' meetings defending themselves.

They're not trying to hold the line. Hold the line? Bullshit. We're going to create something. We're going to build community centers. We're going to put beef in the schools. We're going to work on historic buildings. We're going to invite people in to talk about soil.

Milton thinks that prosperity in agriculture requires the ability to get along with the government.

I like working with the government. I have friends with different points of view. But it's a fine line. It all depends on how you engage. I like to see a plan—as long as it wasn't too burdensome or proscriptive—that if you're going to get (help) from a government program, you've got to do basic soil monitoring, showing you're sustaining the capacity of your soil. I've even heard people say you shouldn't be allowed in the door of an NRCS [Natural Resources Conservation Service] office unless you're willing to pass a benchmark of basic soil health.

Milton is suspicious of eliminating what he sees as essential government participation. "Sure, let's get rid of the FSA [Farm Service Administration] or the NRCS. Let's do that. Any sort of subsidized crop or drought insurance? Nah. Well, guess what? This land will be owned by Kanye West or people like that. He's going to build a house bigger than the White House. Is that what we call liberty?"

I ask Milton, "What other measures of success are there for agriculture besides yield?" He replied, "Is your soil getting better or worse? Is your landscape getting healthier? Are you supporting more or less wildlife?

Are you, in fact, having more or less ranchers on the landscape? Are you having fun yet?"

Twenty Different Crops . . . and Cows

Northwest of Winnett, across the Missouri River Breaks, the land dips, twists, and then flattens to create classic dry farm grain country. It's part of the Montana Hi-Line, so called because the Great Northern Road (now Burlington Northern Santa Fe) laid down track high up in the northern part of the state in 1890. Hill County is one of Montana's leading winter and spring wheat producers. It still struggles with agricultural fallout. In five years, from 2012 to 2017, Hill County lost over one hundred farms/ranchers. During the same time, the average farm grew by 357 acres.

After a losing streak of thirty years, Hill County's population is now slowly recovering, led by its county seat, Havre.

North of Havre, about ten miles from the Canadian border, sits a farm run by a couple who'd like to see the demographic trend continue, preferably in the context of stewardship agriculture. Doug Crabtree and Anna Jones-Crabtree started Vilicus Farms with 1,280 acres in 2009. Now they farm 12,500 acres, all organic. They've added livestock to help build soil health and provide additional revenue streams. Yet they both say their most important crop is new farmers.[59]

Vilicus Farms grows about twenty crops on a seven-year rotation plan, including chickling vetch, Emmer wheat, heavy feeding grains, broadleaf (flax or hemp), and, increasingly, oats.

Molds didn't just get broken during the formation of Vilicus Farms; they got smashed. The operation is big, isolated, and started by a couple who, at the time of origin, happened to both be about forty years old.

For Doug, the creation of Vilicus began decades ago as he emerged from the belly of conventional farming. Doug comes from a long line of farmers in Ohio. He saw his family's grain operation collapse in the 1980s. He began his own farm in Indiana but became disillusioned. His training as an agricultural economist made him question the business model of agriculture, which relied on expensive chemicals. He quit farming but immersed himself in the study of organic agriculture. During that time, he worked as an agricultural systems researcher in the Midwest. He went back to school for a master's in plant science then became the program manager for Montana's Organic Certification program.

Anna has no agricultural background—although she grew up in rural places, surrounded by farms—and continues to work as the director of data governance for the Forest Service. She has a doctorate in civil engineering with a specialty in sustainable systems. Before they bought the farm, Anna and Doug set up a "vision board" to help them manifest the ideal organic operation. Finally, they found the property north of Havre. They utilized every financial tool they had at their disposal: savings, money from retirement funds, and USDA Beginning Farmer loans to get the operation off the ground.

From the start, they began soliciting apprentices.

"We have two guiding stars," said Doug.

First and foremost, get as much of the land off drugs as soon as possible or, in other words, how do we entirely avoid applying poisons to the soil? In order to do that, we need more stewards and they're not being trained. We came up with this idea to train people in the idea of stewardship agriculture and not by formula, either, but the way we do things. The "why" and philosophical aspects matter.

At first, they aimed to recruit young team members. They still do, but they increasingly seek men or women who have some exposure to agriculture and a vision for themselves. Employment at Vilicus has multiple tracks to entry. One is through Quivira, which lasts eight months. Another involves apprentices with longer terms. Finding themselves coming up short for help, Doug and Anna are exploring hiring South Africans and older workers interested in a second career.

Thus far, there's been only one employee from Montana. "Farmers trained in traditional ag are much less open to organic agriculture," said Doug. "One of our biggest learning experiences: organic farmers are, and will continue to be, college-educated, and most of them are less likely to be educated in agriculture. Most of my compatriots got degrees in philosophy, education, or music."

This means adjusting assumptions about who is coming through the agricultural pipeline. "The received wisdom is that the next generation of farmers will come out of families that practice agriculture. That's not true," said Doug.

> It (conventional agriculture) embeds a tendency for sameness and an unchanging approach and an incestuous approach to the idea of community. Yet, agriculture and communities prosper in diversity. The problem with giving kids an ag degree is that there's so few openings for them in traditional agriculture. An ag degree is seen as a path *from* the farm. They go work in other parts of the food system. The message we get from students with degrees in agriculture is the absolute disdain their (degree holding) institutions have for alternative agriculture.

Yet, like Milton, Vilicus Farms seeks community collaboration. "We're also interested in symbiosis," said Anna. "To be a totally independent farmer is not part of the goal. Rather, it's to be part of a functioning community. But you have to have people willing to commit to a place."

Agriculture has to accommodate even more change, said Anna, but that burden should not be solely placed upon the farmer. That's too siloed. "As a society, we need to think differently about the farmer. The shifts in agriculture can't be done in isolation. There are requests for people to fundamentally change the way they farm. Well, OK. But they're not requesting changes in farm policy and logistics. Changes can come about only if everyone participates in changing the system."

"Farms need to be more profitable," asserted Doug. "Right now we pay for the privilege of farming." The USDA data shows that 89 percent of producers make less than $350,000 (gross) annually. This sector counts on most of its disposable income coming from off-farm jobs.[60]

Vilicus relies "heavily" on Anna's salary from the Forest Service. The farm also has an array of associated enterprises, including custom grazing, custom farming, direct (value-added) sales, and occasional speaking fees. As much as they'd like to minimize any federal government input, Vilicus is enrolled in USDA programs to support conservation, crop insurance, and direct farm income subsidy. Some of these, Doug said, feel like a distraction or "mission creep."

Crop insurance in particular makes him feel uncomfortable. "I have often referred to (federally) subsidized crop insurance as the biggest perversion in agriculture. It's an uncomfortable dichotomy, to say the least. While the model is fundamentally flawed, the variability of crop production and revenue makes crop insurance a necessary evil for most farms that grow 'commodity crops' at scale."

As a metric, yield is of minor importance. "It's a dead-end quest," he says. "It's just the opposite of how natural systems work. The production mindset, with its imperative to expand as the only means of survival, pits farmer against farmer and family against family. When a farmer dies in commodity farm country, there's a jostling at the funeral to who is going to be the first in line to talk to the widow."

Doug and Anna are skeptical of the idea that "anything we have to buy to make us 'better' farmers" makes sense. "There is no one single solution. What works for us might not work for the neighbors. Diversity is THE answer is what nature shows us. There's no recipe. Every farm has to come up with their own solutions. Right now, we're addicted to external solutions. Instead, we need to think about associative economies."

Yet, said Anna, "we can't go back to a system of farming the land with horses. We need a better relationship with natural systems. We describe ourselves as a teaching farm. We also want to be researchers. We also see ourselves as stewards of the land. We want to see ourselves as a problem-solving university."

Who works at Vilicus Farms?

In the neatest, most well-organized shop I've seen in recent memory, I wait for Ben Clark, Vilicus Farms mechanic and all-around fix-it whiz. A well-used GMC pickup sits in the bay. Written in yellow pencil on the windshield: *Gauge problems. Transmission issues.*

Ben, who is lean, tan, and wiry, arrives after going to Havre to get groceries. He scrounges up a pair of lawn chairs; we sit in the shade of the second shop. We face the Sweetgrass Hills, forty miles off in the distance. Ben offers me a room temperature hard kombucha. Ben is from Massachusetts and not from a farming background. Family conflict rendered schisms in his family. He ran away from home when he was seventeen, often staying with friends. He drifted toward staying with a friend, whose dad had a small backyard farm. "His mom owned a cafe and used to serve the produce in the cafe."

Ben saw what he liked and apprenticed at an organic farm north of

Boston for two years. He also played music, mostly piano. He then transitioned to a farm that raised beef and pork in the Berkshires. Next to it was a raw milk dairy farm. "It was basically checking off the boxes. I knew how to raise vegetables; I knew how to raise beef and pork; I know how to work on a dairy."

But farm work and music proved a killer combination.

Play until 3 AM then up at 6 to milk cows. Plus, the pay: Miller Lite in the back room. Only one of these jobs has a future, I thought.

The thing is, I discovered that many of these operations were always dependent on a bigger farm somewhere else, like getting grain from Canada. I wondered: what would it be like if we didn't have to do that? There are a few grain farms in the northeast, but it was tough to get jobs at them. So, I started putting out feelers. Doug and Anna were the only ones out there, really. It's funny because when I interviewed with them, I said to myself: I've heard about these guys somewhere then realized afterwards I'd read about them in the *Lentil Underground*. I'm interested in the idea of re-integrating cattle into grain agriculture. When I heard they were exploring this, I got super excited. But I told them: I'm looking for a long-term steady job. I've already been an apprentice.

"What do you want? Why are you here?" I ask.

I don't know. Agriculture is changing and I want to make that change happen. So, I started servicing equipment. You ask me: how does a diesel tractor work? I couldn't tell you. I've got no experience in mechanics. But I'll find out. I want to learn from it and the integration of machinery in the field. This is incredibly cliché, but I learned a lot from *Zen and Art of Motorcycle Maintenance*, particularly that line of you're always afraid of what you don't understand. I was in the music hippie world. Jam bands. Grateful Dead and Phish. It was easy for people to say, "we should be barefoot, flower-wearing simple societies."

That worldview did not sit well with Ben.

I got very frustrated with that. So, for me, that meant looking at food and food systems. I read a lot. I discovered that grain used to be one of the most expensive crops to raise. The labor involved in planting, tending, harvesting and storing made it very costly. Then came the internal combustion engine. Grain rapidly became the least expensive crop to raise. That up-ended agriculture. That up-ending is playing out before our eyes. I suppose it might come down to an existential question: are we going to be here if we don't figure this out? I push myself to understand everything I can. I am not afraid of this world. My passion isn't mechanics. My passion is understanding, and understanding the tools we need to take care of this world.

After his first stint at Vilicus Farms, Doug and Anna asked him to stay; they wanted him to sign a three-year contract. "That was a big ask. I told them I'd need to think about that. But I did it. I've poured myself into this place. That's what we do here. We work really hard. Many twelve-hour days. But I'm very content with my decision."

Gabe Brown

Gabe Brown does not merely talk about regenerative agriculture. He is the discipline's chief evangelist.[61]

Regenerative agriculture, says Brown, is a farm system that focuses on the whole chain: soil health, plant health, animal health, and human health. Nutrient density is important in regenerative agriculture, he says. "It gets the farmer and rancher closer to the consumer, to the end user, and those consumers are willing to pay for that."

It also benefits the community. "There is a direct correlation to their health and the health of the land that surrounds their community," he says.

There is also a direct economic connection. Brown's Ranch, located east of Bismarck, has spun off seventeen different enterprises. Brown estimates these have created about fifty new jobs. Brown Ranch and its marketing arm, Nourished by Nature, are pioneers in direct marketing.

To teach others about regenerative agriculture, Brown became involved in two separate entities run under the same roof in Ft. Payne, Alabama: Soil Health Academy, a nonprofit focused on teaching, and Understanding Ag, a consulting firm. "Understanding Ag has signed a contract with General Mills to teach farmers about regenerative agriculture. We're on ninety farms. They want a steady supply of these regenerative grains."

Transparency is part of his plan. "Anybody can go on our ranch and look around. That builds trust."

Listening to Brown address an audience, you realize you're dealing with a force of nature. He's sixty-six years old, built like a fireplug, and sports a ball cap. Relaxed yet radiating energy, Brown delivers his message with a combination of data and down-home storytelling. Most of it relates to his own Job-like experience with farming.

One additional attribute: Brown is blunt—sometimes very blunt. "Some folks call me an arrogant ass. Maybe I am. But if I don't say it, who will? All those problems with conventional ag? I've experienced them and lived to tell the tale."

He considers most conventional agricultural wisdom to be filled with holes, including this county's infatuation with yield and the "feed-the-world" narrative.

"Agriculture, since WWII, or when fertilizer came cheap, has focused on mass production. More pounds, more yield. Under this mantra, we have to feed the world. Well, last statistics I looked at, which were 2017, there were 7.1 billion on this planet. We produced enough food for 10.2 billion. Producing food is not the problem. The problem is with logistics, government and corruption in getting it to the masses."

"It's pounds over profits," says Brown. "And the rural economy has suffered because of it. I tell anyone who will listen: I'll take profit over pounds and yields any day."

He doesn't believe that distance from an organic hot spot (or any urban market willing to pay higher prices) should hinder your agricultural aspirations, even if it's selling perishable foods. "Isolation is not a reason not to sell your products. We sell our products (through direct marketing) in Florida and Texas."

He also bucks the assumption that producing crops that turn into healthy food requires organic origin. He hasn't used a chemical on his crops since 2009 but refuses to chase after organic certification. Soil health, he says, is more important.

Brown has six general principles for regenerative farming: no till (soil needs an armor, he says); plant cover crops; minimal chemical application; plant diversity, including having a living root in the soil most of the time; animal and insect integration; and context—that is, regenerative practices will differ region to region.

The largest impediment—the most antagonistic force—to regenerative farming: the USDA farm program, Brown says. "Most farmers require an operating loan. Their bank won't lend them the money unless the farmer participates in a USDA program (such as crop insurance)."

"Farmers and ranchers are paid based on past history, pounds, and yield. They are not paid for ecological services and soil health. The more yield they have, the more revenue insurance they can buy. They are almost guaranteed that. I think that's ridiculous. We're not guaranteeing ma and pa's restaurant, are we? Why are we guaranteeing farmers?"

Like Quinn, Brown regrets the shift away from research by land grant universities. Few outside agriculture realize that private investment, not universities, drives agricultural research. As Paul Heisey, an economist with the Economic Research Service, wrote, "Both private and public sectors help fund agricultural research and development (R&D), but due to its rapid growth, private spending is now much greater than public spending—which fell in real terms between 2006 and 2014. Private research spending on agricultural input R&D alone—not including food research—surpassed total public spending in 2010."[62]

"What company is going to fund research at land grant universities when you're working with nature [that is, using few chemicals or genetically engineered seed]?" asks Brown.

He also shares a stewardship farmer's endorsement of inclusivity. Brown calls himself a Libertarian Christian. On the Brown's Ranch website, he declares, "We believe that faith, family and working with the natural resources that God has provided allows us a meaningful life."

Yet in a letter he wrote to *Successful Farmer*, he expressed exasperation after testifying on February 25, 2021, before the US House Agriculture Committee. The congressmen "were missing a genuine opportunity to unite for the common good." Brown continued that his primary consulting firm, Understand Ag, believes that "we are all in this together. Political beliefs, religion, race, creed, none of those should divide us. Rather, we should focus on what is best for society and our planet."[63]

Like many involved in stewardship agriculture, Brown did not grow up driving a tractor. He was raised in Bismarck, married a farm girl and eventually bought her family's place. He describes it as a pretty conventional farm: plowing, chemical fertilizers and herbicides, and monoculture. He raised spring wheat, oats, barley, and raised livestock, too. In 1993, after extensive research on no-till, he sold his plow and all tillage equipment. Since then, his ground has never been tilled.

Then he hit a rough patch. In 1995, he lost his entire crop—1,200 acres—of spring wheat to a hail storm. No hail insurance. Nature pulled the same nasty stunt in 1996: hail took 100 percent of his wheat crop. He was $2 million in debt. Then came a blizzard that killed many of Brown's cattle. "I was flat broke," he said. "Had a pile of debt."

It was a singular moment for Brown. "I said, boy, I better try something different. How am I going to make this ranch productive without buying all these inputs?" He began alternative rotations, planting rye and hairy vetch, triticale, and peas. Brown and wife took off-farm jobs to pay the bills. His banker believed in him, even though 1997 saw a major drought, but wouldn't lend him any more money. "Never combined an acre." The fourth year, 1998, they lost 80 percent of their crop to hail. "So, we had four years in a row with basically no income."

With the hard times came minor revelations. "I noticed that with the no till and smashed wheat on the ground, I was building up an armor on the soil. Earthworms. My soil was more aggregated, so when it did rain, my soil held more water."

"Thanks to crop failures, I changed the way I look at our land. Unfortunately, the Good Lord had to slap me four times before I woke up," he wrote in *Dirt to Soil*.[64] Encounters with National Resource Conservation Specialist Jay Fuhrer and USDA microbiologist Kris Nichols fundamentally changed the way Brown looked at farming. Nichols, for example, told him to quit using synthetic fertilizers. They prevented critical mycorrhizal fungi from doing their job. Then Brown heard Brazilian agronomist Ademir Calegari talk about the multispecies cover crops, not just two varieties planted at once, but seven or eight. Ray Archeleta, an NRCS agronomist from North Carolina, came to visit Brown on his farm. The two became friends and, eventually, business partners in Understanding Ag.

Next came adjusting his cattle production away from weight gain to toward forage adaptability. This meant breeding a small animal and mimicking nature's birth cycle. Calves were born in warm April and May rather than freezing February. This has not hurt Brown's bottom line. "In 2018, I cleared $1,467 per beef animal. That includes all costs: pasture, transportation, processing, labor, storage and delivery. What is the average net profit for most ranchers? $100, maybe?"

In North Dakota, "the average net return in 2021 was $102.12 per cow, which is an increase of $70.67 per cow from 2020," according to the *Dakota Farmer*.[65] In Idaho, a cow-operator could expect to clear $29 in 2020.[66]

The Baton Theory of Agriculture—Pass the Farm onto Your Children—Is on Its Last Legs.

Brown recalls a speaker asking the audience: How many of you have a son, daughter, or relative taking over or planning to take over your operation? Out of two hundred people only Gabe and one other person raised their hand. How come? Brown began asking people. The answer: not enough income and the cost of entry was simply too expensive. Brown's son, Paul, didn't need much encouragement, says his father. But he understands why young people aren't following in their parents' footsteps. "There is no room in the commodity market for young people to come in," Paul said. "Look around you. There are people farming millions of acres, all doing the same thing. You have to make yourself different from your neighbors, otherwise you'll just get thrown into a slew of a never-ending commodity cycle."[67]

Paul wanted to join the ranch as soon as he graduated from high school. Paul's parents insisted on college. He attended a local community college and then transferred to North Dakota State University (NDSU), where he majored in ranch management.

Was what he learned at NDSU helpful to what he does now, which is to run the direct marketing for Brown's Ranch? "No, not really," he said. "It was great from a social aspect but that's about it."

It was about this time he started reading books about regenerative agriculture and its connection to direct marketing. Paul always aimed to return to the farm. "My parents encouraged me, but only if I wanted to be there. They didn't pressure me. I saw that we had to free ourselves from the commodity market. I didn't want to make a living off taxpayer subsidies. That didn't seem very satisfying."

It began small. "I started off with laying hens in 2010. A guy who ran a CSA [community supported agriculture] garden let me sell eggs along with this produce in the back of a pickup. Lamb followed. Next it was pork. All pasture raised and no confinement; i.e, open grazing for cattle, lamb, and chickens."

The family started Brown's Marketing, LLC. Next came Nourished by Nature, a direct marketing program with its own website. Run by Paul, it sells everything raised on Brown's Ranch. While profitable under normal conditions, demand soared 500 percent during the Covid-19 pandemic. Many products sold out.

"We have about 17 different enterprises. 137 products. That makes us very resilient. We become price makers, not price takers," said Gabe. Paul agrees with this father: Brown Ranch and Nourished by Nature are not unique. "Anyone can do this. You just have to think out of the box."

Is There a Takeaway?

I've dedicated this chapter to this very aspiration: How do we encourage 89er commodity agriculture—those producers concentrating on livestock and grains/pulses—to consider a different path moving forward? How do we encourage more first adaptors? How do we—as a society—promote stewardship agriculture in all its forms? Conventional agriculture shows no promise of being able to promote the kind of society envisioned by the authors of the 1889 constitutions. It conjures up, in fact, a terrible paradox. The residents of 89er country identify, however, so strongly with agri- culture. Yet year after year, we hear more bleak news: consolidation, the barrier to entry for young producers, and the economic and demographic struggles of regions dependent on agriculture. According to the USDA, farmers and ranchers received "14.5 cents per dollar spent on domestically produced food in 2021—a decrease of 1.0 cent from a revised 15.5 cents in 2020—to the lowest recorded farm share value in nearly three decades."[68]

Regenerative/stewardship ranching is neither a black-and-white ap- proach nor a quick path to riches. Montana rancher and co-founder of the Old Salt Co-op Cole Mannix said that a lot of his neighbors in the Blackfoot Valley try to be good managers, but they end up selling into the commodity food chain.

That commodity supply chain is built to squeeze down our margin. And the less margin we all have, the less time we can think about ecological practices. Instead, we're reduced to cutting costs, such as the labor essential to stewardship, just to survive another year. And so, when no money is flowing to stewardship and you're squeezed thin, you're not going to be putting mental bandwidth to, "How do I manage bird habitat a little bit differently?" or "How's our soil monitoring program going?" I think we really get wrapped around the wrong axles in the whole regenerative agriculture movement. It's not just about better practices in a vacuum, it's about a food system built to sustain those practices.

Cole added,

Old Salt Co-op is really trying to avoid drawing a bright line between regenerative agriculture versus conventional, although we care deeply about better agricultural practices. It's a spectrum, and at the end of the day we need system wide food change that returns more value back to all producers. Regenerative practices must be supported by regenerative customers and everything in between. Regionalization of the food system![69]

This struggle to accommodate creates tremendous pressure on society's sense of identity. Repairing it begins with what educator and sociologist Shawn Ginwright advocates: moving from problem fixing to solution creating.[70] Concentrate on what you want, not what you don't want. We want vital and resilient rural communities. Yet agriculture regions in the Great Plains and Northern Rockies face the same demons they dealt with 125 years ago: monopoly and overproduction of an undifferentiated product.

It didn't start out that way. In 1870—territorial times for the 89ers—rural American farm communities were the source of stability, despite a colonial economy based on exporting raw products and outside capital. "But however much they actually relied on the outside world, they still managed to retain the sense of living largely to themselves," writes historian Robert Wiebe. "With farms generally fanning around them these communities moved by the rhythms of agriculture: the pace of the sun's day, the working and watching of the crop months, the cycle of the seasons."[71]

And, continues Wiebe, there was a rural-town bond, as there is today in Winnett.

Relatively few families lived so far from town that they did not gravitate to some degree into its circle, and there people at least thought they knew all about each other after crossing and re-crossing paths over the years. Usually homogeneous, usually Protestant, they enjoyed an inner stability that the coming and going of members seldom shook. Even when new towns were established in fresh farm country, the gathering families brought the same familiar habits and ways so that a continuity was scarcely disturbed.

Those sleepy towns have mostly faded away. Stewardship agriculture keeps them from fading further. The proposed solutions may strike some as banal, but without variations of them, agriculture is stuck on the treadmill. Taken as an aggregate, they make a difference:

- Stop buying your beef, chicken, lamb, pork, and eggs at the grocery store. Patronize a local regenerative or organic farmer/rancher instead. Often you can find them at farmer's markets. If none in your area, there are literally dozens of producers who offer products online.
- Support regional ranchers and farmers striving to build local slaughterhouses. Even small operations are expensive. We're talking $1 million per facility at least. Sometimes this requires state economic development funding.
- Buy your grains or flour from mills that support organic or regenerative agriculture. The best choice—the one with the greatest overall regional impact—is to buy flour from local producers. If that's not available, even the big boys are in the regenerative game. By 2030, General Mills has committed to supporting over one million acres of grain grown regeneratively.
- There's a political angle. Stewardship agriculture is a bottom-up movement. "You don't change Washington, it's broken," says Gabe Brown. "The only way this happens is ground up. It's going to be from the farmers."[72] This remains true even as the USDA rolls out programs that encourage new agriculture practices, such as Partnerships for Climate Smart Commodities. As the name suggests, climate change—not stewardship or reviving small agriculturally based communities—drives this program.

- Make production agriculture more attractive to the young farmer or rancher. Create a support system for young farmers. The Natural Resource Conservation Service already attends to this but has a budget ($14.6 million in grants in 2020), a pittance when compared to crop insurance. Crop science majors and budding FFA members no longer play any significant role in production farming.

- Access to credit. Poorly structured loans, many using variable interest rates, buried many farmers in the 1980s. Not having access to credit wasn't an option. What they don't need is a handout, to wit: so do away with crop insurance. As currently designed, crop insurance does stewardship agriculture no favors. "Crop insurance and other bailouts are well-intentioned programs but [they are] perhaps the biggest dam in the regenerative river," said Cole Mannix.[73] Roughly 74 percent of American farm acres, or 290 million acres, are covered by crop insurance. The US taxpayer covers 60–70 percent of crop insurance costs.[74] "The billions of dollars paid to insurance companies to subsidize crop insurance could, instead, be paid to farmers to provide basic income and support practices that build soil and encourage community. Crop insurance does the opposite," said Doug Crabtree.

- The federal Whole-Farm Revenue Protection (WFRP) program, which insures a farm's entire production, not individual crops, has shown promise in promoting a different agricultural narrative. But the financial incentives need to shift from yield to soil health and crop diversity. Currently, most USDA conservation programs, such as the Environmental Quality Incentives Program (EQIP), are voluntary. Other pilot programs, such as the Soil Health and Income Program, are basically a glorified land set-aside, similar to the Conservation Reserve Program.

- Support transition programs for organic or regenerative agriculture. The Natural Resource Conservation Service offers funding for certified organic producers through the Conservation Activity Plan (or CAP 138), which supports organic transition.

- Encourage states to step up to the plate. Many states, such as Montana's Growth Through Agriculture program, do this but they don't provide nearly enough financing for two key elements of stewardship farming: transition from conventional to regenerative/organic agriculture and serious financial backing to get young farmers into production.

• Bolster the participation of land trusts or private financing with interests in stewardship agriculture, such as Iroquois Valley Farms, which is a farmland REIT (Real Estate Investment Trust). Portland-based Steward advertises itself as "the first lending platform built exclusively to support the growth of generative farmers."[75] Groups like the Compeer Financial Organic Bridge Loan also offer services. California Certified Organic Farmers offers up to $10,000 to California farmers transitioning from conventional to organic agriculture.

And finally, land grant schools, so revered by the authors of these 1889 constitutions, need to up their game. "Imagine after the establishment of the gasoline engine and automobile, and the majority of our (land grant) research budget was on how to perfect the stagecoach?" asked Bob Quinn. "That's where we are now."[76]

4

Deadwood, Dakota, December 6, 1877: "Kitty Leroy a jig dancer, well known throughout the country, and particularly in the west, was shot and instantly killed this morning, and her murderer instantly afterwards destroyed his own life with the same pistol. Kitty came to Deadwood from Texas, with one Raymond, six months ago. Soon they fell out, and she took up with Samuel Curley, a well-known Faro dealer in the west, and a few weeks ago they were married by the justice of the peace here. Curley subsequently went to Sydney, leaving his wife, when her friendship with Raymond was restored, and criminal intimacy followed. Curley returned on yesterday, and, learning of the affairs between his wife and Raymond, declared his intention of killing her and himself. After supper, tonight, he went upstairs, at the Lone Star Hotel. Meeting with his wife in the front room, he drew a Smith and Wesson 444 pistol, and instantly fired, the ball entering her breast between the nipples. She fell a corpse, whereas he put the pistol to own temple for the second shot and fell by the side of his wife, dead. The deceased woman was about 28, and a great favorite as a dancer and had achieved considerable popularity."
—*Daily Press and Dakotian, December 9, 1877*

Modern America both revels in and recoils at the violence of the old West towns. We largely romanticize and mythologize these places, the fodder for Hollywood creations. But generally—as a spot for our home—westerners don't like towns. We'd rather live in the country. Yet in 1889, we weren't talking about any sprawling metropolis sullying the northern plains and Rockies. According to the 1890 Census, the largest municipalities in the region were Butte (10,723), Sioux Falls (10,177), and Cheyenne (11,690). By contrast, Chicago, New York, and Philadelphia each had over one million souls in 1890.[1]

Still, many westward migrating citizens carried the stigma that towns were to be avoided. Some sought to cement ill thoughts of municipalities into statute. One Midwesterner, John Forest Dillion, spent most of his career casting calumny on anything urban, particularly small cities and towns. Dillion, Chief Justice of the Iowa Supreme Court, gained fame for his 1868 Dillon's Rule, a legal interpretation that restricts the powers of municipalities.

Dillion thought ill of the people running village society, saying, "Those best fitted by their intelligence, business experience, capacity and moral character" do not run local governments. The conduct of municipal affairs was generally "unwise and extravagant."[2]

Admittedly, a number of 89er cities—and a few counties—did not enjoy stellar reputations. Bismarck had a particularly dark reputation. One block of Fourth Street, the haunts of saloons and gambling halls, was known as "Bloody Fourth."

Some problems could be chalked up to economic naïveté, not gunplay, brothels, and gambling. Yankton County, Dakota Territory (which encompassed the city of Yankton), got itself into trouble with railroad bonds.[3] In 1871, the county—with voter approval—donated $200,000 worth of bonds to the South Dakota Railroad Company. But they refused to pay the interest on these bonds, even when the US Supreme Court said they must. Creditors were not amused and flexed their muscles in Washington. When South Dakota petitioned Congress for statehood in 1882, Senator Eugene Hale of Maine, a Republican no less, testily squashed the effort. He "objected to conferring statehood upon a territory whose people took their financial obligations so lightly."[4]

This blunder reinforced the idea that lower political subdivisions were not to be trusted. Constitutional delegates remembered this in 1889. Ever since statehood, legislatures of the Great Plains and Northern Rockies have restricted the ability of urban regions to raise revenue.

The Wyoming Association of Municipalities, exasperated with this servitude, published a report in 2016 stating, "Restrictions on local taxation authority and municipal access to the local tax base cause Wyoming cities and towns to have the least local fiscal authority and the highest reliance upon State resources among the 50 States."[5]

This trend to restrict the power of municipalities is growing, particularly in Montana. A study by the National League of Cities revealed that acts of preemption—that is, using legislation to usurp the powers of a lower political subdivision—are on the rise. Of all states, "Montana passed the most laws that limit local authority (five) and was the only state that passed laws across the four grouped domains (employment, housing, firearms and municipal broadband)."[6]

Despite handicaps, towns proved critical. Even in territorial times, it turns out that farmers, ranchers, loggers, and miners needed banks, courts, and other professional services, like surveyors and doctors. The larger the urban area, the greater the opportunity. During the Great Depression, larger 89er cities grew modestly in population. Bismarck's population doubled from 1920 to 1940. Small towns began to fade.

Rural Exceptionalism

It's a good time to think differently about urban areas. For many in rural areas, the term "cities" conjures images of a sprawling megalopolis burdened by traffic-clogged roads, pollution, high taxes, and rising crime rates. Yet cities in 89er country, many with under fifty thousand people, such as Helena, Montana, and Minot, North Dakota, have few—or at least fewer—of these problems. They punch above their weight when it comes to jobs and revenue streams. The bigger the city, the more powerful the punch. For example, the total assessed valuation for Ada County, Idaho (Boise), for 2022 was $35 billion. That is nearly three times the assessed valuation for the *entire* state of Wyoming in the same period, which was $12.6 billion.

Yet, to paraphrase Rodney Dangerfield, cities don't get no respect. Problems arose over a century ago from a skewed social contract. Remnants of what Fredrick J. Turner called the *forest philosophy*—the virtue of a rural society—remained.[7] While citizens came to see municipalities as necessary evils, this grudging acceptance came only if towns stayed in their place and didn't get uppity. Towns and cities would serve the needs of the rural constituency. Not the other way around. By restricting taxing powers, legislatures discouraged municipalities from operating independently; that is, cities for their own sake. Banks and legal firms serviced the farming, ranching, and energy industries. Cities supported land grant universities. These institutions educated students in the educational, engineering, and agricultural arts, all with the aim of creating a more prosperous rural society. Legislatures in state capitals tended to the needs of their farming, ranching, or mining constituents.

Cities grew anyway. Cultural institutions such as museums or opera houses helped diversify the economy. So did churches, hospitals, and federal offices. Still, Fargo, Billings, Casper, and Sioux Falls were reactive and based on a colonial economy with little diversification. When commodity busts arrived, cities survived but suffered.

WWII relegated 89er towns into three categories: thrivers, survivors, and goners. Towns with under five thousand people began a slow and sometimes terminal decline. Cities with over twenty-five thousand people grew in fits and starts; their economies still connected to the commodity index. From 1960 to 1970—a slow time in the energy industry—the population of Casper, Wyoming, grew only 1.1 percent. The following decade it grew by 30 percent when oil, gas, and coal boomed.[8]

It's hard to pinpoint the exact date but sometime in the late 1970s and early 1980s, certain parts of the 89er country began to consistently thrive. Others did not. In general terms, the winners were cities that encouraged diversification from commodities and regions that capitalized on their scenic amenities. Places like Teton County, Idaho, went from having forty years of negative population growth to 23 percent growth from 1970 to 1980. In the same time period, Flathead County, Montana, had 32 percent growth in population, its biggest leap ever.[9] From 1980 to 1990, Sioux Falls metropolitan statistical area (MSA) grew by 24 percent in population, despite a brutal agricultural recession.

Why some rural or isolated towns have flat (or no) growth and others prosper has been analyzed ad infinitum.[10] Little I could say here would add to the conversation, although the Covid-19 pandemic and shifting job patterns have changed matters.

For some small cities, pandemic or not, exuberant growth was foretold. Bozeman, Montana, has gone from having 21,600 people in 1980 to 56,495 in 2022. An abundance of amenities—natural beauty, easy access to national forests and Yellowstone National Park, a hip land-grant university, being close to an interstate, and commendable air transport—made its rise almost inevitable.

Not all cities and towns have a similar trajectory. While Bozeman grew, Jamestown, North Dakota, Thermopolis, Wyoming, and Hot Springs, South Dakota, shrank. How come? Both Thermopolis and Hot Springs, as their names imply, have thermal springs open to the public. While these two places may not offer scenic grandeur—like the Tetons or the Beartooth Mountains—they have their own beauty and offer easy access to public land. Three colleges exist within a twenty-five-mile radius of Jamestown, yet it has fewer people than it did in 1980.

For Hot Springs and Thermopolis, demography and a dependency on government and energy isn't doing these cities any favors. Neither of these occupations are known for innovation. Moreover, these places are filled with the middle-aged. The average age in Fall River County, South Dakota (home to Hot Springs), is 54.4 years. In Hot Springs County, Wyoming (home to Thermopolis), it's 46 years old. The average age in the United States is 38.1.

Both places are also overly dependent on non-labor income: investments, pension payments, rents, social security, Medicare, and Medicaid.[11] For Fall River County, 50 percent of personal income comes from nonlabor sources. For Hot Springs County, it's 41 percent of personal income.

Having residents rely on nonlabor income can be a boon; it all depends on their generosity. But in 242 89er counties, all but a handful receive at least 30 percent of their revenue from non-labor income. Typically, what you have is a middle-aged population unconcerned about wealth creation. Instead they seek wealth preservation, which is not a recipe for vitality.

Jamestown is different. It's got a young-ish population, with the median age right at the national average: thirty-eight. It's fortunate enough to have a strong manufacturing sector. It has an abundance of affordable housing. In 2023, you could purchase a cute home in Jamestown for under $150,000. But, says North Dakota demographer Kevin Iverson, it's got old Dakota challenges. "I have always found Jamestown to represent the most 'typical' city in North Dakota. It is kind of a bellwether of what is happening with the state's cities."

Jamestown's lack of vitality stems from a dependency on agriculture. Of North Dakota's 244 cities, or Census Designated Places, 61 percent saw no growth or a reduction in population. "Thirty of the State's 53 counties lost population," said Iverson. "All tend to have agricultural based economies, and have been losing population for decades. The vast majority of the State's growth happened in the state's largest cities and counties and in the west where oil development had a major impact."[12]

Bigger cities also impact Jamestown's prosperity. The "gravity" of Fargo and Bismarck, "both much larger than Jamestown, and their ability to pull individuals for employment, has impacted Jamestown, as both MSAs are straight down Interstate 94 in opposite directions," Iverson said.

Fundamental Issues Challenging Historic 89er Values: Polarization, Adjusting to Post-Covid, and Roadblocks for Women

In the 89er region, a Montana husband-and-wife team, Mark and Julia Haggerty, offer some pragmatic ideas as to improving the fate of rural cities and towns.[13] They include the importance of local institutions and prudent fiscal policy choices.[14]

But analysts rarely discuss the importance of cultural identity. Most 89er towns have commodity roots. Successful ones have moved away from a dependence on oil, gas, timber, and agriculture. But, if they can help it, they don't give up these occupations entirely. Doing so threatens a region's cultural identity and causes a host of problems, mostly fueling a polarization between the "old" and the "new" West. The Sagebrush Rebellion and wise use movement, both rooted in rural anger over commodity restrictions on public lands, are just two examples of this dynamic.

By the same token, communities that make successful transitions to diverse economies avoid one critical reaction: they don't hunker down and wait for the next boom. Nor do they petition various governmental agencies, mostly the federal government, for a lifting of restrictions; that is, allowing more drilling on federal land or permitting a higher timber cut or additional grazing on the National Forest. Moreover, protesting the closing of a coal-fired power plant rarely guarantees its survival.

Instead, they adapt and look forward. They lean in on concepts of cooperation and collaboration. It's a predictable, well-documented path. Towns and rural areas begin working together. Streets get turned into walkable neighborhoods. Buildings get makeovers. Cities encourage in-building and discourage massive expansion projects at a town's edge. Anyone unfamiliar with this narrative should read Charles Marohn's *Strong Towns: A Bottom-Up Revolution to Rebuild American Prosperity.*[15]

One of the most profound observations on community prosperity comes from the pen of architect and visionary Christopher Alexander: "We must first recognize that what a town or building is, is governed, above all, by what is happening there. The life of a house, or of a town, is not given to it, directly, by the shape of its buildings, or by the ornament and plan—it is given to them by the quality of the events and situations we encounter there."[16]

What does Alexander mean by *what is happening there*? This statement goes to the heart of the question: What do we expect out of our communities? Alexander implies that we can build community, regardless of locale or external circumstances. Yet if we do everything "right," what kind of community is the result?

There is no correct answer, of course. Communities are forever in flux. But I think what Alexander is emphasizing is the necessity of *cooperation*, *innovation, risk taking,* and *mentoring.* Are residents engaged? Are they proactive in tackling challenges? Do their occupations embrace and engage the changes that an ever-shifting world demands? Are they teaching the next generation how to thrive in the world? Are they waiting for the arrival of an economic savior or do they take responsibility for their town's future? Or, by contrast, are they determined to keep the world as the world was—or how they think it was: fighting tax increases, voting down school bonding issues, and rebelling against innovation.

So, what's our ideal? A multiage, gender-balanced demographic engaged in a diverse economy and culture that supports financial resiliency, both municipal and individual?

Maybe. But that's a cold, bare-bones definition that could apply to any place, regardless of locality or political orientation. It doesn't talk about important intangibles, like safety or scenic amenities. Something more basic often gets ignored. Successful communities focus on the next generation. This does not mean ignoring the needs of retirees. It does require, however, an emphasis on young families and the needs of working women. And that's a problem, as, in recent years, 89ers cities and towns have become havens for retirees seeking a low-tax climate. Yet they demand services.

In addition, just as commodities are on the wane in most vital 89er communities, manufacturing, as a percentage of GDP, is slipping. This is not true of all cities, but it's the trend. In its stead comes services. In 2021, "the professional and business services industry" in Montana, for example, was "the largest contributor to the overall gain in real GDP . . . with gains in 2021 of more than $575 million over its 2020 level."[17]

"These service sector jobs are agglomerated in cities," said Haggerty, in an Aspen Institute talk on "Public Land and the Rural West." In the Pacific Northwest, Seattle, Portland, and Boise created 73 percent all new jobs and income, said Haggerty.[18]

Once again, as a century ago, cities matter. This time—with services on the ascendant—they really matter.

Lastly, the Covid-19 epidemic sent seismic shock waves throughout the world of work. According to the Pew Research Center, only 23 percent of Americans say they "teleworked frequently before the coronavirus outbreak." By 2022, nearly 60 percent said they worked almost exclusively from home.[19]

This jump toward home-based employment is made possible through work in professional services, as opposed to manufacturing, restaurant, or resource-based jobs. However, while this trend affirms that people can work from anywhere, including less populated areas, rarely do workers move to very remote areas.[20] Still, the 89ers, however rural, are included in this work trend.

In addition, over three million people retired earlier than expected during the pandemic. This meant a greater percentage of the population joined the nonlabor income constituency. Retirees seeking new places to live put tremendous pressure on housing, including in 89er communities. If your town had any sort of scenic amenity, prices really soared. In tiny (population, 2,134) Red Lodge, Montana, the average home value, circa

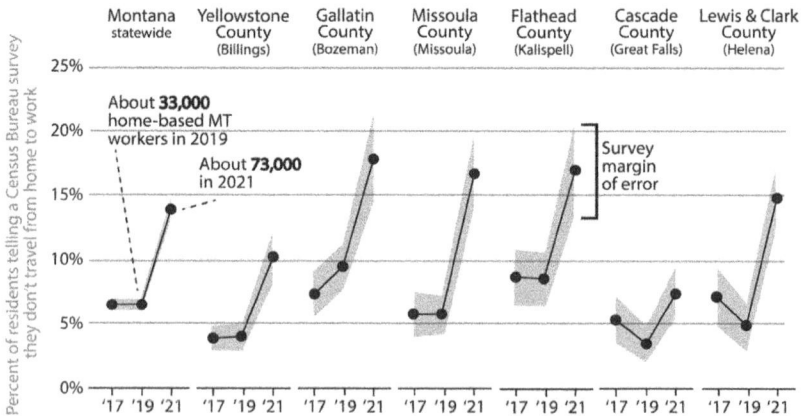

Figure 4.1. Working at home in Montana. Courtesy of *The Montana Free Press.*

2022, was $419,353, a 20 percent increase from the previous year. Just over the border in Wyoming, the median price of a home in Cody jumped 27 percent during the same period to $433,641.[21]

In fact, according to the U.S. Census Bureau and Zillow, housing prices in three 89er states, Idaho, South Dakota, and Montana, have experienced higher increases than many other states. Nationally, Montana leads the pack with a 60 percent increase in housing cost since February 2020.[22]

This trend does little to encourage a community of young families and women. Hence any city or town that isn't paying attention to American educational and cultural shifts is smoking crack. Women are shellacking men, numerically, in almost every category of advanced education.

Wall Street Journal writer Douglas Belkin made this case in a 2021 article titled "A Generation of Men Give Up on College: I Just Feel Lost."

> At the close of the 2020-21 academic year, women made up 59.5% of college students, an all-time high, and men 40.5%, according to enrollment data from the National Student Clearinghouse, a nonprofit research group. U.S. colleges and universities had 1.5 million fewer students compared with five years ago, and men accounted for 71% of the decline.[23]

For the first time in history, women make at least half of full-time MBA students at five top business schools: Penn State, University of Pennsylvania, University of Oxford, Johns Hopkins and George Washington University.[24]

On the national average in 2021, according to the US Bureau of Labor statistics, women occupied 53 percent of the positions in the banking industry (70 percent if you include credit unions); 61 percent of all insurance business; 52 percent of the real estate business; 57 percent of legal services; 64 percent of the accounting industry; 74 percent of educational services; 75 percent of all medical services, and 81 percent of all veterinary jobs.[25]

"You can't be naïve about the unequal distribution of gender in education," said economist Samuel Wolkenhauer of the Idaho Department of Labor. "I don't see this reversing anytime soon."[26]

"Professionals marry professionals," said Wolkenhauer.

I repeatedly hear the following story: companies or municipalities in Idaho want to hire talent from out of state. If it's a man, the job candidate will ask: "what would be the job opportunities for my wife? She's a professional with a career." And so often, the candidate will not take the job because his wife can't find meaningful work. You have to have a job for both members of the family.

A Worried Piece of Paradise

Yet one 89er city—and its surrounding region—until very recently, had managed to keep its traditional industries, diversify its economy (including tech, manufacturing, and recreation), attract and retain an eclectic workforce, including women: Sandpoint, the county seat of Bonner County, Idaho. If the definition of political pragmatism is an agenda based on practical considerations rather than theoretical ones, then this region—until recently—fit the bill.

The county's entrepreneurial zeal, doggedness in the face of economic troubles, and quality of life make it unique. In the 1980s, Bonner County survived a significant downturn in its central industry: timber. The region also weathered the tough times of one of its main employers, Schweitzer Mountain Resort, which went into bankruptcy in 1997. It managed to ride out the Great Recession, even when another one of its primary employers, Coldwater Creek, a retailer specializing in women's clothing, went out of business in 2014.

The fact that Schweitzer Mountain and Coldwater Creek existed in such a small community is a testament to Bonner County. Most rural, relatively isolated areas, rooted in commodities, rarely have such diversity. Those that do break away cash in on a single attribute: scenic amenities. Sun Valley, Vail, and Aspen were washed up mining towns. They ended up with another single-driver economy—high-end recreation-resort tourism—which has its own set of problems.

Commodities put Sandpoint on the map. The 1888 discovery of silver- and gold-bearing ore in the Pend Oreille Mining District brought prospectors to what is now Bonner County. While initially promising enough to build a smelter at Sandpoint, mining eventually fizzled out by 1927. The Idaho Inspector of Mines estimated $2 million in metals had been extracted.[27]

For the longer term, timber underwrote the prosperity of Sandpoint: millions of acres of old growth timber, including especially valuable western red cedar. The Humbird Lumber Company moved in around 1900 and quickly took over smaller mills. Funded in part by the Weyerhaeuser Syndicate, Humbird built its own mill. It burned down in 1907. Never mind that—Humbird constructed an even larger one. By the 1920s Humbird employed at least 500 men, turning out two hundred thousand board feet every twenty-four hours.[28] The Great Depression, however, revealed that not even the mighty are immune from market forces. By 1931, low demand silenced the mill. Liquidation came next.

As it did for so many commodity-driven towns, WWII broke the slump that had settled over Bonner County. The nation at war needed timber. One individual answered the call in an unusual way. In 1939, Jim Brown Jr., using his car as collateral, borrowed $500 and started the Sand Creek Lumber Company. He got his raw material from the thousands of sunken logs ("deadheads") that collected at the bottom of Pack River and Lake Pend Oreille. He changed his company's name to the Pack River Timber Company and soon purchased mills in nearby Colburn and Dover.

Pack River expanded, buying more mills and land and went on to become a major economic force in northern Idaho, Montana, and Washington. It brought Brown wealth; he eventually sold his timber holdings in 1979 for $105 million.[29]

But Brown was no ordinary entrepreneur, gifted with hustle and an eye for opportunity. Born eighty miles south of Sandpoint in the timber town of Harrison, Brown graduated from Gonzaga University in 1938 with a degree in philosophy. He took a lifetime interest in the commonweal. In 1982, he bought out the shareholders of Schweitzer Mountain, a small area started in 1963 by Jack Fowler, a Spokane dentist and ski aficionado. According to Fowler's 1991 book, *Looking Back on Schweitzer*, Fowler said Brown was adamant about a cardinal rule on any new amenity at Schweitzer Mountain: "It must be for children."[30]

Brown and his family would pour $50 million into improving Schweitzer Mountain. Unfortunately, after Brown's death in 1989, a series of bad decisions created unsustainable debt. Schweitzer Mountain was sold to Harbor Properties in 1998 for a reputed price of $18 million. The Seattle-based McCaw Investment Group now owns the resort.

The heart of this narrative is neither Brown's ascent to wealth nor missteps made in the managing of Schweitzer Mountain. It's that a man, born in small-town Idaho, who made millions in commodities recycled that wealth into a recreation economy. It was, moreover, in the same place that brought him his fortune. He was a locally grown entrepreneur that wasn't afraid to take big risks.

That is a singular story and, if replicated, is one of the most potent ingredients to achieve a vibrant economy for small towns. By contrast, look at other areas driven by a ski-area economy: Sun Valley was started by an Austrian royalty, Count Felix Schaffgotsch. A Chicago industrialist named Walter Paepcke founded the Aspen Ski Company in 1950. Peter Seibert, a 10th Mountain veteran from Massachusetts, masterminded the creation of Vail.

As Schweitzer Mountain expanded, timber faltered. At one point in the 1970s, Bonner County had approximately eleven sawmills.[31] Most shuttered their doors. The ones that survived remained financially troubled but would, thanks to technology and better markets, revive. That's another part of the secret sauce, too; these three mills helped Bonner County keep its cultural identity.[32]

In contrast to employment in most commodity sections, which either yo-yo to boom and bust or shrink due to technological advances, the timber industry in Bonner County offers steady employment. This includes both the number of jobs and wages. And yet, overall, these mills play only a small role in Bonner County's economy, employing only 359 people out of a labor force of 22,944.[33]

The highest occupational wage in northern Idaho is not a sawmill worker, for example; it's a nurse. A mill worker's median wage is $17.71. A nurse earns $33.41.[34]

Still, the idea of the land providing a sustainable commodity remains engrained. For example, the Sandpoint-based Kaniksu Land Trust owns 180 acres (with the purchase of additional acreage in the works) of forested land just west of town. The original idea was that the Pine Street Woods would provide a multipurpose recreation area with hiking and cross-country ski trails. Then, in 2020, a windstorm knocked down hundreds of trees, many of which had to be yarded out of the woods to clear trails. "We ended up with about six log trucks worth of trees," said Katie Egland Cox, executive director of the trust. "It turns out the mills didn't want the pine. So, what to do?"[35]

The answer soon arrived: purchase a small Norwood portable sawmill and teach people how to mill logs into lumber. Some of the lumber was used in construction outbuildings of the Pine Street Woods. The remainder was sold, with the proceeds going back to the trust.

The Bonner County Soil, Water, and Conservation (BCSWC) district got involved in the purchase of the mill. "Timber is always going to be a piece of our identity," said Sarah Garcia, the district administrator for the BCSWC.[36] "We're still a logging community, despite the changes we're seeing toward being a recreation economy. We saw this project as a chance to forward this (timber) identity in perpetuity. That's what drew the board into being involved."

Who Lives in Bonner County?

If you look at the population trends, it reveals a curious pattern. Just when the timber industry was in major decline (1970–1980), Bonner County experienced a huge population boom, growing by 55 percent.[37] That is the opposite of what usually happens during a bust in most commodity-dependent areas. Attracted by the quality of life and affordability, the young and adventurous moved in.

In 1977, $10,600 would buy you a condo at Schweitzer Mountain; a house in Sandpoint went for as little as $17,000; a two-bath, six-room house with lake frontage and a boat dock was listed for sale at $45,000. Raw land in the county could be had for under $1,000 per acre.[38]

These new residents, according to interviews, had a more relaxed vision of life. They were typically recreation-oriented, relying on seasonal work. But they were also teachers, administrators, and carpenters, and low-level managers after a certain quality of life. Attracted by the low price of housing and cost of living, they sometimes bought houses but took out mortgages.

The region also attracted creators. In 1995, the Spokane *Spokesman-Review* ran an article titled "Town Draws Artists; Sandpoint Area Home to An Astonishing Number of Major Artists."[39]

But residents also participated in venerable 89ers value: live and let live. This era is remembered, somewhat nostalgically, as the period when "hippies and loggers got along," said Susan Drumheller.[40]

Drumheller, who directs the local field office for the Idaho Conservation League, expressed this sentiment in a column for the *Bonner Daily Bee*. In the column she condemned the pushing and shoving fracas in Bonner County over mask policy during the Covid-19 pandemic. She called Bonner County as "the friendliest community we've known and loved."[41]

"Sandpoint is a kind of melting pot of cultural differences, from hippies to loggers, professionals to hermits living up in the woods, and young families to retirees," she wrote. "Sandpoint boasts a little of everything. The bottom line is that people here are genuine, not afraid to speak their mind and yet still willing to hear what someone else might have to say."

From 1990 to 2000, Bonner County's population grew by 31 percent. The newer residents had a different agenda than those newcomers of the past. Northern Idaho has a reputation for attracting adherents of conservative and anti-government beliefs. Often called the American Redoubt Movement for its embrace of an anti-urban and defensive view of life, Bonner County has become a preferred location for them.[42] Sandpoint is home to Flee the City, a real estate firm specializing in finding homes for the "common bond" of its customers.[43] That bond is characterized by a "deep respect and reverence for the U.S. Constitution and Bill of Rights, ultimately providing for a common defense from tyranny," according to Flee the City's website.

My phone calls and emails to anyone connected to northern Idaho's American Redoubt Movement went unanswered. This included trying to contact founder James Wesley Rawles—or Flee the City real estate representative Todd Savage or the editor of the *Redoubt News*, which advertises itself as "news and opinion online publication featuring the Christian conservative culture around, and important to, the American Redoubt."[44]

What I wanted to ask them was: are the pragmatic commonwealth ideals found in the state's 1889 constitution still embraced in northern Idaho?

If so, the evidence is scant. "Sandpoint is changing dramatically. It began about ten years ago," said Trish Gannon, editor of *Sandpoint Magazine*.[45] "We've become Republican and an extreme form of Republicanism at that. The curious thing is that women are at the forefront of this change. Women like Heather Scott (who now represents Bonner County in the state legislature) were involved in the Tea Party movement."

Timber may not have the clout it once did, said Gannon, who lived in Sandpoint most of her adult life. But "we now have a different kind of extraction economy. We're extracting our way of life. All this high-end housing and gated communities? They are extracting our natural amenities."

Drumheller and Cox model another ingredient of Sandpoint's economic durability: the area attracts people who can reinvent themselves. Repeated interviews with Sandpoint residents showed this to be a common trend.

Drumheller and Cox, for example, adapted their professional careers in order to stay in Sandpoint. Drumheller, a former reporter for the *Spokesman-Review*, now works in the conservation field.

> I was working as an editor out of the Coeur d'Alene office. I was driving back and forth each day, burning the candle at both ends. It was not sustainable. So, when the Conservation League opened up a field office in Sandpoint, I took a close look. I was prepared and lucky. I can tell anyone's story clearly and concisely. I've covered so many beats. I've rubbed shoulders with so many different types of people.

Drumheller also said her philosophical mindset toward humans helped her make the transition. "We typecast so quickly. People are more complex than that. I give people the benefit of the doubt. There are a lot more values we have in common than you might think."

Cox received a master's in architecture from the University of

Washington. In her professional career, she strove to design buildings that "gathered community."

When she moved to Sandpoint, she struggled to find work that fulfilled this desire. "Had to do work on decks and additions," she admits. Then she became part of a fundraising campaign to buy what would become the Pine Street Woods.

> We (the Kaniksu Land Trust) were successful but then the director left. I was asked if I'd looked at the job description. I hadn't. Well, I read the job description and realized I could gather community with this work. I threw my hat in the ring and was given the job. I do more to gather community with the land trust than I ever could with architecture. The foundation of our work is conservation focusing on how we connect people with the land they live on. My job, as executive director, is to listen, listen to the concerns of the community.

In the 1980s, Sandpoint became home to a couple who reinvented themselves in a big way. In 1984, Dennis and Ann Pence moved to Sandpoint. Two New Yorkers with backgrounds in commerce (her: Macy's) and marketing (him: Sony), they started a mail-order women's clothing company. Using $40,000 in savings and credit cards, the couple worked out of their small apartment, doing most of the layout and marketing themselves. A local newspaper printed their first catalog. It had eighteen items.[46]

By 1985, the enterprise had a name: Northcountry, which was changed shortly afterwards to Coldwater Creek.[47] The Pences focused on quality advertising but used no models. Instead, they cashed in on a sense of place, including photos of northern Idaho, creating a narrative of beauty and romantic isolation that appealed to the affluent urban female.

They began hiring and, over the next ten years, spent millions modernizing the company, using the latest data processing and communication technology. By 1991, the company grossed $11 million. Coldwater Creek opened a call center in Coeur d'Alene. Brick-and-mortar stores began popping up in places like Jackson Hole and Seaside, Oregon—then in Japan and Canada. By 1997, net sales reached $145 million. The company went public. In 2007, it had 306 stores and over $1 billion in gross revenue. All run out of Sandpoint.

The 2000s were not kind to retail. Economic trends eventually brought even giants like Sears to their knees. The same meteoric trajectory at which Coldwater Creek rose to prominence mirrored its demise. By 2014, the company filed for bankruptcy. In Sandpoint alone, three hundred jobs disappeared.

Sandpoint shuddered but soldiered on. Coldwater Creek's employees took their talents to other locally based employers. Jill Bentley, who worked in Coldwater Creek's HR department, took a job with a budding software company, Kochava. She is now head of the firm's HR department.

Shannon Barnes worked for eight years at Coldwater Creek, eventually becoming divisional vice president of human resources. Barnes said she saw the writing on the wall in 2014 and left Coldwater Creek before it folded. "I knew I wanted to stay in Sandpoint. It's just one of the most magical and beautiful places on earth. I'm a super outdoorsy kind of person and made it a priority to keep on living here."[48]

Barnes took several HR jobs before becoming Chief Human Resource Officer at Bonner General Hospital. "This is home," she said. "We've always had diversity in Sandpoint." Although she doesn't see eye to eye with some of the community's newest conservative residents, she understands why they came to Sandpoint.

It's no accident that the majority of these adaptable citizens are women. Throughout 89er history, women have supplied the community glue: they have taught school, performed administrative work in public offices, and ran institutions like community and senior centers.

Women of this era lacked political power, but more than a few of the 1889 constitutional conventioneers could see that changing. In some larger cities, such as Chicago, "nearly one-half of the clerical force are women," said Hiram Knowles of the Montana constitutional convention. Women are writing books, practicing medicine and law, preaching in church, and have almost "monopolized education," Knowles ventured. "I do suppose that the people of Montana territory have not yet advanced to the point where they are willing to say that women may take part in public matters, but the time may come," said Knowles, who represented Silver Bow County. "Public sentiment may change upon that matter. The world is moving."[49]

Well, it's taken a while. Women in Bonner County have gained some economic and political power, although they are still underrepresented.

There is only one woman on the board of the Bonner County commissioners. Out of the six members of the Sand Point city council, two are women.

Encouragingly, Idaho is only second to Montana in 89er states with the highest percentage of women in their state legislature, with 30.5 percent in 2024. Wyoming is the lowest, with 22.7 percent of the state house and senate made up of women in 2024.[50]

But even with educated, flexible, and community-oriented residents, Bonner County's formula for success is fraying. Maybe it's reached that point of no-return, particularly with the advent of Covid-19.

Sandpoint-based land planning consultant Jeremy Grimm (elected mayor in 2023) described what he calls the "Sandpoint/Bonner County transect." It's a blueprint, really, on how rural communities reinvent themselves only to become victims of their own success.[51]

Most of the jobs in Bonner County are in incorporated townships. Three out of four jobs in Sandpoint are held by residents outside the city, making it an economic hub for the region.[52]

As Grimm describes it, the timeline starts when a vision for a community arises after an extended patch of bad economic news. For Bonner County, it was the collapse of the timber industry in the late 1970s. Sometimes, new ideas are fueled by a collective memory of the commodity boom-and-bust cycle and a willingness to put such cycles behind them. "This is a 'look in the mirror' moment when there is buy-in, and people say let's change/diversify," Grimm said.

This meant boosting the region's recreational attributes (Schweitzer Mountain, Lake Pend Oreille) and promoting a healthy business climate. A business group called Sandpoint Unlimited printed a poster of a man in an armchair speaking on the phone. He's looking out his window at Lake Pend Oreille. Recreation gear, skies, mountain bike, and fishing gear litter his office. The caption reads: "Sandpoint Idaho, USA: We mean business . . . but don't forget your toys!"

People outside Bonner County began getting the message. "Some who vacation in the area realized they could relocate or start a business here," said Grimm. "The area's identity is changing, and the numbers prove it, like workforce, (new) businesses, prove it." Schweitzer Mountain underwent a dramatic expansion. By 2005, it became the largest ski area in Idaho. Companies already established in Sandpoint, such as Litehouse

Foods, famed for their salad dressings, expanded. Other locals started new companies, such as John and Mary Snedden, who, in 1991, began a line of manufactured dental products under the name of Unicep Packaging.[53] Before competitor Silgan Holdings bought the company in 2021, Unicep had sales of $45 million.[54] In 1991, missionary pilot David Voetmann and aircraft designer Tom Hamilton formed Quest Aircraft with the goal of building the ultimate single-engine aircraft. The firm went through various changes, including ultimately being bought by the French conglomerate Dahler. In December 2021, the company made its three hundredth delivery.[55]

The companies kept coming. Thorne Research, a nutritional supplement maker owned by Al and Kelly Czap, arrived from Seattle in 1990.[56] The firm did well enough to build a 60,000-foot headquarters in neighboring Dover. It still couldn't keep up with orders. Its success attracted outside attention; in 2005, WestView Capital Partners of Boston bought Thorne. In 2018, WestView sold their interest in Thorne Research to the Japanese-based firms Mitsui & Co. Ltd. and Kirin Holdings Company Ltd.

In 2011, Charles and Kimberly Manning started the software company Kochava, which creates attribution platforms for real-time data solutions for mobile and connected devices. It tracks people's location data and sells it to other companies. Advertisers use Kochava's products to measure the extent to which their mobile marketing affected sales. As of 2021, Kochava has 171 employees.

By now, "the entire local workforce is changing," said Grimm. "Maybe local government is funding an economic development position to respond to inbound calls. Maybe applying for site specific grants to support new businesses. There is cross-pollination—maybe—employees (with sufficient new skills in the community) come together to form new businesses." Housing goes off on a tear. The number of housing units in Bonner County rose from 15,152 units in 1990 to 19,646 in 2000 and 24,669 in 2010. But of the 2010 figure, 35.5 percent were vacant.[57]

Home values begins to climb, although slowly at first. As of 2013, the estimated median home value in Bonner County stood at $222,200. In 2015, it was $230,000. By 2017, the median price had reached $273,000.[58]

Bonner County, however, fell prey to a trend common to so many places of rural beauty in the West. Even though the cost of housing was

New Parcels Each Year

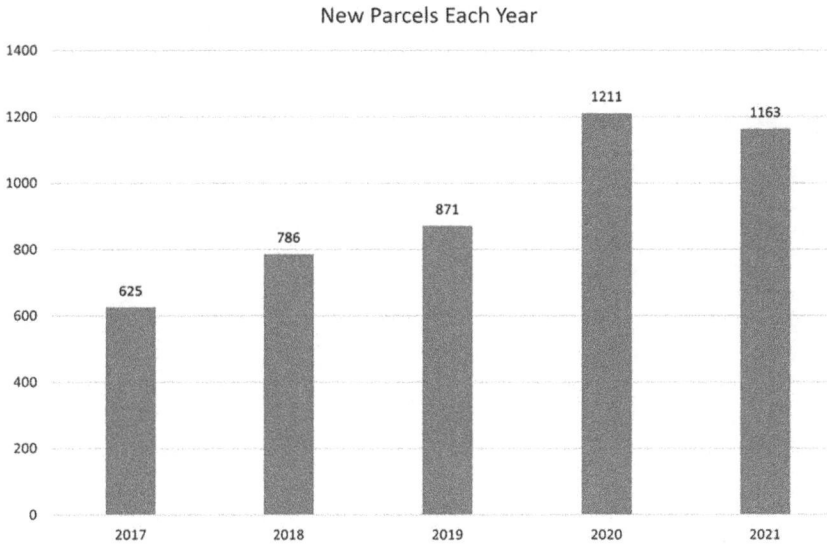

Figure 4.2. New parcels in Bonner County. Data by Bonner County Assessor. Graphics by Gage Graphics, Bozeman, MT.

climbing only modestly, it was too expensive for some. People sought lots and homes outside of town. By 2012, 72.4 percent of Bonner County's population lived outside urban areas.[59] Combine this dynamic with the American Redoubt movement, whose adherents seek rural living, and you have the ingredients for a zoning blowup, which is what happened in Bonner County.

The county exacerbated this trend in 2016 by creating a "Minor Land Division." This procedure grants land splits with only minor regulatory restraints—including no public hearing—if it offers four or fewer contiguous lots under common ownership. As a way to create raw land properties, it worked like a charm.

In three years, the number of new lots available in Bonner County doubled. Then came the pandemic and with it, an exploding demand for housing. By April 2020, the median price for a house in Sandpoint had jumped to $750,000; the median price in the county was only slightly less: $740,000. Costs and liabilities come to the fore, such as housing, infrastructure, and zoning complications.[60]

For example, in 2021, a development company called Pack River Partners asked the county commissioners to rezone a 714.23-acre rural parcel

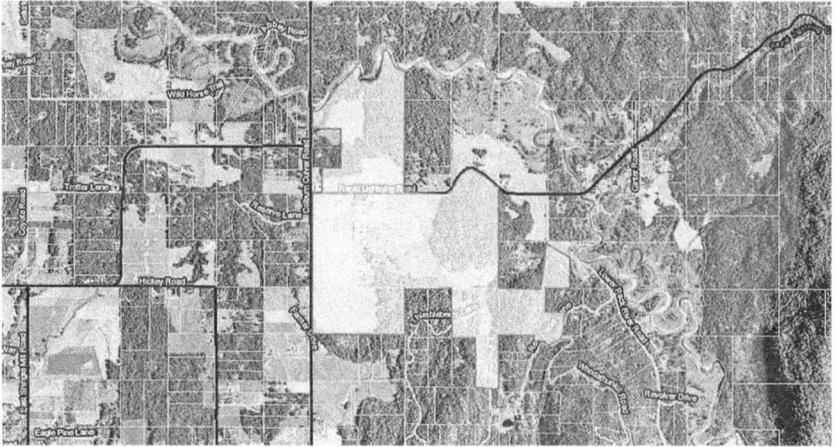

Figure 4.3. New land parcels in the Selle Valley. Courtesy of Bonner County Planning.

in the Selle Valley from a 20-acre minimum to a 10-acre minimum, hence effectively doubling the density. The county denied the request; then, on May 4, 2022, it changed its mind.[61]

One look at the landscape around the Selle Valley shows that it's already carved into residential parcels. The photo above shows the Pack River Partners parcel. In 2021, Bonner County created 608 new lots. The county also issued 661 housing permits, including 166 multifamily permits; 117 new residential units were issued in Sandpoint, including apartments.

This zoning-palooza adds accelerant to an already complicated growth narrative. "I will tell you that when the taxes rocket through the sky due to the increased cost of services for all these new residents living 20-mile from town, they will know their error," said Grimm in an email. A housing shortage remains a serious issue. "The local employers are struggling to attract workers," said Grimm. "Greater demand for services (healthcare, leisure & hospitality, landscaping, snow plowing) reflected by the demand from retirees' VRBOs (Vacation Rentals by Owner), and even more tourists. Local businesses relocate or invest in other facilities where the challenges are not as significant."

As of January 2023, Grimm said Bonner County contractors are building roughly four hundred to five hundred new apartments, hoping to ease the shortfall. Still, will it be enough?

Litehouse Foods, long an economic mainstay in Sandpoint, has expanded again. But it's not in Bonner County. In 2017, it bought a food processing facility in Lowell, Michigan.[62] The same year, Litehouse invested $40 million in a new facility in Hurricane, Utah.[63] In 2019, Litehouse invested another $46 million in a facility in Danville, Virginia.[64]

Keeping Litehouse Foods strong in Sandpoint "is going to be a challenge," said CEO Kelly Prior in a phone interview. "Challenges on all levels, including recruiting and retention. We've had people interested in our company, but when they start looking at the cost of housing, that talent starts to look elsewhere."

Yet, said Prior, "all services are experiencing similar struggles, be they restaurants, auto repair, or home maintenance."

Prior said, however, that Litehouse takes its prominent place in the community seriously. "We continue to talk with housing councils and developers about long-term solutions. We haven't come up with any yet, but we continue to have conversations."

Some companies didn't have the same commitment. In 2018, Thorne Research left Sandpoint for South Carolina, taking one hundred jobs with them.[65]

A troubling migration trend helps none of this. The young are leaving—or what economist Samuel Wolkenhauer calls a "demographic breakdown," in which, despite northern Idaho's record rate of population growth, "there are more deaths than births," he said.[66] "It's created a real tangle." Wolkenhauer said that the population growth for those aged twenty-five to fifty-five is now in the negative numbers. Retirees who may have once had a vacation home in Bonner County are now making it their primary residence. According to 2017 data, a remarkable 55 percent of Bonner County's personal income comes from nonlabor sources. Compare this with Ada County, home to Boise, where only 34 percent of the county's personal income comes from nonlabor forces.[67]

Part of the problem, says Wolkenhauer, "is that much of northern Idaho is heavily forested and mountainous. It's kind of like San Francisco, hemmed in by the sea. There's limited geography for new housing." About 40 percent of Bonner County's land base is privately owned, while the remainder is federal (44.4 percent) and state (15.2 percent).

"Man or woman," said Gannon, "I wouldn't move here unless you bring your own dough."

All this worries Grimm. A humming manufacturing sector has singled Bonner County out from other prosperous rural towns. But these manufacturers need young workers. They're leaving due to high housing costs. "In their departure, do these places (like Sandpoint) lose their authentic vibe? Do we just become vacant, generic mountain towns filled with trust funders? No more local music? Local art? Effectively 'Service Centers' with little sense of community? Who's going to the little league games? Staffing the community organizations?" he asks.

Not Exactly Part of the Commonwealth

Bonner County's challenge, in part, lies in the fact it's located in Idaho, a state with a long history of division. Dennis Colson, who wrote the seminal work· *Idaho's Constitution,* the state's constitution, said the mountainous north versus the agricultural Snake River plain to the south is at least partially to blame. "These great landmarks produced strikingly diverse settlement patterns in the various regions of Idaho," Colson wrote in the preface to his book. "The radical differences in topography, culture, religion, law and economics constantly push the state toward disunity rather than cohesiveness."[68]

Idaho struggled from its inception, wrote Colson, especially after its territory was severed from Washington Territory. Stranded, it was promptly torn asunder by the creation of the Montana and Wyoming territories. Thus, the state "was created, as it were, by amputation, nearly died of fragmentation, and was saved by a shotgun marriage (joining of north and south interests)."

Another handicap: since territorial times, prejudice and racism have burdened Idaho to a greater degree than the other 89ers. Many residents of early Idaho did not take kindly to the Republican agenda of equality for African Americans. The first Idaho territorial officials, most of them Radical Republicans who hailed from Oregon, faced a tough political battle with their constituency. Denunciation of their agenda they "became a favorite indulgence of the Confederate Democrats who continued to fight the Civil War in Idaho years after Jefferson Davis and Robert E. Lee had conceded the military issue in Virginia."[69]

One of Idaho's first mining camps was named Dixie. Former Confederate captain John Stanley discovered a gold strike in 1863/1864 on the Yuba River. He called it the Atlanta Lode. Later, the town of Stanley was named after the captain. As early as 1863, miners sought to keep Chinese and African Americans out of their industry in Bannock City.[70]

On July 8, 1865, a member of the editorial board of the *Idaho World*, likely Henry Clay Street, the paper's co-owner and Southern sympathizer, wrote this in an editorial: "The leading political issue which is likely to arise in the next session of the Legislature, will probably be on negro suffrage," wrote Street. "When negroes are admitted to the ballot box the time will be short until the Chinamen and Indians are admitted to equal privileges." He concluded by urging the voice of Boise County to "forever hush the whisperings of negro equality in Idaho."[71]

Thus, perhaps it is no accident that 125 years later, Idaho continues to attract those with exclusive agendas, including political ones. In March 2023, Bonner General Hospital closed its obstetrical unit. Due to the decreasing number of young parents in the area, the hospital delivers fewer infants. The low volume discourages pediatricians and OB/GYN specialists. "Highly respected, talented physicians are leaving. Recruiting replacements will be extraordinarily difficult," said Bonner General Health President Ford Elsaesser in a press release. "In addition, the Idaho Legislature continues to introduce and pass bills that criminalize physicians for medical care nationally recognized as the standard of care. Consequences for Idaho Physicians providing the standard of care may include civil litigation and criminal prosecution, leading to jail time or fines."[72]

This does little to help Sandpoint embrace the adaptation needed to help it remain a vibrant community. Yet, "adaption," says Kelly Prior, "is something very much part of our community. The ability to get along is still there but our current political climate continues to divide us. Sandpoint," he pauses, "is in a state of flux."

DISMANTLING THE CULT OF COMMODITY PROSPERITY
Breaking the Cycle of Victimhood and Resentment

5

On April 22, 1889, at high noon—signaled by a cannon's boom—thousands bolted from Fort Reno (now the town of El Reno, Oklahoma) toward Oklahoma Territory's Unassigned Lands. This nearly two million acres, purchased (more like hornswoggled, really) from the Muskogee, Seminole, Cheyenne, and Apache tribes, contained the last of the best "unoccupied" territory in the West. It was all about harnessing the land: land to farm, graze, mine, and build on. It was to form the foundation of Oklahoma's natural resource economy: first in agriculture, then in oil and gas.

When compared to the rest of the West, especially in 89er country, Oklahoma was late in the boom game. The Great Dakota Boom, an epoch when one hundred thousand people had poured into the Northern Great Plains, had ended three years earlier. The Homestake Mine, located near present-day Lead, South Dakota, was already fifteen years old. Montana's Alder Gulch bonanza, discovered in 1863, was long played out. In Wyoming, geologists and drillers had a pretty good idea that oil could be found around Salt Creek.

Thus by 1889, these newly formed states of the Great Plains and Rockies had to decide on the degree of their dependency on these natural resources. They went all in. Community, the constitutional conventioneers decided, could be built through mining, oil, logging, and especially agriculture.

Oklahoma has diversified but still struggles. According

to the Oklahoma Department of Commerce, of the top ten employers, 60 percent are related to the government or American Indian tribes. The mineral company with the largest number of employees, Phillips 66, ranks fifty-ninth in terms of employment. The state's wealthiest county on a per capita basis, Roger Mills, is losing people. It's dependent on agriculture, oil, and gas.[1]

This dovetails with Haggerty's research. "Half of all the counties that have high GDP per capita in the west are non-metro counties. A third of them are rural," he said. "The counties are also losing population."[2]

Likewise, the 89ers continue to grapple with diversification and government dependency. In all these states, government—local, state, and federal—remains the top employer.[3]

The rural narrative envisioned by the authors of the 1889 constitutions has largely failed. The lightly peopled places of the 89ers region are not places of self-sufficiency and independence. Instead, they rely heavily on government jobs, nonlabor income, federal appropriations, commodity price supports, and, in Wyoming and North Dakota, wealth transfer policies of energy-funded trust funds. In all five of these states, rural counties survive on a thread. The majority of the property taxes, a key source of local income, are paid by city dwellers or mineral companies, not those living in the hinterlands. More than in any other part of the United States, the political and economic are connected in 89er country. Again, the cultural connection—the sense of identity—with traditional 89er industries carries more clout than the paycheck.

The commodity-based community focuses on grievance peddling, not recreating the future. "The federal government won't let us" begins a familiar phrase during a conversation about grazing, logging, or mining coal on federal land—or *any* restrictions on commodity extraction in general, whether privately or federally owned land. Either that or "those damned environmentalists and greenies just don't care about ordinary people."

On pre-election day in 2022, *New York Times* reporters Katherine Miller and Adrian Rivera queried a group of Wyoming residents about various questions concerning their state, including the election of Liz Cheney. When the reporters asked "James" about his biggest concerns about Wyoming, he replied,

I think that we feel a little bit as if we don't have control of our own destiny. Government regulation comes down on oil and gas in every part of the state of Wyoming. They make the rules in Washington, and this dramatically changes our tax base and who we are as a community.[4]

There may be elements of truth to Washington's sentiments, although "indifferent" might be a more accurate term. Yet participants in the commodity index can't hide from the forces of technology, shifting political forces, and climate change.

The Cult of Extractive Prosperity

There is a book of Scripture, read and revered by the chosen few in the trans-Mississippi River region of the United States. Its central tenant: a cultish focus on natural resources. It's rooted in the conviction that if we just removed government regulations on mining, agriculture, oil and gas, and logging, we'd have perpetual prosperity.

When I use the word "cult," I mean a belief system that relies on cultural identity spliced with fantasy, nostalgia, and, in this case, opportunism. It's not so much blind devotion to an individual leader, although that's possible (William Jennings Bryan came pretty close in the 1890s), as it is to a rigid ideal. This cult thrives outside the realm of reason. It ignores the metrics usually employed to measure the pulse of commodities, such as supply and demand or shifts in government policy. For example, in 1850, wood composed 91 percent of America's fuel base, wrote authors Sam Schurr and Bruce Netschert; coal composed 9 percent. "By 1895, coal's share had increased to 65 percent and the share of wood had declined to 30 percent."[5]

After peaking in 2007 when coal provided roughly half the nation's energy supplies, coal accounted for just 22 percent of the electricity produced in the United States in 2021. Natural gas produced 38 percent. The same year, renewables produced 20 percent of all electricity, double what it did in 2010.

The idea behind this cult has a storied history in America, beginning with agriculture. After all, didn't Thomas Jefferson say that cultivators of the earth are the chosen people of God? That message has been tweaked

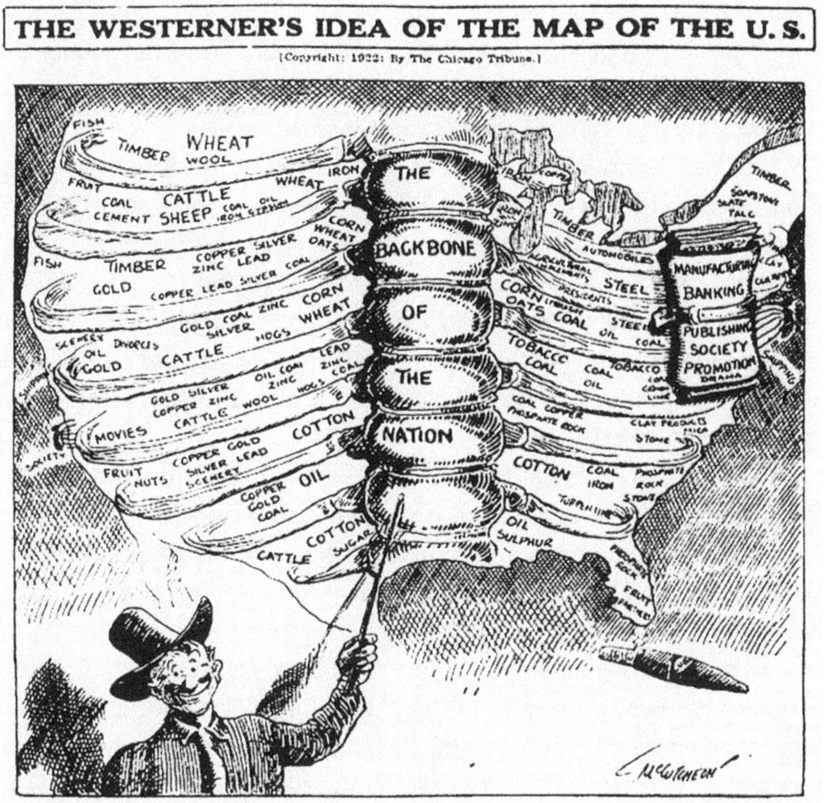

THE WESTERNER'S IDEA OF THE MAP OF THE U. S.

[Copyright: 1922: By The Chicago Tribune.]

Figure 5.1. "The Westerner's Idea of the Map of the US" (1922), *Chicago Tribune*. From author's collection.

over the centuries to include all commodity production. It demands that extraction or production is justified, no matter the consequences, because we'll soon run out of food or oil or iron ore. Regulations, a secular invention, need to go away.

It thrives on anthemic and simplistic credos, such as "We Feed the World," "Ban Mining: Let the Bastards Freeze in the Dark," or "The Sierra Club Sucks." The savvy producer sees through the shallowness of these slogans but is smart enough not to say so in front of a live microphone. Once, while interviewing Wheat Montana—a grain, flour, and bread company—founder Dean Folkford, I mentioned one of these slogans: *no farms, no food*. Folkford practically vaulted across his desk and pointed his index finger at me. "No," he said, "that's not true. Farmers do not produce food. They produce a commodity. And the sooner the agricultural community understands that, the better."

That's the anti-cult speaking, a voice in short supply.

Circa the twentieth century, this cult thrived in the American West. From furs to cattle to coal to oil to gold and silver, every 89er state has their economic roots in commodities. Look at their state seals: South Dakota is my favorite, with a smelter, riverboat, grazing cattle, and a farmer tilling his field. Montana, ever the 89er child yearning to be different, sports a blatant banner: "Oro y Plato," with an image of a plow, shovel, and pickaxe; yet it devotes half the seal to natural wonders, such as the waterfalls at Great Falls and mountain splendor.

Importantly, this belief system feeds into the narrative of American West individualism. The federal government sold land and minerals for $1.25/acre to *any* individual with enough gumption and savvy to file a claim under the Homestead Act and The General Mining Act of 1872. Again, let no one underestimate the grit required to homestead. Laura Ingalls Wilder conveniently left out, or at least sanitized, many darker details of her family's famous journey, including near destitution, bankruptcy, infant death, and drought. Imagine, if you will, putting up with a swarm of grasshoppers nearly two hundred thousand square miles in size, made up of 3.5 trillion insects. The 1875 swarm ranged from Texas to Saskatchewan (Canada).[6]

This narrative, however heroic in nature, has plenty of inconsistencies. Thousands of ranches become holders of section after section by buying abandoned homesteads for pennies on the dollar. Mining corporations, not plyers of the gold sluicing pan, rapidly capitalized on the 1872 mining law.

No matter that boom and bust and the practices of conventional agriculture have shattered hundreds of 89er communities—the cult and its *idee fixe* with scuttling regulations lives on.

For example, on May 6, 2022, Wyoming's state Republican convention voted to dismantle the Environmental Protection Agency and the Bureau of Land Management. Both agencies have a direct influence over commodity extraction, particularly on federal land.[7]

Year after year, the Washington delegates from these states fight regulations against commodities. They stuck closely and persistently to the narrative that the regulations promulgated under President Barack Obama killed the coal industry. No matter that peer-reviewed studies showed that technology, primarily fracking, dethroned king coal.[8] Now renewables push a further demotion of the bituminous.

We forget this during boom time. On the surface, Wyoming and North Dakota have benefited tremendously from energy-based commodities. Wyoming is in possession of a mineral trust fund currently worth roughly $10 billion. North Dakota's Legacy Fund has assets of $6.2 billion.

Wyoming and North Dakota might do well to heed what happened in Alaska. Natural resource income, primarily oil, drives its economy. Funded by years of production from Prudhoe Bay, Alaska's Permanent Fund tops $80 billion. In 2021, it provided $3.1 billion in interest to fund Alaska's liabilities.[9]

But the state still cannot pay its bills. In May 2022, after agreeing to a $16 billion budget, Republican senator Bert Stedman of Sitka said "something is seriously wrong" if the budget is not balanced with crude oil prices over $100 a barrel.[10]

The budget included a $3,284 dividend payment to each Alaskan. Yet, in 2020, Alaska cut its ferry service, critical to communities, by 30 percent. As of April 2023, only half of the eight ferries owned by the Alaska Marine Highway System were running.[11]

Mineral trust funds don't necessarily build stability. These energy-based trust funds are really state-owned banks. They were created to not only build infrastructure and fund education, but to help balance budgets when the commodity prices hit a rough patch. In reality, they've created a welfare state.

Wyoming's sovereign fund has contributed over $5 billion to the state's general fund. According to the Wyoming Taxpayers Association, a three-person family who pays $3,770 in taxes gets $28,280 in services.[12]

This does not exactly promote regional independence or self-determining communities; in addition, the states have little incentive to diversify. Trust fund protection has put a moat of money around state legislatures. It keeps out new ideas. Why bother with new ones? All the bills are getting paid, right? Reaching the bottom creates solutions. When there's money afloat, few want to change.

Trust fund distribution distorts the ways and means of community revenue. Fiscal democracy happens when individual taxes are collected by voter consent, with voter-approved rates, and are spent on entities that have also been approved by the voter. They are distributed by people who are put in those positions by the voters.

Something else subscribers to the cult of commodity prosperity don't want to admit: commodities makes residents more dependent on the government, not less. Again, this is particularly true for agriculture. If your economic stability comes from growing corn, soybeans, or wheat, then you are wedded at the hip to federal agricultural policy and financial support.

At the very bottom of this polarization, beyond a debate about economics or identity or some combination of the two, and what keeps the idea of community at bay, lies the concept of tribalism: the genetically built-in tendency to view the world in terms of us vs. them. Tribalism is a form of political monoculture. Without the benefit of repression, entities governed by a single party don't thrive in the long term. To the contrary, democracies work best when they serve the interests of the many, not the few. James Madison figured out that these competing political opinions are what kept democracy viable. *Divide et impera*, he called it.[13]

The greater the monoculture, economic or demographic, the more likely a populace will embrace tribalism. This is particularly true of extractive societies; they struggle to build what is at the heart of their most critical narratives: family and prosperity.

Tin Cup Economics and Volatility for Cities

A dependency on commodities complicates a municipality's revenue stream. As Haggerty points out, taxation and expenditure limitations (TELS) are the state's way of curbing costs.[14] Moreover, as we've discussed, state legislatures actively limit the ability of cities and towns to impose taxes. These policies make fine fodder in political speeches but hinder the ability of cities and towns to raise revenue for critical institutions and infrastructure.

Sometimes, during smooth economic sailing, municipalities can function under TELS and legislative limitations. Eventually, however, cities and towns resort to "tin cup economics": they go to the federal government or state capitals and petition for additional funds.

During commodity booms, state legislatures can be generous. For example, in 2019, the North Dakota legislature passed House Bill 1066. Operation Prairie Dog, as it is called, allocates up to $250 million per biennium to fund municipal infrastructure projects.[15] Wyoming has given over $1 billion to its cities and towns since 2004, much of it from mineral production.[16]

Boom time in the energy patch also elevates local property tax income; oil and gas wells, in addition to coal mines, are subject to *ad valorem* taxes (a tax based on the value of a transaction or property). Efforts toward diversification lag. Energy booms, with their high-flying revenues, "crowd out" alternative economic agendas.[17]

But then the bust shows up. Property tax income shrinks. Legislatures develop a cautious attitude toward distribution. But the basic needs of municipalities don't go away. Police and firemen need to be paid. Schools need repairs. Hospitals, in a constant need for revenue, begin to cut costs. In other words, unless a community diversifies away from commodities, it becomes dependent on these cycles.

Women and Commodities

Historically, commodity production has been the prerogative of men. Flip through historical photographs of 89er residents as they ranch, farm, log, or mine; mostly men crowd the frame. Women are pictured performing domestic duties, such as preparing meals, collecting eggs, milking the cows, mopping the floors, or other tasks of drudgery. Sometimes they're seen balancing the books by the light of a kerosene lamp.

"Even if a Dakota woman was married to a man who called himself boss, chances were that she called him that, too," wrote Catherine Stock in *Main Street in Crisis*, which documented the disruption of the middle class in the Great Plains during the Depression. "However much they produced for sale in eggs, butter, or home-grown chickens, women rarely owned property in their own names or fully shared in decisions about the distribution of profits."[18]

Fortunately, that's changed—at least for agriculture. In 2019, more than half (51 percent) of all farming operations in the United States had at least one women operator, according to the 2019 Agricultural Resource Management Survey (ARMS).[19]

Agriculture is the exception, however. Data about women's participation in modern commodity production in the Northern Rockies and Great Plains are in short supply. On a national scale, we know that only 3.8 percent of the coal mining workforce is made up of women. According to the Bureau of Labor Statistics, women occupy about 15 percent of positions in all mining industries.[20]

This figure warrants exceptions. Women have made considerable inroads in the coal mines of Wyoming's Powder River Basin. Jessica Smith Rolston documented the shift in her book *Mining Coal and Undermining Gender*.[21] Rolston states that in the average Powder River Basin mine, women make up 20 percent of the workforce.

Despite improvements, mines are not necessarily easy places for women to work. "A woman in a coal mine has to be above average. There's not a lot of room for error," said Debra Vokenroth, who retired after working in various coal mines around Gillette since 2008. "A mining company can just take so many excuses for you not showing up for your shift, even if it is about your kids."[22]

Vokenroth, who describes herself as mechanically inclined and never "destined for nursing school," said there is prejudice against women,

> but you can do it. You gotta be crass and bold. They will train you. They have maternity leave. I've seen women work until just about the day before they have their baby. There's always going to be more men than women. The last crew I worked on there were thirty-four men and two women. But, there was another crew on the mine who had about a 50/50 ratio, men to women. The reason they had so many women was probably the supervisor, who supported the idea of women working in mines. So, if you're a woman and you want to be a miner, you better have your life setup. You better have a spouse or can take care of the kids or have a nanny who is as dependable as you are.

The women who rise to the top, said Vokenroth, like being shovel operators and are usually lesbians or don't have kids.

> When you get on at a mine, you better start planning your retirement right away. For one, these jobs don't last forever. Secondly, if you work until you're, say, fifty-five, you're not going to be in the best physical

DISMANTLING THE CULT OF COMMODITY PROSPERITY | 139

shape. Chances are you'll be severely overweight. There's not going to be a second career for you. But working in the mines is a good career. Like I said: save hard and save enough to hire a good nanny.

Wallowa County: An Alternative Stewardship Model

I had to travel out of 89er country to find an isolated resource-based community that is successfully forging a path to stewardship prosperity. While Winnett and Petroleum County indeed qualify, I wanted to find a community not solely dependent on agriculture that had made progress in their relations with Indigenous Americans. I say *forging* because Wallowa County, Oregon, is a work in progress. Like every other isolated county that is 65 percent publicly owned and historically based in ranching and logging, it has challenges; yet it has fewer than most counties in the same boat. Residents have learned to address challenges proactively. I heard the phrase "we thought maybe we could get ahead of a few problems" repeatedly during my interviews in Wallowa County.

Critically, this approach did not threaten the cultural identity connected to a resource economy. Ranching and logging remain economic mainstays. In short, this is a county that thrives on a pragmatic approach to getting things done.

Wallowa County occupies the extreme northeast corner of Oregon. By western states' standards, it's modest in size—3,153 square miles—and home to unique topography: Hells Canyon and the Wallowa Mountains. In theory, someone could walk from the apex of Sacajawea Peak (9,838 ft.) to the bottom of Hells Canyon (7,993 feet from the top of the rim) and record a 17,845-feet drop in elevation. In the United States, only the mountains in Alaska feature such a descent.

It's isolated. From Enterprise, the county seat, it's 65 miles to Interstate 84. The city has a small airport with no regularly scheduled service. The runway is dicey for small jets (visual landing only) and out of the question for commercial aircraft. The closest airport that accommodates major airlines is Lewiston, Idaho, 87 miles distant. This trip requires navigating Rattlesnake Grade, a winding, steep, switchback-ridden chunk of pavement worthy of its name. The closest major city is Boise, 232 miles away. Portland, in good weather, is five hours away.

Wallowa County had a railroad but it ceased service in 1996. "No freight to haul in, no freight to haul out," said Nels Gabbert, a resident with a life-long interest in renewable energy, fostering local economies, and invigorating education.[23]

But once upon a time it exported plenty—mostly lumber. By 1911, the county had a dozen sawmills. The numbers waxed and waned, depending on the markets. Timber drove the economy. Boise Cascade once owned three hundred thousand acres in northeast Oregon, including in Wallowa County.

Yet the county embraces a clear-eyed but optimistic view of their future. In 2021, for example, the Wallowa County Commissioners hired the Bend-based PARC Resources to examine their economy.[24] The report pulls no punches. "The income levels in Wallowa County have lagged behind state levels for decades and there is no reason at this juncture to suspect that will change." One-third of the population is over sixty years old. The report projects a slowly decreasing population. Like in Bonner County, Idaho, young people are disappearing. "People are not moving to the County at rates high enough to offset those leaving," the report noted.[25]

Cities and towns, unsurprisingly, are doing better. Populations in its two largest urban areas, as it were, Joseph and Enterprise, are predicted to rise. The enrollment in these towns' school districts has been rising. It's the population and enrollment in the county's smaller towns, Lostine and Wallowa City, that can expect decreases; the same trend applies to unincorporated areas of the county. And yet, the PARC report does not advocate any radical economic development shifts. "Any consideration of Wallowa County and its economic engines must begin with agriculture. Historically, forestry and lumber would have been co-equal, but today, there are more cows than people in the county."[26]

"That's true," affirms Nils Christoffersen, executive director of Wallowa Resources, a local non-profit that encourages innovation and collaboration in agriculture, logging, and fisheries. "The biggest employer here is the public sector, but if you take that away, agriculture is really important, especially because it protects our scenic values. A lot of producers here are paying attention to the way they graze, their animal husbandry methods, and taking care of the water. They're forming co-ops."[27]

Christoffersen came to Wallowa County in 1999 after working in re-source-based jobs all over the globe: tending sheep in Australia, fishing off the coast of Norway, and working on a kibbutz in Israel. His last series of jobs before moving to Oregon were in eastern and southern Africa. There, he worked with communities directly involved in resource management. Both his children were born in Botswana. Somewhere between these tasks, he acquired a master's in forestry from Oxford University in 1990.

He came to Wallowa County because he was "looking for a commu-nity that was ready to think about a new relationship, a new social con-tract—move beyond the production and export of low-cost commodities (extraction of natural capital) to one committed to long-term steward-ship—investing in the health of the land, and producing high-value / value-added food, wood products, renewable energy, etc.," Christoffer-sen wrote in an email. "In essence, maintaining the working relationship with the land, with the clear intent and investment on building soil health, restoring salmon, restoring forest health, etc."

If Wallowa County approaches matters differently than other resource-based places, it is because they've adopted a pragmatic path with collabora-tion at the center. Collaboration, however, can pack water for all sorts of crusades. It's sometimes regarded with suspicion because the organizers of such a process can, as Christoffersen says, "set a table for their own friends."

Christoffersen entertains no fantasies about collaboration as the perfect tool. He still sees it as a way to solve problems and not involve the courts.

We're trying to find a social construct. It looks a little different in differ-ent places. Depends on the stakeholders. For example, when we work in collaboration with the tribes, we've got to be careful we don't interfere with their government to government relations. Basically, however, we try and create an inclusive process with stakeholders who have a clear interest in working this way. We need respectful behavior, good com-munications. Participants can't be disruptive to the process.

Salmon and Tribal Inclusivity

No action more clearly demonstrates collaborative power in Wallowa County than the agreement between two tribes, the local irrigation district, and the state of Oregon over the rebuilding of the Wallowa Lake dam. Wallowa County has five primary salmon-bearing rivers: Snake, Wenaha, Grand Ronde, Imnaha, and the Wallowa.

At one time, Wallowa Lake, fed by the Wallowa River, had a run of sockeye salmon, an event culturally and economically important to the Umatilla and Nez Perce tribes. In 1916, the Wallowa County Irrigation District built a dam at the lake's outlet. Residents spotted the last sockeye salmon below the dam in the early 1930s. In 1978, the US Army Corps of Engineers found structural problems with the dam and labeled it a "high hazard." The Corps recommended a reduced storage capacity. Ever since then, the Wallowa Lake Irrigation District has sought ways to make repairs and increase storage capacity.

Talks began in the late 1990s between the Wallowa Lake Irrigation District, the Confederated Tribes of the Umatilla Reservation, and the Nez Perce tribe. In June 2020, these parties, in conjunction with the Oregon Department of Fish and Wildlife, hammered out a memorandum of understanding concerning a new dam. It declared the parties have "a mutual interest in restoring, protecting and enhancing anadromous and resident fish species, wildlife, economic, and cultural resources affected by the Wallowa Lake Dam; and providing long-term water management solutions for the Wallowa and Grand Ronde River Basin."[28]

The Oregon legislature appropriated $14 million for the restoration. In November 2022, the US Fish and Wildlife Foundation, a nonprofit public/private organization, granted the Nez Perce and Umatilla tribes $5 million for the project, which begins in 2024.

It turns out fish restoration often drives the stewardship/collaboration narrative for the commodity-driven economies of the West. For example, as the Razorback Sucker disappeared from the Colorado River, the Colorado Water Congress (CWC), a Denver-based nonprofit dedicated to finding solutions to challenges facing the river, decided to get ahead of the endangered species listing. The CWC enlisted over ten stakeholders, including upstream states, the Nature Conservancy, the Western Power Administration, various water users' associations, and federal entities like the Bureau of Reclamation and US Fish and Wildlife.

These organizations, on a voluntary basis, figured out how to promote a habitat for the Razorback Sucker. The fish is no longer a candidate for listing. During the process, there was no litigation, no lawsuits, and "no water project was halted or delayed because of the CWC's actions," said Margie Nelson, who runs the EPA's Endangered Species Protection Program out of Denver. The plan worked, said Nelson, because the CWC saw that "the people with the most to lose had particularly valuable ideas." Also, she said, "it's not just about the fish, it's about all the players and stakeholders."[29]

The Big Hole Watershed Committee, a nonprofit based out of Divide, Montana, took a similar approach. Droughts began creating extremely low water levels (including sections that totally dried up in the torrid summer of 1988) in the Big Hole River.

Not only did these conditions create perilous conditions for irrigators, but they threatened the existence of the Arctic grayling. The Big Hole is the only river in the lower forty-eight states to have the grayling. To prevent a listing, anglers and ranchers got together and agreed on the plan of "shared sacrifice, shared success." Low flows meant less water for the irrigators but also restrictions on fishing. Thus far, no listing.

For Wallowa County, this was the second time around concerning salmon-driven restoration. In 1992, the EPA put the Chinook salmon on the endangered species list. The EPA identified logging, which can increase water turbidity and elevate stream temperatures, as a cause for the salmon's decline. The Forest Service drastically reduced the cut on national forests surrounding Wallowa County. Federal timber sales accounted for roughly 70 percent of the available feedstock for local sawmills. In 1994, two of the county's biggest mills—both located in Joseph—shut down, eliminating 120 jobs.

The closings attracted the era's flag-bearing leaders of the commodity cult. In September 1994, angry locals held a rally in Joseph. The local newspaper, the *Wallowa County Chieftain*, co-sponsored the event. Attendees heard from wise use leader Ron Arnold, William Perry Pendley, then director of the Rocky Mountain Legal foundation (which advocates the selling of public land), and Wayne Hage, the Nevada rancher who believed he had the right to grazing cattle on public land without a permit.

The following day, citizens burned effigies of Ric Bailey of the Hells Canyon Preservation Council and Andy Kerr of the Oregon Natural Resources Council.

No apologies from newspaper editor Rick Swart. "There's a message to be heard that is not being heard, about people having lives and jobs and job security. People here are not used to lights, cameras and having to engage in debate with Andy Kerr. We wanted to send the message that it's okay to be loggers and ranchers in a small town."[30]

The mill closures and public anger might have created yet another chapter in the book of extractive prosperity. Yet enough people in Wallowa County didn't want that to become the permanent narrative. In fact, they were already ahead of the curve. Two years prior, the members of Nez Pierce tribe, county commissioners, local merchants, millworkers, loggers, federal and state agency officials, and ranchers joined together to form the Wallowa County Salmon Recovery Strategic Committee.

The creation of this body, focused on salmon recovery, created a template. It eventually led to the formation of another panel: Wallowa County Natural Resources Advisory Committee (NRAC). This body oversees, in an advisory capacity, all natural resource provisions of the Wallowa County Comprehensive Land Use Plan. The committee has twenty members, representing many of the same stakeholders as the previous committee.

Rich Wandschneider has lived in Wallowa County for fifty years, observing and documenting the history and changes of the region. He founded Fishtrap, a group that promotes western writers. He now heads the Josephy Library of Western History and Culture in Joseph. He's seen a significant shift in the county regarding attitudes toward the federal government and the Nez Perce. "There's a lot of borders being broken down right now. The hard-core anti-government is beginning to realize maybe the government isn't so bad after all."[31]

When it comes to tribal inclusivity, Wandscheinder points to a certain evolution. "We have this annual event called Chief Joseph Days. It used to be one big drunk with fights between locals and Indians. Now, we have the annual Nez Perce festival [the Tamkalilks Celebration] and have tribal members sitting on nonprofits and participating in salmon restoration. We also have a Nez Perce Wallowa Homeland established in the county, complete with a longhouse."

The Homeland, as it is called, is a 320-acre parcel in the City of Wallowa located on the banks of the Wallowa River.

Joe McCormack, a Nez Perce tribal member and fish biologist, again points toward salmon restoration as an avenue for greater cooperation between the nonnative and tribal communities. In the 1980s, said McCormack, the Nez Perce began monitoring smolt run on the local rivers.

> Eventually, this monitoring led us to believe we could reopen a tribal fishery, especially on the Imnaha. Well, that led to a lot of interest from other agencies that maybe could open up the river to sportfishing. (The Imnaha is currently open for a three-week salmon season of sport fishing). The community thought that was a great thing and achievement by the tribes. We, the tribes, bring about two million assets in Wallowa county annually. I think that's success.[32]

The annual Tamkalilks Celebration, which McCormack calls a "friendship feast," has "been responsible for a lot of reconciliation around here," he said. "There was a time in Wallowa County when no Umatilla or Nez Perce would publicly call themselves an Indian. That's changed."

Wallowa Resources originally concentrated on a restoration economy: "restoration of our streams, forests, and range," said Christoffersen. "We still do that. But we realized that was too short-term. What we're actually after is a stewardship economy, which is generational. In fact you might say we're devoting 100 percent of our effort to prepare the next generation of land managers."

The reigning approach to county government, said Wandschneider, is pragmatism. "Sure, there are some conservatives among the Wallowa county commissioners but by and large they're non-partisan in their approach and pretty pragmatic."

The anger at Washington hasn't gone away. "There is still anti-fed speak and talk about not complying with the federal government," said Franz Goebel, Wallowa County's director land planning. "But, in general, it's mostly venting as opposed to people wanting to take action."[33]

Timber Still Matters. Heartwood Biomass: Combining Stewardship and Restoration

In the late 1990s, alarming reports appeared concerning forest health in northeast Oregon. Fire suppression and drought, which led to wildfires—combined with increased pest activity—had put the landscape into a tailspin. On the Wallowa-Whitman National Forest, tree mortality exceeded new growth by 30 percent.[34] The Forest Service began offering stewardship contracting—logging focused on restoration. In 2009, Congress passed the Collaborative Forest Landscape Restoration Program, which funded restoration in eight different national forests.

Much of this work focused on thinning out the understory. But what to do with these small diameter (under seven inches) trees? Remaining regional sawmills were not set up for such puny feedstock.

The solution: build a mill that uses logs nobody else wants. In 2000, Wallowa Resources' for-profit subsidiary, WR Community Solutions, in combination with the Joseph Timber Company, joined forces to build such an operation. It produced dimension lumber, post and poles, and chips for pulp. It lasted two years before Joseph Timber decided to liquidate all its operations.

The idea wouldn't die, however. The mill was revived under the name Community Smallwood Solutions. Over the next twenty years, the operation often ran on a wing and prayer. It went through various names and numerous owners, including sixteen parties/investors from Wallowa County. "Wallowa Resources, in particular Nils Christoffersen, were valuable allies and supporters throughout this time," said CEO David Schmidt.[35]

In 2019, a fire broke out in the mill. Denied insurance money (the mill sued and eventually won), "we limped through the next few years," said Schmidt. During this time, Schmidt, his wife Jesse, and Christoffersen sought—and gained—a new set of investors. In 2021, the mill was renamed Heartwood Biomass. Today, it employs twenty-five people, produces kiln-dried firewood, trellis poles for orchards and hop yards, two grades of chips for pulp, and a small amount of veneer. It's experimenting with a new product called Woodstraw, a patented wood-strand mulch. In addition, Heartwood Biomass has received a grant to produce small amounts of bio-char, a soil amendment.

Schmidt saw Heartwood Biomass through its ups and downs, although with typical humility he says his wife Jesse is the chief reason for the mill's success. "She's the rock," he said.

Visiting the office of Heartland Biomass, I was greeted by a seven-month-old doodle-something named Rex and a shy third grader named Dirk. Daycare hadn't worked out that morning, so Dirk had come to work with his parents.

This dovetails with something Christoffersen said: "In this community, kids come first, no matter the job or the political persuasion. You gotta sick kid and can't come to work? You have to bring them to work or have to stay home? We understand that."

Schmidt gives me a tour of the mills, with Dirk in tow. Lean and fit as a rock climber, Schmidt emanates energy and enthusiasm for his operation. The idea of making forest products from trees no one else wants clearly thrills him, as does the idea of change and adaptation. "It was terrible when we had that fire in 2019 and had to fight the insurance companies. But it forced a change in our trajectory, especially when it came to financing. We're in much better shape now than we were before the fire."

When I say trees nobody else wants, I mean literally. Heartwood has bid on eight Forest Service timber sales over the last few years. According to Schmidt, they were the only ones bidding.

I ask him, "On a scale of one to ten, what's your relationship with the Forest Service?"

"Oh, it's a ten," said Schmidt. "We've got a great relationship, although we still have problems we need to work out."

Schmidt relies on and encourages a cooperative model. For example, when one of their primary competitors, a Canadian company—was forced to shut down temporarily, Heartwood fulfilled their orders. "They reciprocated when we had our fire," said Schmidt.

When I ask about the mill's core principles, Schmidt lists four: kindness/empathy, everyone shovels no matter your position, zero waste, and innovation.

This philosophy has been noticed. Last year, the Forest Service approached Schmidt and his team, asking if they would consider building a similar mill near Sonora, California. "Design and permitting now, breaking ground in spring of 2023, and planning to be fully operational by spring of 2024," said Schmidt. "Before we said yes we had a meeting with the local officials and met the general public. We absolutely had to have community buy-in before we would sign off on this project."

Compare this attitude of inclusivity to a sawmill that concentrates on dimensional lumber (2x4s, 2x8s, etc.), which is what the Wallowa County mills traditionally produced. They had little production differentiation, but instead relied on market whims, improvements in efficiency, and an ample timber supply. For over one hundred years, their lifecycle varied little: working on the assumption that no community wouldn't want a sawmill, they came. They built. They sawed. They shut down. They re-opened. They shut down, permanently. The communities were left with unemployment and hulking, empty buildings.

Such mills operated under the rules dictated by the cult of commodity prosperity: fight regulation and demand primacy of a resource—that is, forests are there to supply mills, not offer recreation or protect salmon. When they shuttered their doors, they resorted to grievance peddling. The federal government caused their demise.

What remains in Wallowa County is a mill grounded in economic and social reality. That is to say: Heartland Biomass understands that a National Forest can supply just so much timber, or that a hotter climate has ecological consequences, especially in the drier regions of eastern Oregon, and that excess timber cutting and conventional logging is hard on salmon. Instead, Heartland sees that *opportunity* lies within this new framework. Instead of blaming the government, Heartland Biomass leans into what a changing regulatory framework has to offer. Innovation and breaking convention remain the order of the day. Orchards in hotter climate require shade. Why not fill this niche by using small trees to create trellises? Logs come in, forest products come out. But it's not a saw*mill*.

And yet, Heartwood Biomass made this adaption in a rural, isolated community. It built on and embraced existing values. Yet producing firewood, trellis poles, and pulp didn't threaten anyone's cultural identity. That may be their strongest product.

EPILOGUE

When reading the various 89er constitutional convention notes, one senses that worries over geographic isolation and economic uncertainty were never far from the delegates' minds. These men represented a region hundreds of miles from markets, short on capital and cash, and dependent—by necessity and cultural inclination—on commodities.

Jilted by territorial administrations, the delegates put the emphasis on an active state government. "They wanted that government to be the voice of the West in Congress; the enforcing arm of popular will; a peacemaker between labor and capital; the protector of residents from the irrigation company, railroad, or mine; and the protector of the many from the distant, indifferent, and predatory few."[1]

This philosophy has deep roots in western ideals on what constitutes community. Look no further than the writings of John Locke:

> The only way whereby any one devests himself of his natural liberty, and puts on the bonds of Civil Society is by agreeing with other men to join and unite into a community, for their comfortable, safe, and peaceable living one amongst another, in a secure enjoyment of their properties, and a greater security against any that are not of it.[2]

This may strike the modern political mind as abject paternalism. Yet these ideals extoll commonwealth or republican values embraced by independent, generally conservative men who saw themselves, their constituents, and their communities as vulnerable.

That exposure remains among rural, resource-based economies. As I hope this book has demonstrated, this is not an inevitable outcome. On the contrary, places that have embraced a stewardship economy are more protected and resilient. They have, in a twenty-first century way, embraced the pragmatism and commonwealth values of the 1889 constitutions.

However. This book has not mentioned a core—and complicated—historical American value: defiance, particularly in association with the concept of liberty. America did not care for Britain's dominance and responded with textbook defiance. Thomas Jefferson, in a 1787 letter to William Smith, who was serving as an American diplomat in London, rebuffed what the British called "anarchy"—that is, America's fight for independence. Instead, Jefferson called it an honorable rebellion. "God forbid we should ever be 20 years without such a rebellion. . . . What country can preserve its liberties if their rulers are not warned from time to time that their people preserve the spirit of resistance."[3]

Reduced to its most basic form: no government or authority can tell me what to do or how to run my affairs. Nor will I tell my neighbor, or even a corporation, how to run their affairs.

In an ideal world, this form of raw liberty has enormous appeal. In general, however, society has discovered that, while it may—in some cases—benefit the individual and especially corporations, such liberty delivers mixed results for the commonweal. The history of democracies can be writ large in terms of the effort to balance liberty and state police powers. Examples choke American case law. Forcing corporations, such as Atlantic Richfield, owners of the defunct Anaconda Smelter in Anaconda, Montana, to clean up public resources, like rivers and streams, might be an obvious example.

This book questions the projected idyll of absolute liberty in 89er country. Specifically, how does categorically defying all governmental authority lead to "freedom"? Few 1889 constitutional delegates embraced blank-check liberty for this fundamental reason: they saw how it had led not to personal freedom but corporation domination.

This realization has not changed the minds of many in the rural West, where the concepts of freedom carry water for crusades large and small. The yearning to return to a less restricted era when sawmills, mines, and agriculture played central roles in small towns has not died, along with the "traditional values" that allegedly accompanied these epochs.

To that end, places like Wallowa County and Winnett are not out of the woods, even with innovative organizations like the Winnett ACES or the attitude of former Wallowa county commissioner Tom Hayward. Hayward explains:

> There's a general consensus in Wallowa County that it's harmful to ignore land. Don't pay attention to a forest and it burns up. Don't pay attention to the land and suddenly you've got a huge weed infestation. Say somebody wants to build a house on ten acres. There's slope involved. NRAC [Natural Resources Advisory Committee] might say, "you know, if you build the house over here as opposed to your original site, you're going to have less impact on the fish species, less runoff." Most people have found that helpful and not a significant hardship.[4]

This attitude represents the merging of stewardship and commonwealth values; telling someone the placement of their home might lead to runoff into a stream does not necessarily violate anyone's property rights. Zoning laws have affirmed this a thousand times over. Such an attitude merely takes in the bigger picture. Community, pragmatism, stewardship economies, and commonwealth values go hand in hand.

Still, Wallowa must deal with the likes of the Greater Idaho Movement, which seeks to make eastern Oregon, including Wallowa County, a part of Idaho. Driven by anti-city and pro-gun ideology and a vision of commodity-driven prosperity, it rejects what it sees as Oregon's liberal political process. It's absolutely focused on the victim narrative of extractive economies. "Oregon's rural residents carve out a resource-based living on marginal farm ground and the leftovers of Oregon's economic growth, infrastructure, and technological innovation," claims its website.[5]

Movements for secession—or their variants—focus on creating a region of like-minded people. They have been around since America's founding. Almost all fail. This did not stop Wallowa Country voters from approving a measure that obliges county commissioners to discuss relocating Idaho borders to include Wallowa County. The measure passed in June 2023 by a margin of seven votes: 1,752 people for, 1,745 people against.[6]

Winnett must deal with a different form of discontent, although the root issues differ little. Petroleum County has no land owned or leased by the American Prairie, an organization dedicated to forming a reserve that favors bison over cattle. Still, the concept has few fans in Winnett. American Prairie now owns or leases 460,000 acres in north central Montana.

Cattlemen see it as an existential threat. They, and a movement called Save the Cowboy, throw up legal roadblocks to American Prairie expansion and the leasing of federal land to graze bison. Like the Greater Idaho Movement, cattlemen have had only limited success in advancing their cause.

And like the Greater Idaho Movement, opponents of American Prairie object that their elected officials—and their appointees in positions of power—aren't listening to them. They speak about disappearing family ranches and elites and donors controlling large tracts of land. Yet they seemingly have no objections to the Farris family, who owns 640,000 acres in Montana, or the Texas-based Wilks Brothers, who own or control 672,000 acres of Montana land.[7] Rupert Murdoch owns 380,000 acres of the Beaverhead Valley. Various Belgian firms control 222,716 acres.[8]

Save the Cowboy and the Greater Idaho movements may be fringe, but their stories must be heard and, to some extent, acted on. How does society do that? The problem is that their movements incorporate the worst aspects of the 1889 constitutions: an emphasis on commodities, championing rural exceptionalism, and discouraging anything urban. In short, a recipe for continued economic and cultural colonialism. Such organizations reject the genius of these founding documents: egalitarianism, adaptability, a measured inclusivity, and, above all, the belief that pragmatic ideals and individual liberty remain compatible.

The constitutional delegates attempted big-tent pluralism, a live-and-let-live policy that included those seeking a society within a society, like the Mormons and the Hutterites. That meant subscribing to the concept of freedom of conscience, the liberty to worship—or not to worship—in your own way, to marry whom you please, and to speak your mind, as long as you didn't yell fire in a crowded theater. You got to vote your conscience, not the party.

Yet freedom of conscience has fallen out of favor in 89er country. As mentioned earlier, state legislatures of the Northern Rockies and Great Plains now shun or eliminate any solon who does not tow the party line. Loyalty has replaced a considered libertarianism, which included those who dared to be a tad different. In fact, loyalty is now morphing into its ugly stepchild: obedience. Whoever packaged loyalty and obedience and

sold it as freedom may be a marketing genius, but it is authoritarianism—
the ultimate anti-89ers value—in disguise.

Bridges points out that those who occupied the convention halls in
August "were, and understood themselves to be, citizens of the periphery
of the United States. Delegates to the conventions hoped to shield their
states from the worst possible outcomes of the peripheral relationships and
foster the best ones."[9]

That physical nineteenth-century periphery is gone. The relationships
remain, however, as do the original values, although they've been badly
manhandled the last decade or so. It's up to residents of the Northern
Rockies and Great Plains to restore them, in a twenty-first century way,
and put them in play in daily civic life.

NOTES

PREFACE

1. Tom Lubnau, Cowboy Daily, August 8, 2022, https://cowboystatedaily
.com/2022/08/08/tom-lubnau-no-one-wants-to-starve-children-eat-humans
-or-steal-your-firearms.

2. James Mitchell Ashley, *HarpWeek*, https://15thamendment.harpweek.com
/HubPages/CommentaryPage.asp?Commentary=06Bios01.

3. Rebecca E. Zietlow, "James Ashley's Thirteenth Amendment," *Columbia
Law Review* 112, no. 7 (2012): 1697–1731, http://www.jstor.org/stable/41708162.

4. Jennifer Helton, "*So Great an Innovation*," https://www.sdhspress.com
/blog/201cso-great-an-innovation201d-women-suffrage-in-wyoming; see also
Lori Ann Lahlum and Molly P. Rozum, eds., *Equality at the Ballot Box: Votes
for Women in the Northern Great Plains* (Pierre: South Dakota Historical Society
Press, 2019), 39.

5. FindLaw staff, "Wyoming Organic Act" FindLaw, https://codes.findlaw
.com/wy/wyoming-organic-act/wy-st-organic-act.html.

6. Shalom H. Schwartz, "An Overview of the Schwartz Theory of Basic Values," *Online Readings in Psychology and Culture* 2, no. 1 (2012), http://dx.doi.org
/10.9707/2307-0919.1116.

7. Carson Vaughan, "Saddle Up with Badger Clark, America's Forgotten
Cowboy Poet," *Smithsonian,* October 2020, https://www.smithsonianmag.com
/arts-culture/saddle-up-badger-clark-americas-cowboy-poet-180975770.

8. Joseph Schuman, "The Righteous Mind: Moral Foundations Theory," *Divided We Fall,* July 15, 2018, https://dividedwefall.org/the-righteous-mind-moral
-foundations-theory.

9. Martin Sandbu, *The Economics of Belonging: A Radical Plan to Win Back the
Left Behind and Achieve Prosperity for All* (Princeton: Princeton University Press,
2020).

10. Sandbu, *The Economics of Belonging*, 46–49.

11. Rebecca Solnit, "Why Republicans Keep Falling for Trump's Lies," *New
York Times*, January 5, 2022.

12. Email, March 26, 2023.

13. Nick Bowlin, "Joke's on Them; How Democrats Gave Up on Rural America," *Guardian*, February 22, 2022.

14. Richard Florida, "Some Rural Counties Are Seeing a Job Boom, Too,"
Bloomberg, September 25, 2018.

15. Corey Robin, *The Reactionary Mind: Conservatism from Edmund Burke to Sarah Palin*, Second Edition (New York: Oxford University Press, 2017).

16. Eric Dietrich, "The Viz: Are In-migrating Montanans Making Their Relocation Decisions Based on Political Identity?" *Montana Free Press*, September 9, 2022, https://montanafreepress.org/2022/09/01/are-new-montanans-deepening-partisan-divides.

17. Email correspondence, April 14, 2023.

18. G. Alan Tarr, "The Montana Constitution: A National Perspective," *Montana Law Review* 64 (2003): 2.

INTRODUCTION

1. Jeffrey Ostler, *The Plains Sioux and U.S. Colonialism from Lewis and Clark to Wounded Knee* (Cambridge: Cambridge University, 2004), 6.

2. *Saturday Pioneer*, Aberdeen, South Dakota, January 3, 1891.

3. Michael Lawson, *Dammed Indians Revisited: The Continuing History of the Pick-Sloan Plan and the Missouri River Sioux* (Pierre: South Dakota State Historical Society Press, 2009), Introduction.

4. Frankie Barnhill, "Why Idaho's Racist History Matters," July 30, 2020, https://www.boisestatepublicradio.org/show/idaho-matters/2020-07-30/why-idahos-racist-history-matters-part-1.

5. Elizabeth Cady Stanton, "Progress of the American Woman," *The North American Review* 171, no. 529 (December 1900): 907.

6. Rebecca Hein, "Those Damn Women: Louise Graf and Women on Wyoming Juries," *Wyohistory.org*, October 3, 2016, https://www.wyohistory.org/encyclopedia/those-damn-women-louise-graf-and-women-wyoming-juries.

7. Abe Streep, "How Montana Took a Hard Right Turn Toward Christian Nationalism," *New York Times Magazine*, January 15, 2023, 24.

8. Holly Meyer "How a South Dakota Priest Inspired 125 Years of Direct Democracy—and the Fight to Preserve It," *Associated Press*, October 27, 2023, https://apnews.com/article/ballot-initiatives-south-dakota-catholic-priest-ohio-abortion-b638b25795b951af3f5a3e65182c7b36.

9. Jon Lauck, *Prairie Republic: The Political Culture of Dakota Territory, 1879–1889* (Norman: University of Oklahoma, 2010), 18.

10. Thomas Frank, *What's the Matter with Kansas: How Conservatives Won the Heart of America* (New York: Picador, 2004), 66–67.

11. Ross Benes, *Rural Rebellion: How Nebraska Became a Republican Stronghold* (Lawrence: University of Kansas Press, 2021), 169.

12. Catherine McNicol Stock, *Rural Radicals: Righteous Rage in the American Grain* (New York: Penguin Group, 1996), 22.

13. Catherine McNicol Stock, *Nuclear Country: The Origins of the Rural New Right* (Philadelphia: University of Pennsylvania Press, 2020).

14. Amy Bridges, "Managing the Periphery in the Gilded Age: Writing Constitutions for the Western States," *Studies in American Political Development* 22, no. 1 (Spring 2008): 32–58.

15. Bridges, "Managing the Periphery," 32.

16. Bridges, "Managing the Periphery," 32, 36.

17. Interview, March 21, 2019.

18. Email correspondence, August 31, 2019.

19. Wyoming, Constitutional Convention (1889), *Journal and Debates of the Constitutional Convention of the State of Wyoming: Begun at the City of Cheyenne on September 2, 1889, and Concluded September 30, 1889* (Cheyenne: The Daily Sun, 1893), 353.

20. *Proceedings and Debates of the Constitutional Convention: Held in the City of Helena, Montana, July 4th, 1889, August 17th, 1889* (Helena: State Publishing Company, 1921), 82.

21. *Proceedings and Debates of the Constitutional Convention of Idaho* (Caldwell: Caxton Printers, 1912), 947.

22. "All corporations and limited liability companies, except as otherwise provided in this chapter, are prohibited from owning or leasing land used for farming or ranching and from engaging in the business of farming or ranching. A corporation or a limited liability company may be a partner in a partnership that is in the business of farming or ranching only if that corporation or limited liability company complies with this chapter" (N.D. Cent. Code § 10–06.1–02).

23. Robert Putnam, *Bowling Alone: The Collapse and Revival of American Community* (New York: Simon and Schuster, 2000), 372.

24. Tomas Nonnenmacher, History of the U.S. Telegraph Industry, EH.net, https://eh.net/encyclopedia/history-of-the-u-s-telegraph-industry.

25. Josiah Strong, *The Twentieth Century City* (New York: Baker and Taylor, 1898), 181.

26. Stanley Buder, *Capitalizing on Change: A Social History of American Business* (Chapel Hill: University of North Carolina Press, 2009), 172.

27. Congressional Budget Office, "Trends in the Distribution of Family Wealth, 1989 to 2019," Summary, https://www.cbo.gov/system/files/2022-09/57598-family-wealth.pdf.

28. Henry Gannett, "Proportion of Foreign Born to Total Population of the

United States at the Twelfth Census 1900," in *Statistical Atlas of the United States, 1900* (Washington, DC: United States Census Office, 1901).

29. John Higham, *Strangers in the Land: Patterns of American Nativism, 1860–1925* (New Brunswick: Rutgers University, 1955), 111.

30. Philip Bump, "Americans See an 'Invasion' at the Border. But What Does That Mean?" *Washington Post*, August 18, 2022, https://www.washingtonpost.com/politics/2022/08/18/immigration-border-republicans.

31. Nuance and multiple interpretations riddle the subject of values. Generally, scholars agree that core values only shift due to shock or trauma. However, young adults—under the right conditions—seem able to shift their core values. See Colin Foad, Gregory Maio, and Paul Hanel, "Perceptions of Values Over Time and Why They Matter," *Journal of Personality* (November 2020), https://onlinelibrary.wiley.com/doi/10.1111/jopy.12608.

CHAPTER 1. A RECKONING IN AUGUST

1. R. M. Tuttle, *Official Report of the Proceedings and Debates of the First Constitutional Convention of North Dakota, Assembled in the City of Bismarck, July 4th to Aug. 17th, 1889* (Bismarck: Tribune, State Printers and Binders), 410–411.

2. Department of the Interior, *Report on the Statistics of Agriculture in the United States, Eleventh Census* (Washington, DC: GPO, 1895), https://agcensus.library.cornell.edu/census_year/1890-census.

3. Donald Worster, *A River Running West: The Life of John Wesley Powell* (New York: Oxford University Press, 2001), 468.

4. Tuttle, *Official Report of the Proceedings and Debates of the First Constitutional Convention of North Dakota*, 103.

5. Frank Hagerty, *The Territory of Dakota, The State of North Dakota, The State of South Dakota; An Official Statistical, Historical, and Political Abstract, 1889* (Aberdeen: Daily News Print, 1889), 71.

6. William Culp Darrah, *Powell of the Colorado* (Princeton: Princeton University Press, 1951), 304.

7. Tuttle, *Official Report of the Proceedings and Debates of the First Constitutional Convention of North Dakota*, 112.

8. Jon K. Lauck, *Prairie Republic: The Political Culture of Dakota Territory, 1879–1889* (Norman: University of Oklahoma Press, 2010), 89.

9. Howard R. Lamar, *Dakota Territory: 1861–1889* (New Haven: Yale University Press, 1951), 78.

10. In 1870 there were 1,720 farms in Dakota Territory with an average size of 176 acres. In 1880 this had increased to 17,435 with an average size of 218 acres.

By 1890, there were 27,611 farms in North Dakota with an average size of 277 acres. See https://www.history.nd.gov/hp/PDFinfo/Farms-in-North-Dakota-Part1.pdf, 14.

11. Douglas Dowd, "A Comparative Analysis of Economic Development in the American West and South," *The Journal of Economic History* 16, no. 4 (1956): 564.

12. R. F. Pettit Jr., *Maxwell Land Grant, in: Taos-Raton-Spanish Peaks Country* (Sorocco, NM, 1966), Northrop Guidebook, 17th Field Conference, 66–68.

13. *The New York Times*, February 6, 1882, 2.

14. Curiously, the Native Daughters of the American West, a women's historical society with a conservative bent, sought for years to glorify the years of Spanish settlement. See https://www.latimes.com/archives/la-xpm-2006-aug-16-me-bells16-story.html.

15. Damian Bacich, "Land Grants in Alta California," California Frontier Project, https://www.californiafrontier.net/land-grants-in-alta-california.

16. Marsha Baum and Christian Fritz, "American Constitution-Making: The Neglected State Constitutional Sources," *Hastings Constitutional Law Quarterly* 27, no. 2 (Winter 2000): 208.

17. B. F. Potts, *Montana: Report of the Governor of Montana Territory, 1878*, H.R. Exec. Doc. No. 1, 45th Cong., 3rd Sess. (1878), 1108.

18. Brian Albright, "Iron Production," *Encyclopedia of Greater Philadelphia*, https://philadelphiaencyclopedia.org/essays/iron-production.

19. Lance E. Davis and H. Louis Stettler III, "The New England Textile Industry, 1825–60: Trends and Fluctuations," in *Output, Employment, and Productivity in the United States after 1800* (Washington, DC: National Bureau of Economic Research, 1966), 213–242.

20. Larry McFarlane, "British Agricultural Investment in the Dakotas, 1877–1953," *Business and Economic History*, vol. 5 (Cambridge: Cambridge University Press, 1971), 112–126.

21. Doane Robinson, *South Dakota Constitutional Convention, Constitutional Debates* (Huron, SD: Huronite Printing Company, 1907), 293.

22. James B. Thayer "The Origin and Scope of the American Doctrine of Constitutional Law," *Harvard Law Review* 7, no. 3 (October 25, 1893): 129–156.

23. Steven Calebresi, "Originalism and James Bradley Thayer," *Northwestern Law Review* 116, no. 6 (2019): 1419.

24. Herbert Meschke and Lawrence Spears, "Digging for Roots: The North Dakota Constitution and the Thayer Correspondence," *North Dakota Law Review* 65, no. 3, article 2 (1989).

25. T. C. Atkeson, *Semi-Centennial History of the Patrons of Husbandry* (New York: Orange Judd, 1916), 46.

26. Doane Robinson, *South Dakota, Vol. 1* (Indianapolis: B. F. Bowen and Co., 1904), 317.

27. Caroline Fraser, *Prairie Fires: The Dreams of Laura Ingalls Wilder* (New York: Metropolitan Books, 2017), 160.

28. Robert Weibe, *The Search for Order* (New York: Hill and Wang, 1967), 58.

29. *Proceedings and Debates of the Constitutional Convention of Idaho* (Caldwell: Caxton Printers, 1912), 889.

30. Alan Tarr, "The Montana Constitution: National Prospective," *Montana Law Review* 64 (2003): 3.

31. *Journal and Debates of the Constitutional Convention of the State of Wyoming: Begun at the City of Cheyenne on September 2, 1889, and Concluded September 30, 1889* (Cheyenne: The Daily Sun, 1893), 390–393.

32. *Journal and Debates of the Constitutional Convention of the State of Wyoming: Begun at the City of Cheyenne,* 390–393.

33. The 1876 law was not well followed. See Michael Katz, *A History of Compulsory Education Laws* (Bloomington: Phi Delta Kappa Press, 1976), 20.

34. *Proceedings and Debates of the Constitutional Convention of Idaho,* 377.

35. Education Data Initiative, "U.S. Public Education Spending Statistics," June 15, 2022, https://educationdata.org/public-education-spending-statistics.

36. Associated Press, "War on Public Education in Idaho Causes Businesses to Rethink Locating, Expanding There, Leaders Say," December 16, 2021, https://www.oregonlive.com/education/2021/12/war-on-public-education-in-idaho-causes-businesses-to-rethink-locating-expanding-there-leaders-say.html.

37. Carlos Schwantes, *In Mountain Shadows: A History of Idaho* (Lincoln: University of Nebraska Press, 1991), 140.

38. World Population Review, "U.S. Literacy Rates by State 2022," https://worldpopulationreview.com/state-rankings/us-literacy-rates-by-state.

39. Lori Ann Lahlum and Molly P. Rozum, *Equality at the Ballot Box: Votes for Women on the Northern Great Plains* (Pierre: South Dakota Historical Society Press, 2019), 13.

40. *Idaho: Proceedings and Debates of the Constitutional Convention of Idaho,* 692.

41. John D. Hicks, *The Constitutions of the Northwest States,* vol. 23, issues 1–4 (Lincoln: University Studies of the University of Nebraska 1923), 31.

42. *Official Report of the Proceedings and Debates of the First Constitutional Convention of North Dakota,* 481.

43. Digital Public Library of America, "Boom and Bust: The Industries That Settled Montana," https://dp.la/exhibitions/industries-settled-montana/mining/becoming-territory?item=1144.

44. For a discussion of Montana's territorial debts, see Michael P. Malone,

Richard B. Roeder, and William L. Lang, *Montana: A History of Two Centuries* (Seattle: University of Washington Press, 1991), 107–109.

45. From a speech given by Doane Robinson on November 2, 1922, at the celebration of the thirty-third anniversary of South Dakota's at Mission as a state. Quoted in the introduction to Patrick M. Garry, *South Dakota State Constitution* (Oxford: Oxford University Press, 2014), 30.

46. Ronald Limbaugh, review of *In Mountain Shadows: A History of Idaho* by Carlos A. Schwates and *Idaho's Constitution: The Tie That Binds* by Dennis C. Colson, *The Western Historical Quarterly* 23, no. 2 (1992): 257–258, https://doi .org/10.2307/970477.

47. Wyoming Constitutional Convention (1889), 723–725.

48. Wyoming Constitutional Convention (1889), 724.

49. Wyoming Constitutional Convention (1889), 724.

50. Gordon Bakken, *Rocky Mountain Constitution Making* (New York: Greenwood Press, 1987), 24.

51. Ross Cotroneo, "Northern Pacific Officials and the Disposition of the Railroad's Land Grant in North Dakota After 1880," *North Dakota History* 37, no. 2 (1970): 77–103.

52. Elywn Robinson, *The History of North Dakota* (Lincoln: University of Nebraska Press, 1966), 226.

53. T. A. Larson, *History of Wyoming* (Lincoln: University of Nebraska Press, 1990), 29.

54. James R. Kane, "Populism, Progressivism, and Pure Food," *Agricultural History* 38, no. 3 (1964): 163.

55. Kenneth Carey, "Alexander McKenzie, Boss of North Dakota 1883–1906" (master's thesis, University of North Dakota, 1949), 18.

56. "From Magnet to First Pardon," *Bismarck Tribune*, December 1, 2011.

57. Connie DeVelder Schaffer, "Money Versus Morality: The Divorce Industry of Sioux Falls" *South Dakota State Historical Society* 20, no. 3 (1990), https: //www.sdhspress.com/journal/south-dakota-history-20-3/money-versus-morality-the-divorce-industry-of-sioux-falls/vol-20-no-3-money-versus-morality .pdf.

58. George D. Mueller, "The Severe Drought of 1919 and Its Effect on Central Montana," Montana Memory Project.

59. Tuttle, *Official Report of the Proceedings and Debates of the First Constitutional Convention of North Dakota*, 411.

60. J. W. Powell, "Institutions for Arid Lands," *Century Magazine*, May 1890, 111–116.

61. Powell, "Institutions for Arid Lands," 111–116.

CHAPTER 2. THE POISON SEED

1. The South Dakota State Archives in Pierre house Todd's scant documents. These include a military journal written during the Harney Expedition (1855), scattered speeches, and assorted (and very short) biographies.

2. Howard Lamar, *Dakota Territory 1861–1889* (New Haven: Yale University Press, 1956), 68.

3. Thomas Donaldson, *The Public Domain, Its History with Statistics* (Washington, DC: Government Printing Office, 1884), 678.

4. George W. Kingsbury, G. W. Smith, and G. Martin, *History of Dakota Territory* (Chicago: S. J. Clarke, 1915), 193.

5. Richard Slotkin, *The Fatal Environment: The Myth of the Frontier in the Age of Industrialization, 1800–1890* (New York: Atheneum, 1985), 203.

6. Patrick Coleman, "A Rare Find: The Treaty of Washington, 1858," *Minnesota History Magazine*, http://collections.mnhs.org/mnhistorymagazine/articl es/59/v59i05p197-199.pdf.

7. National Park Service, "Struck By The Ree," https://www.nps.gov/peo ple/struck-by-the-ree.htm.

8. Grant Anderson, "The Politics of Land in Dakota Territory: Early Skirmishes—1857–1861," *South Dakota State Historical Society* 9, no. 3 (1979): 212, https://www.sdhspress.com/journal/south-dakota-history-9-3/the-politics-of -land-in-dakota-territory-early-skirmishesa1857-1861/vol-09-no-3-the-politics -of-land-in-dakota-territory.pdf.

9. William E. Lass, "The First Attempt to Organize Dakota Territory," in *Centennial West: Essays on the Northern Tier States*, ed. William L. Lang (Seattle: University of Washington Press, 1991), http://www.minnesotalegalhistoryproj ect.org/assets/Lass.pdf. See also "Excluded Part of Minnesota, Minnesota," *Historical Society*, 1923, http://collections.mnhs.org/MNHistoryMagazine/articles /5/v05i03p205-207.pdf.

10. Robert J. Forrest, "Mythical Cities of Southwestern Minnesota," *Minnesota History Magazine* 14, no. 3 (1933): 243–262.

11. Samuel J. Albright, "The First Organized Government of Dakota," *Minnesota Legal History Project*, 8, http://www.minnesotalegalhistoryproject.org/as sets/First%20Organized%20Govt-Dak.--MMM.pdf.

12. Albright, "The First Organized Government of Dakota," 14.

13. Anderson, "The Politics of Land in Dakota Territory," 221.

14. *Congressional Globe*, 36th Congress, 1st session, May 12, 1860, 2080.

15. Howard Lamar, *Dakota Territory, 1861–1889: A Study of Frontier Politics* (New Haven: Yale University Press 1956), 49–50.

16. *Congressional Globe*, 35th Congress, 2nd session, February 8, 1859, 877.

17. Charles Albright, "The First Organized Government of Dakota," *Minnesota Legal History Project*, 16.

18. *Congressional Globe*, 36th Congress, 1st session, May 11, 1860, 2074.

19. Kingsbury, Smith, and Martin, *History of Dakota Territory*.

20. U.S. Congress, House, *Congressional Globe*, 36th Cong., 2nd sess., 15 February 1861, 897.

21. James Blaine, *Twenty Years in Congress, Volume 1* (Norwich, CN: Henry Hill Publishing, 1884), 270.

22. Treaty of 1863. The Nez Perce refer to this as the "Thief Treaty."

23. Taft Alfred Larson, *History of Wyoming* (Lincoln: University of Nebraska Press, 1965), 65.

24. John O'Sullivan, "Introduction," *The United States Magazine and Democratic Review* 1, no. 1 (1837): 6.

25. Genevieve K. Croft, "The U.S. Land-Grant University System: Overview and Role in Agricultural Research," *Congressional Research Service Report R45897* (August 9, 2022): 2.

26. Donaldson, *The Public Domain*.

27. John C. Lacy, "The Historic Origins of the U.S. Mining Laws and Proposals for Change." *Natural Resources & Environment* 10, no. 1 (1995): 17, http://www.jstor.org/stable/40923428.

28. George Crook, *General George Crook: His Autobiography* (Norman: University of Oklahoma Press, 1949), 229.

29. Mark Brown, *The Plainsman of the Yellowstone: A History of the Yellowstone Basin* (Lincoln: Bison Books, 1977), 436.

30. "Report of the Commissioner of Indian Affairs for the Year 1866" (Washington: Government Printing Office, 1866), 181.

31. *Yankton Press,* August 17, 1870.

32. *Dakota Herald*, August 25, 1874: "Honorable W. A. Burleigh yesterday sold 2500 acres of his large farm in the neighborhood of Bon Homme. The buyer is a group of Russian-Germans who have united after the fashion of Apostolic Communists. Of the purchase price of 25,000 dollars, they pay 17,000 dollars cash, the balance they pay on time."

33. George H. Phillips, "The Indian Ring in Dakota Territory, 1870–1890," *South Dakota History* 2, no. 4 (1972): 353.

34. US Department of Agriculture, Bureau of Statistics, 1903 (Washington: Government Printing Office, 1904).

35. "Report of the Commissioners of Indian Affairs for the Year 1866" (Washington: Government Printing Office, 1866).

36. *Sweetwater Mines*, May 30, 1868, volume 1, number 24.

37. John Pope, (Untitled) *The Journal of the Armed Forces* (1877–1878), July 27, 1878, 827.

38. Earl Pomeroy, *The Territories and the United States, 1861–1890: Studies in Colonial Administration* (Philadelphia: University of Pennsylvania Press, 1947), 36–37.

39. *Journal and Debates of the Constitutional Convention of the State of Wyoming*, 520.

40. Kermit Hall, "Hacks and Derelicts Revisited: American Territorial Judiciary, 1789–1959," *The Western Historical Quarterly* 12, no. 3 (1981): 273–289.

41. Merle W. Wells, "David W. Ballard, Governor of Idaho, 1866–1870," *Oregon Historical Quarterly* 54, no. 1 (1953): 5, http://www.jstor.org/stable/20612088.

42. Ulysses S. Grant, "Seventh Annual Message," December 7, 1875, https://millercenter.org/the-presidency/presidential-speeches/december-7-1875-seventh-annual-message.

43. Karl Landstrom, "Reclamation under the Desert-Land Act," *Journal of Farm Economics* 36, no. 3 (1954): 500–508.

44. Email correspondence dated August 17, 2022. See also https://reports.blm.gov/reports/LR2000.

45. Donaldson, *The Public Domain*, 537.

46. "Annual Report of the Commissioner of the Land Office for the Year 1885" (Washington: Government Printing Office, 1885), 54.

47. Harold Dunham, *Government Handout: A Study in the Administration of the Public Lands, 1875–1891* (Ann Arbor: Edward Brothers, 1941), 64.

48. "Annual Report of the Commissioner of the Land Office for the Year 1885," 55.

49. US Department of the Interior, "Annual Report of the Secretary of the Interior" (Washington, DC: G.P.O., 1886–1887), 4.

50. Paul Wallace Gates, "The Homestead Law in an Incongruous Land System," *The American Historical Review* 41, no. 4 (1936): 652–681, https://doi.org/10.2307/1842606.

51. *New York Times*, December 7, 1886, 8.

52. Carlos Schwantes, *In Mountain Shadows* (Lincoln: University of Nebraska Press, 1991), 133.

53. John Use, *The United States Forest Policy* (New Haven: Yale University Press, 1920), 123–124.

54. USDA, *Benefits to the People*, Bighorn National Forest, 2, https://www.fs.usda.gov/emc/economics/documents/at-a-glance/benefits-to-people/rockymtn/BTP-Bighorn.pdf.

55. Use, *The United States Forest Policy*, 125.

56. National Museum of Forest Service History, *Case 1: Forest Reserves*, https://forestservicemuseum.org/exhibits/case-number-one/forest-reserves.

57. W. L. Dutton, "History of Grazing Fees," *Journal of Range Management* 6, no. 6 (1953): 393.

58. John Clayton, "Conservation Politics: 'Triple A' Anderson and the Yellowstone Forest Reserve," *Wyohistory.org*, July 25, 2017.

59. Amie Thompson, "Homestead Act Had Huge Economic Impact on Montana's History," *Great Falls Tribune*, November 1, 2014.

60. Charles V. Stern and Anna E. Normand, "Bureau of Reclamation: History, Authorities, and Issues for Congress," Congressional Research Office, April 3, 2020, 20.

61. In 1870, there were 1,720 farms in all of Dakota Territory, with an average size of 176 acres. This grew tenfold in one decade to 17,435 farms by 1880, the average size growing modestly to 218 acres. The number continued to grow until 1910, by which time there were 74,360 farms in North Dakota, averaging 382 acres each. The number of farms in North Dakota has never grown substantially above this figure and has been declining since 1950. See https://library.ndsu.edu/fargo-history/?q=content/dakota-territory-growth.

62. Reynold M. Wik, "Henry Ford and the Agricultural Depression of 1920–1923," *Agricultural History* 29, no. 1 (1955): 15–22.

63. Elwyn B. Robinson, *History of North Dakota* (Lincoln: University of Nebraska Press, 1966), 399.

64. Ann Marie Low, *Dust Bowl Diary* (Lincoln: University of Nebraska Press, 1984), 65–67.

65. Margaret S. Gordon, *Employment Expansion in Population Growth: The California Experience, 1900–1950* (Berkeley: University of California Press, 1954), 4–6.

66. Hathaway likely overstated the state's dire circumstances. In his book, *The Paradox of Plenty*, former governor David Freudenthal demonstrated that the state had $5 million in the general fund at the time.

67. Dennis Farley, "The Lonesome Land," *The Wall Street Journal*, October 3, 1969, 3.

68. Rep. John Wold, Government Printing Office, Extension of Remarks, 29767, https://www.govinfo.gov/content/pkg/GPO-CRECB-1969-pt22/pdf/GPO-CRECB-1969-pt22-2-3.pdf.

69. Low, *Dust Bowl Diary*, 183.

70. Robert Righter, *Crucible for Conservation: The Struggle for Grand Teton National Park* (Jackson: Grand Teton Association, 2008), 83.

71. Laurie Hinck, *Waiting for Wilderness: The Corporate Genesis of Grand Teton National Park, 1927–1965* (PhD diss., University of New Mexico, 2009), 90.

72. Jayson Lusk, "The Evolution of American Agriculture," June 27, 2016, http://jaysonlusk.com/blog/2016/6/26/the-evolution-of-american-agriculture. See also USA Facts, "Federal Farm Subsidies: What the Data Says," September 29, 2020, https://usafacts.org/articles/federal-farm-subsidies-what-data-says/.

73. Bill Ganzel, "Shrinking Farm Numbers," *Living History Farm*, https://livinghistoryfarm.org/farminginthe50s/life_11.html.

74. Harry Thompson and Herbert Hoover, *A New History of South Dakota* (Sioux Falls: Center for Western Studies/Augustana College, 2009), 247.

75. Committee for Economic Development, "An Adaptive Program for Agriculture. A Statement on National Policy," 1962, https://babel.hathitrust.org/cgi/pt?id=mdp.39015008782123&view=1up&seq=31&skin=2021.

76. Thompson and Hoover, *A New History of South Dakota*, 245.

77. May Peters, Suchada Langley, and Paul Westcott, "Agricultural Commodity Price Spikes in the 1970s and 1990s: Valuable Lessons for Today," *Amber Waves*, March 1, 2009.

78. May Peters, Suchada Langley, and Paul Westcott, "Agricultural Commodity Price Spikes in the 1970s and 1990s: Valuable Lessons for Today," *Amber Waves*, March 1, 2009.

79. Farm Credit Association, History of the FCA, https://www.fca.gov/about/history-of fca#:~:text=For%201985%20and%201986%2C%20FCS,for%20any%20U.S.%20financial%20institution.

80. Pamela Riney-Kehrberg, *When a Dream Dies: Agriculture, Iowa, and the Farm Crisis of the 1980s* (Lawrence: University Press of Kansas, 2022), 8–9.

81. Riney-Kehrberg, *When a Dream Dies*, 95.

82. Catherine M. Stock, *Main Street in Crisis: The Great Depression and the Old Middle Class on the Northern Plains* (Chapel Hill: University of North Carolina Press, 1992), 209.

83. Amanda Rees, "The Buffalo Commons: Great Plains Residents' Responses to a Radical Vision," *Great Plains Quarterly* 188 (2005).

84. Wyoming Mining Association, *The Concise Guide to Coal Mining*, http://www.wyomingmining.org/wp-content/uploads/2013/11/2013-14-Concise-Guide-to-Wyoming-Coal.pdf.

85. US Energy Association, "Petroleum and Other Liquids," https://www.eia.gov/dnav/pet/hist/LeafHandler.ashx?n=pet&s=f000000__3&f=m. See also Jad Mouawad, "Oil Prices Pass Record Set in '80s, but Then Recede," *New York Times*, March 3, 2008.

86. Bill Sniffin, "Remembering Malcolm Wallop and His Unlikely and

Amazing Victory in 1976," *Cowboy Daily*, February 27, 2020. See also https://kingfm.com/how-a-port-o-potty-changed-wyoming-politics-forever-video.

87. Ronald Arnold, *Wise Use Agenda* (Belleview: Merril Press, 1988), https://s3.amazonaws.com/s3.documentcloud.org/documents/1349160/cdfearn old00089.pdf.

88. Clay Jenkinson, "Federal Money Boosts North Dakota," *Bismarck Tribune*, August 16, 2015.

89. Nate Schweber, *This America of Ours: Bernard and Avis DeVoto and the Forgotten Fight to Save the Wild* (Boston: Mariner Books, 2022), 182.

90. David Stockman, *The Triumph of Politics: How the Reagan Revolution Failed* (New York: Harper & Row, 1986), 152.

91. U.S. Department of the Interior News Release, "FY 2021 Disbursements, Providing Important Funds for States, Tribes and Conservation Initiatives," November 23, 2021. https://onrr.gov/press-releases/Fiscal_Year_2021_Disburse ments_Press_Release.pdf.

CHAPTER 3. YIELD AND POUNDS DO NOT A COMMUNITY MAKE

1. Caroline Fraser, *Prairie Fires: The American Dreams of Laura Ingalls Wilder* (New York: Metropolitan Books, 2017), 144.

2. Fraser, *Prairie Fires,* 166.

3. Paula Nelson, "Everything I Want is Here; The Dakota Farmer's Rural Ideal, 1884–1934," *South Dakota State Historical Society* 22, no. 2 (1992): 110.

4. Suggested readings about McM: Jesse Newman, "Two Brothers, Tied to the Land, Face Wrath of America's Farm Bust," *Wall Street Journal*, December 18, 2017; Mikkel Pates, "McMartin Discloses Financials," *Agweek*, September 29, 2017; Jim Mundorf, "Update: The Wall Street Journal Profiles Bankrupt Farmer and Forgets to Mention That He Is Living in a Million Dollar House and Is Charged with Fraud," *Lonesome Land*, January 9, 2018.

5. Environmental Working Group Subsidy Database, https://farm.ewg.org /addrsearch.php?search_input_text=58276.

6. Marvin Riley and Darryll Johnson, "South Dakota Farm Facts from 1964 Census of Agriculture," Cooperative Extension, South Dakota State University, 1967; Thomas Foulke, Roger Coupal, and David Taylor, "Trends in Wyoming Agriculture, Size of Operation (1935–1977)," University of Wyoming College of Agriculture, Cooperative Extension Service, October 2000. See also: USDA Agricultural Census—1935, "Montana County Tables," https://agcensus.libra ry.cornell.edu/wp-content/uploads/1935-Montana-COUNTY_TABLES-15 14-Table-01.pdf; USDA, 1969 Census of Agriculture, "Idaho All Farms—481,

Table 01," https://agcensus.library.cornell.edu/wp-content/uploads/1969-Ida ho-All_Farms-481-Table-01.pdf; USDA Agricultural Census—1935, "North Dakota State, Table 03," https://agcensus.library.cornell.edu/wp-content/uplo ads/1935-North_Dakota-STATE_TABLES-1513-Table-03.pdf.

7. Thorstein Veblen, "The Price of Wheat Since 1867," *Journal of Political History* 1, no. 1 (December 1892): 157.

8. Lynwood Oyos, "Farming: Dependency and Depopulation," in *A New South Dakota History* (Sioux Fall: Center for Western Studies, 2005), 227.

9. Frank Bavendick, *Climate and Weather in North Dakota* (Bismarck: U.S. Weather Bureau Office and North Dakota State Water Conservation Commission, 1952), 13.

10. Candice Savage, *Prairie: A Natural History* (Vancouver, Greystone Books, 2004), 72.

11. The U.S. Climate Resilience Toolkit, site managed by NOAA's Climate Program Office, https://toolkit.climate.gov/regions/northern-great-plains.

12. National Drought Mitigation Center, https://droughtmonitor.unl.edu /CurrentMap/StateDroughtMonitor.aspx.

13. USDA, NASS, 2021 State Agricultural Overview, Iowa, https://www.na ss.usda.gov/Quick_Stats/Ag_Overview/stateOverview.php?state=IOWA.

14. All figures from Statistia.com.

15. Idaho Farm Bureau Federation, "Drought, Heat Will Impact Idaho's Barley Production," https://www.idahofb.org/News-Media/2021/07/drought -heat-will-impact-idaho#:~:text=Idaho%2C%20traditionally%20the%20 nation's%20No,at%20110%20bushels%20per%20acre.

16. US Census of Agriculture, 1900, https://www2.census.gov/prod2/decen nial/documents/11350853ch3.pdf.

17. Chris Hurt, "Drought Devastating to Beef Industry; Herd Numbers Drop- ping," Purdue University News, October 25, 2012, https://www.purdue.edu /newsroom/releases/2012/Q4/hurt-drought-devastating-to-beef-industry-herd -numbers-dropping.html.

18. Greg Johnson, "New Zealand's Livestock 'Fart Tax' Is Disastrous Policy Says Wyoming Ag Expert," *Cowboy Daily*, October 12, 2022.

19. NDSU Extension and Ag Research News, "N.D. Net Farm Income Drops 30 Percent," https://www.ag.ndsu.edu/news/newsreleases/2018/may-21-2018 /n-d-net-farm-income-drops-30-percent.

20. Mikkel Pates, "Potential Cattle Profits Follow Years of Real Stress," *Ag- week*, January 31, 2022, https://www.agweek.com/business/potential-cattle-pro fits-follow-years-of-real-stress-1.

21. Lynsey Aberle, "ND Producers' Net Farm Income Up In 2020," *Dakota*

Farmer, June 25, 2021, https://www.farmprogress.com/farm-business/nd-pro ducers-net-farm-income-2020.

22. Kevin Killough, "Wyoming Farmers and Ranchers Have 'Tougher Than Ever' Year," *Cowboy Daily*, September 13, 2022, https://cowboystatedaily.com /2022/09/13/wyoming-farmers-and-ranchers-have-tougher-than-ever-year.

23. Conventional agriculture relies on four foundations: chemicals (herbicides, pesticides, and fertilizers), genetically engineered seeds, support from the federal government (crop insurance and the like), and tillage (breaking the surface of the soil). This last practice is on the decline, however.

24. Climate, Food, and Ag Dialogue, "Recognizing Early Innovators," March 2022, https://climatefoodag.org/wp-content/uploads/sites/9/2022/03/Recogni zing-Early-Innovators.pdf.

25. Willard Cochrane, *The Curse of American Agricultural Abundance* (Lincoln: University of Nebraska Press, 2003).

26. Reuters, "World Food Prices Decline for 10th Month Running in January, Says FAO," https://www.reuters.com/world/world-food-prices-decline-10th -month-running-january-says-fao-2023-02-03/

27. David R. Montgomery, "3 Big Myths about Modern Agriculture," *Scientific American*, April 5, 2017, https://www.scientificamerican.com/article/3-big -myths-about-modern-agriculture1.

28. Economic Research Service, "Feed Grains Sector at a Glance," https: //www.ers.usda.gov/topics/crops/corn-and-other-feed-grains/feed-grains- sector-at-a-glance.

29. H. C. Sherman, "Use of Corn (Maize) As Human Food, *JAMA* 70, no. 22 (1918): 1579–1581.

30. Chad Hart and Lee Shultz, "China's Importance in the U.S. Ag Market," *Agricultural Policy Review*, https://www.card.iastate.edu/ag_policy_review/arti cle/?a=41#:~:text=Roughly%2060%20percent%20of%20US,finds%20its%20 way%20to%20China.

31. H. H. Stein, J. A. Roth, K. M. Sotak, and O. J. Rojas, "Nutritional Value of Soy Producers Fed to Pigs," *Swine Focus004*, 2, https://nutrition.ansci.illinois .edu/sites/default/files/SwineFocus004.pdf.

32. World Wildlife Fund, "Driven to Waste: Global Food Loss on Farms," https://wwf.panda.org/discover/our_focus/food_practice/food_loss_and_was te/driven_to_waste_global_food_loss_on_farms; Elaine Povich, "Waste Not? Some States Are Sending Less Food to Landfills," *Stateline*, July 8, 2021, https: //www.pewtrusts.org/en/research-and-analysis/blogs/stateline/2021/07/08 /waste-not-some-states-are-sending-less-food-to-landfills.

33. Marty Strange, *Family Farming, A New Economic Vision* (Lincoln: University of Nebraska Press, 2008).

34. US Department of Agriculture Summary Report: 2017 National Resources Inventory, Natural Resources Conservation Service, Washington, DC, 2020, 8.

35. David R. Montgomery, *Dirt: The Erosion of Civilizations* (Berkeley: University of California Press, 2007), 3.

36. David Montgomery, "Soil Erosion and Agricultural Sustainability," Proceedings of the National Academy of Sciences, August 14, 2000, https://www.pnas.org/doi/full/10.1073/pnas.0611508104.

37. Dennis Keeney and Richard Cruse, *Advances in Soil and Water Conservation*, edited by F. J. Pierce and W. W. Frye (Ann Arbor, Chelsea, 1998), 185–194.

38. Personal email correspondence, dated March 20, 2022.

39. Environmental Defense Fund, *Banking on Soil Health: Farmer Interest in Transition Loan Products*, September 2021, 19, https://www.edf.org/sites/default/files/content/Banking-on-Soil-Health.pdf.

40. Daniel Hellerstein, Dennis Vilorio, and Marc Ribaudo, *Agricultural Resources and Environmental Indicators*, 2019, https://www.ers.usda.gov/webdocs/publications/93026/eib-208_summary.pdf?v=6654.

41. Daniel Cohan and Lina Luo, "Agriculture Emissions Pose Risks to Health and Climate," *Science Daily*, June 1, 2022, https://www.sciencedaily.com/releases/2022/06/220621091415.htm.

42. Patrick Thomas, "Cattle Ranchers Take Aim at Meatpackers' Dominance," *Wall Street Journal*, March 21, 2022.

43. In 2017, Shawn Williamson, a CPA following farm trends, penciled out how much money it would take a young person to get into farming. Williamson calculations figured in the cost of the minimum amount of land needed (five hundred acres plus a one-thousand-acre lease), the purchase of used equipment, plus the cost of basic buildings, seed, fuel, and fertilizer costs: $5,157,500.

44. Laura Reilly and Andrew Van Dam, "Advocates Hoped Census Would Find Diversity in Agriculture. It Found Old White People," *Washington Post*, April 13, 2019.

45. Elizabeth Ann R. Bird, Gordon L. Bultena, and John C. Gardner, eds., *Planting the Future: Developing an Agriculture that Sustains Land and Community* (Ames: Iowa State University Press, 1995).

46. Kate Silver, "Feeding Our Future," *Politico*, February 2, 2022, https://www.politico.com/sponsored-content/2022/02/feeding-our-future.

47. Matthew Sedacca, "JBS Agrees to Pay Beef Wholesalers $52.5 Million in Latest Price-Fixing Settlement," *The Counter*, February 4, 2022.

48. See Bob Quinn and Liz Carlisle, *Grain by Grain* (Washington: Island Press, 2019).

49. Edward C. Jaenicke, *U.S. Organic Hotspots and their Benefit to Local Economies*, 2016, https://ota.com/sites/default/files/indexed_files/OTA-Hot SpotsWhitePaper-OnlineVersion.pdf.

50. Personal interview, July 30, 2020.

51. Organic Trade Association, "U.S. Organic Grain—How to Keep it Growing," 2019, https://ota.com/sites/default/files/indexed_files/US%20Organic %20Grain_How%20to%20Keep%20it%20Growing_Organic%20Trade%20 Association.pdf.

52. Email correspondence, January 16, 2023.

53. Personal interview, March 18, 2022, with follow-up phone calls.

54. New Agrarian Program, "Supporting Apprenticeship and Mentorship in Agriculture," https://quiviracoalition.org/newagrarian.

55. Milton Ranch, "Eight-Month Cattle Ranching Apprenticeship in Roundup, Montana," https://quiviracoalition.org/milton-ranch.

56. Beginning in 2019, I interviewed Milton numerous times in person, on Zoom, and on the phone.

57. Most of this interview took place on October 23, 2020, with subsequent follow-up phone calls.

58. Interview, February 16, 2022.

59. I spent a week at Vilicus Farms in 2021, plus additional interviews through phone calls and a Zoom session.

60. USDA, Economic Research Office, "Farming and Farm Income, 2022," https://www.ers.usda.gov/data-products/ag-and-food-statistics-charting-the -essentials/farming-and-farm-income.

61. I interviewed Brown at his ranch on August 21, 2021. In addition, I've attended a conference with him as keynote speaker. Also, we've had follow-up phone calls and emails.

62. Daniel Hellerstein, Dennis Vilorio, and Marc Ribaudo, eds., *Agricultural Resources and Environmental Indicators, 2019*, ERS, Economic Information Bulletin Number 208, May 2019, 25.

63. Successful Farming Staff, "What Gabe Brown Learned by Testifying Before Congress," March 9, 2021, https://www.agriculture.com/farm-manage ment/programs-and-policies/what-gabe-brown-learned-by-testifying-before -congress.

64. Gabe Brown, *From Dirt to Soil: One Family's Journey into Regenerative Agriculture* (White River Junction, VT: Chelsea Brown Publishing, 2018), 24.

65. Lynsey Aberle, "2021 Net Farm Income for ND Farmers Soars," Dakota Farmer, June 21, 2022.

66. Ben Eborn and Jim Church, "Cow-Calf Budget: 250-head Northern Idaho Summer on Private Range, Winter Feeding Necessary," University of Idaho Extension, University of Idaho, Moscow, Idaho.

67. Interview, May 25, 2022.

68. USDA, Economic Research Service, "Farm Share of U.S. Food Dollar Reached Historic Low in 2021," November 28, 2022, https://www.ers.usda.gov/data-products/chart-gallery/gallery/chart-detail/?chartId=105281#:~:text=U.S.%20farm%20establishments%20received%2014.5,value%20in%20nearly%20three%20decades.

69. Email, January 18, 2023.

70. Shawn Ginwright, *The Four Pivots* (Berkeley: North Atlantic Books, 2022), 16.

71. Robert Wiebe, *The Search for Order* (New York: Hill and Wang, 1967), 2.

72. Montana Soil Health Symposium, Billings, Montana, February 5, 2020.

73. Email correspondence, January 19, 2023.

74. Congressional Research Office, Federal Crop Insurance: A Primer, February 18, 2020, https://crsreports.congress.gov/product/pdf/R/R46686.

75. Steward Technologies factsheet: https://gosteward.com.

76. Interview, July 30, 2020.

CHAPTER 4. CITIES OF THE PLAINS

1. Fourteenth Census of the United States, "1920, Population: Idaho. Number of Inhabitants, by Counties and Minor Divisions," https://www2.census.gov/library/publications/decennial/1920/bulletins/demographics/population-id-number-of-inhabitants.pdf. See also Twelfth Census of the United States, Census Bulletin, No. 33, January 17, 1901, "Population of Montana by Counties and Minor Division," https://www2.census.gov/library/publications/decennial/1900/bulletins/demographic/33-population-mt.pdf; US Census Bureau, "No. HS-7, Population of the 75 Largest Cities: 1900 to 2000," https://www.census.gov/history/pdf/los_angeles_pop.pdf.

2. State v. Hutchinson, 624 P.2d 1116 (1980) Supreme Court of Utah, December 9, 1980.

3. Stephen Williams, *Reports of Cases Argued and Decided in the Supreme Court, Book 25, First National Bank of Brunswick v. County of Yankton* (Rochester: Lawyers Cooperative Publishing, 1901), 1046.

4. John D. Hicks, *The Constitutions of the Northwest States*, vol. 23, issues 1–4 (Lincoln: University Studies of the University of Nebraska 1923), 9.

5. Wyoming Association of Municipalities, *Municipal Financial Report, 2016*, 24.

6. Christiana McFarland, Julia Bauer, "The Changing Landscape of Preemption," *National League of Cities*, February 14, 2022, https://www.nlc.org/article /2022/02/14/the-changing-landscape-of-preemption.

7. Fredrick Turner, "The Problem of the West," *The Atlantic Monthly*, September 1886, 290.

8. Wyoming Economic Analysis Division, "Historical Decennial Census Population for Wyoming Counties, Cities, and Towns," http://eadiv.state.wy.us /demog_data/cntycity_hist.htm.

9. FRED, St. Louis Federal Reserve, "Resident Population in Teton, Idaho," https://fred.stlouisfed.org/series/IDTETO1POP; FRED, St. Louis Federal Reserve, "Resident Population in Flathead County, MT," https://fred.stlouisfed .org/series/MTFLAT0POP; US Census, "Population of States and Counties of the United States, 1790–1990," 144, https://www2.census.gov/library/pub lications/decennial/1990/population-of-states-and-counties-us-1790-1990/po pulation-of-states-and-counties-of-the-united-states-1790-1990.pdf.

10. In 2021, yet another analysis appeared. The St. Louis Federal Reserve put out a 605-page tome titled *Investing in Rural America*.

11. Headwaters Economics, *Economy Surprisingly Dependent on Non-Labor Income*, August 2017, https://headwaterseconomics.org/economic-development /trends-performance/economy-surprisingly-dependent-on-non-labor-income.

12. Email, May 24, 2022.

13. Mark Haggarty, "Getting Real About Rural Resilience," *Headwaters Economics*, April 16, 2019. See also Julia H. Haggerty, Mark N. Haggerty, Kelli Roemer, and Jackson Rose, "Planning for the Local Impacts of Coal Facility Closure: Emerging Strategies in the U.S. West," *Resources Policy* 57 (August 2018): 69–80.

14. Mark Haggarty, "Fiscal Policy is Failing Rural America: Understanding Barriers to Economic Development, Conservation, and Renewable Energy," *Headwater Economics,* October 2020.

15. Charles Marohn, *Strongtowns: A Bottom-Up Revolution to Rebuild American Prosperity* (Hoboken: John Wiley and Sons, 2020).

16. Christopher Alexander, *The Timeless Way of Building* (New York: Oxford University Press, 1979), 65.

17. Governor's Office, "Montana's Economy 7th Strongest in Nation with Robust Growth in 2021," April 25, 2022, https://news.mt.gov/GovernorsOffice /Montanas_Economy_7th_Strongest_in_Nation_With_Robust_Growth_in_2021.

18. Mark Haggerty, "Tension as Catalyst: Public Lands and the Rural West," March 2020, https://headwaterseconomics.org/economic-development/tension-as-catalyst-public-lands-and-the-rural-west.

19. Kim Parker, Juliana Menasce Horowitz, and Rachel Minkin, "Covid-19 Pandemic Continues to Reshape Work in America," Pew Research Center, February 16, 2022, https://www.pewresearch.org/social-trends/2022/02/16/covid-19-pandemic-continues-to-reshape-work-in-america.

20. Lydia Saad, "Country Living Enjoys Renewed Appeal in U.S.," Gallup, January 5, 2022, https://www2.census.gov/library/publications/decennial/1920/bulletins/demographics/population-id-number-of-inhabitants.pdf.

21. Joshua Montes, Christopher Smith, and Juliana Dajon, "'The Great Retirement Boom': The Pandemic-Era Surge in Retirements and Implications for Future Labor Force Participation," Finance and Economics Discussion Series 2022-081, Board of Governors of the Federal Reserve System (November 2022): 1. https://www.federalreserve.gov/econres/feds/the-great-retirement-boom.htm; https://www.zillow.com/home-values/6705/red-lodge-mt/; https://www.zillow.com/home-values/17504/cody-wy.

22. Andrew Van Dam, "Where We Build Homes Helps Explain America's Political Divide," *Washington Post*, November 24, 2023, https://www.washingtonpost.com/business/2023/11/24/counties-building-new-housing.

23. Douglas Belkin, "A Generation of Men Give Up on College: I Just Feel Lost," *Wall Street Journal*, 2021, https://www.wsj.com/articles/college-university-fall-higher-education-men-women-enrollment-admissions-back-to-school-11630948233.

24. Lindsay Ellis, "Women Catch Up with Men at More Top Business Schools," *Wall Street Journal*, November 3, 2023, https://www.wsj.com/us-news/education/top-business-schools-are-enrolling-more-women-than-men-375913bb?mod=hp_lead_pos11.

25. US Bureau of Statistics, "Labor Force Statistics from the Current Population Survey, 2021," https://www.bls.gov/cps/cpsaat18.htm.

26. Interview, May 14, 2022.

27. Edward Sampson, "Geology and Silver Ore Deposits of the Pend Oreille District, Idaho," Bureau of Mines and Geology, December 1928, https://www.idahogeology.org/pub/Pamphlets/P-31.pdf.

28. Billie Jean Gerke, "Timber Town, USA: The Way It Was In Our Neck of the Woods," Summer 1994, 26.

29. Kevin Keating, "Ski Hill Battle Is Last Resort for Brown Family Fortune," *The Spokesman-Review*, November 30, 1997.

30. Jack Fowler, *Looking Back on Schweitzer: The Story of Schweitzer* (Spokane: Marshall Publishing, 1991), 14.

31. Brand S. Corp., Merritt Brothers Mill, Riley Brothers, Old Tow, Louisiana Pacific, JD Lumber, WI Mill, Crown Pacific, Dover (Pack River Management), Ceda-Pine Veneer (located just over the county line in the town of Samuels), and Arrow Tie. See also: Jeff Opdyke, "Timber Towns Face Bleak Future as More Saw Mills Close for Good," *Wall Street Journal,* December 16, 1998, https://www .wsj.com/articles/SB913750088731340500; Inland Forest Management, "Tree Talk," Vanishing Sawmills, http://inlandforest.com/vanishing-sawmills.

32. Idaho Forest Products, Stimpson, and TriPro Forest Products.

33. Samuel Wolkenhauer, "Bonner County Economic Overview," Idaho Department of Labor, September 2022, https://lmi.idaho.gov/Portals/0/2022/Wo rkforceTrends/BonnerProfile.pdf?v=052022.

34. Bonner County, "Workforce Trends, April 2019," https://www.bonner countyid.gov/media/Planning/Subarea%20Comp%20Plans/Priest%20 River-Oldtown/Draft%20plans%20and%20other%20supporting%20 documents/Workforce%20Trends%202019.pdf.

35. Interview, April 18, 2022.

36. Interview, April 28, 2022.

37. World Population Review, Bonner County, Idaho Population 2022, https: //worldpopulationreview.com/us-counties/id/bonner-county-population.

38. *Sandpoint Daily Bee*, September 28, 1977, 21.

39. Kevin Keating, "Town Draws Artists Sandpoint Area Home to an Astonishing Number of Major Artists," *Spokesman-Review*, November 6, 1995.

40. Interview, April 17, 2022.

41. Susan Drumheller, "Outside Agitators Turn Us Against Each Other," *Bonner Daily Bee*, October 25, 2020.

42. Betsey Russell, "Redoubt Movement Helps Push North Idaho Politics to Extreme Right," *Spokesman-Review*, May 15, 2016.

43. Flee the City, Strategic Relocation, https://fleethecity.com.

44. *Redoubt Report, Conservative News Aggregate*, https://redoubtnews.com.

45. Interview, April 17, 2022.

46. Kevin Taylor, 'Losing Coldwater Creek," *Sandpoint Magazine*, Summer 2014.

47. Encyclopedia.com, "Coldwater Creek, Inc., May 17, 2018," https://www .encyclopedia.com/social-sciences-and-law/economics-business-and-labor/bu sinesses-and-occupations/coldwater-creek-inc.

48. Interview, April 18, 2022.

49. *Proceedings and Debates of the Constitutional Convention*, held in the city of

Helena, Montana, July 4, 1889, August 17, 1889 (Helena, MT: State Publishing Company), 483.

50. Women in State Legislatures, "2023, National Conference of State Legislatures," https://www.ncsl.org/womens-legislative-network/women-in-state-legislatures-for-2023.

51. Interview, April 19, 2022.

52. Sandpoint Comprehensive Plan Update, June 12, 2020, 23, https://www.sandpointidaho.gov/home/showpublisheddocument/14271/637275821044570000.

53. R. J. Cohn, "None Better than Unicep," *Bonner County Daily Bee*, November 11, 2008.

54. Businesswire, "Silgan Acquires Unicep Packaging," September 30, 2021, https://www.businesswire.com/news/home/20210930005994/en/Silgan-Acquires-Unicep-Packaging.

55. "Daher's Kodiak Multi-Role Aircraft: 300 Deliveries and Going Strong!" December 1, 2021, https://kodiak.aero/news/2021/12/dahers-kodiak-multi-role-aircraft-300-deliveries-and-going-strong.

56. Anne Wallace Allen, "Supplement Maker to Leave Idaho for South Carolina," *Idaho Business Review*, November 11, 2016.

57. Bonner County Planning Department, *Bonner County Comprehensive Plan*, July 26, 2023, 4–34, https://www.bonnercountyid.gov/media/Planning/Comp%20Plan%20Update/Housing%20(v.9%20-%2007.26.23)%20-%20Adopted%20Update.pdf.

58. Mark Don McInnes, "Bonner County Market Report 2017," https://www.linkedin.com/pulse/bonner-county-market-report-2017-mark-don-mcinnes/?trk=articles_directory.

59. Bonner County Planning Department, *Bonner County Comprehensive Plan*, Chapter 12: Housing, 15, https://www.bonnercountyid.gov/media/Planning/Comp%20Plan%20Update/Housing%20-%20Suggested%20Update%20(07.06.2015).pdf.

60. Redfin, "Sandpoint Housing Market," September 2022, https://www.redfin.com/city/18403/ID/Sandpoint/housing-market.

61. Lyndsie Kiebert-Carey, "County Upholds 700-Acre Selle Valley Zone Change," *Sandpoint Reader*, May 22, 2022.

62. The Right Place, "The Right Place Assists Litehouse, Inc. with Area Expansion," November 8, 2017, https://www.rightplace.org/news/the-right-place-assists-litehouse-inc-with-area-expansion#:~:text=The%20Right%20Place%20assists%20Litehouse,with%20area%20expansion&text=Business%20

Development%20Projects-,Today%20The%20Right%20Place%2C%20Inc
.%2C%20in%20collaboration%20with%20the,jobs%20at%20its%20Lowell
%20facility.

63. Keith Nunes, "Litehouse Foods Investing $40 Million in Utah Plant," *Food Business News,* May 15, 2017.

64. "Lighthouse Creating 160 New Jobs at Virginia Production Facilities," *Businessfacilities.com*, May 2017.

65. Take Five Daily, "Thorne's Transition to South Carolina," May 24, 2018, https://ca.thorne.com/take-5-daily/article/thornes-transition-to-south-caro lina.

66. Interview, May 14, 2022.

67. Headwaters Economics, "Economy Surprisingly Dependent on Non-Labor Income," August 2017.

68. Dennis Colson, *Idaho's Constitution* (Moscow: University of Idaho Press, 1991), introduction.

69. Merle W. Wells, "David W. Ballard, Governor of Idaho, 1866–1870," *Oregon Historical Quarterly* 54, no. 1 (1953): 3, http://www.jstor.org/stable/20 612088.

70. *The Boise News*, December 26, 1863, 3.

71. "For the Legislature," *Idaho World*, July 8, 1865, 2.

72. Bonner General Health Press Release, "Discontinuation of Labor and De-livery Services at Bonner General Hospital," March 3, 2023, https://bonnergene ral.org/wp-content/uploads/2023/03/Bonner-General-Health-Press-Release -Closure-of-LD-3.17.2023.pdf.

CHAPTER 5. DISMANTLING THE CULT OF COMMODITY PROSPERITY

1. Oklahoma Chamber of Commerce, "Oklahoma's Largest Employers," https://www.okcommerce.gov/wp-content/uploads/2021-Oklahoma-Employ ers-1000-Employees.pdf.

2. Mark Haggerty, "Tension as Catalyst: Public Lands and the Rural West," March 2020, https://headwaterseconomics.org/economic-development/tension -as-catalyst-public-lands-and-the-rural-west.

3. As of 2019 (public sector): North Dakota: 79,300; South Dakota, 7,700; Montana: 89,000; Wyoming: 72,419; Idaho: 124,300.

4. Katherine Miller and Adrian J. Rivera, "These 13 Wyoming Voters Helped Decide Liz Cheney's Fate," *New York Times*, August 16, 2022.

5. Sam H. Schurr and Bruce C. Netschert, *Energy in the American Economy,*

1850–1975: An Economic Study of Its History and Prospects (Baltimore: Johns Hopkins Press, 1960), 41.

6. Jeffrey A. Lockwood, *The Infested Mind: Why Humans Fear, Loathe, and Love Insects* (Oxford, Oxford University Press, 2013): 19–20.

7. Leo Wolfsen, "Wyo Republican Convention: Resolutions Committee Wants End to EPA, BLM," *Cowboy State Daily*, May 7, 2022. See also Emily Holden, "Republicans' New Favorite Study Trashes Biden's Climate Plans—but Who's Behind It?" *Guardian*, March 9, 2021.

8. Walter J. Culver and Mingguo Hong, "Coal's Decline: Driven by Policy or Technology?" *The Electricity Journal* 29, no. 7 (2016).

9. Alaska Permanent Fund: History, https://apfc.org/history.

10. Sean Maguire, "Alaska House Budget Vote Stalls over $5,500 Cash Payments and Deficit Concerns," *Alaska's News Source*, May 12, 2022.

11. Alaska Marine Highway System, Fleet Status, https://dot.alaska.gov/amhs/fleet/fleet_status.shtml.

12. Wyoming Taxpayers Association, "Direct Tax Collections and Public Service Costs 2020," http://wyotax.org/wp-content/uploads/2021/11/Cost-of-Services-2020.pdf.

13. James Madison, letter to Thomas Jefferson, October 24, 1787. Philip Kurland and Ralph Lerner, *The Founders' Constitution, Volume 1* (Chicago: University of Chicago Press, 2000), Chapter 17, Document 22, http://press-pubs.uchicago.edu/founders/documents/v1ch17s22.html.

14. Mark Haggerty, "Getting Real About Rural Resilience," *Headwaters Economics*, April 16, 2019.

15. Jack Dura, "'This Dog Is Digging': Gov. Burgum Signs 'Operation Prairie Dog' Infrastructure Bill," *Bismarck Tribune*, March 20, 2019.

16. Wyoming Legislative Service Office, "Local Government Distributions," October 14, 2016.

17. Mark Haggerty, "Fiscal Policy is Failing Rural America," *Headwaters Economics*, October 2020.

18. Catherine McNicol Stock, *Main Street in Crisis: The Great Depression and the Old Middle Class on the Northern Great Plains* (Chapel Hill: University of North Carolina Press, 1992), 74.

19. Christine Whitt and Jessica Todd, "Women Identified as Operators on 51 Percent of U.S. Farms in 2019," June 7, 2021, https://www.ers.usda.gov/amber-waves/2021/june/women-identified-as-operators-on-51-percent-of-us-farms-in-2019.

20. Zippia, "Coal Miners Demographics and Statistics in the US," https://www.zippia.com/coal-miner-jobs/demographics.

21. Jessica Smith Rolston, *Mining Coal and Undermining Gender: Rhythms of Word and Family in the American West* (Brunswick: Rutgers University Press, 2014).

22. Interview, July 26, 2022.

23. Interview, August 31, 2022.

24. *Wallowa County: Economic Opportunity Analysis, 2021*, PARC Resources, 64644 Cook Avenue, Bend, OR. 97703.

25. *Wallowa County: Economic Opportunity Analysis, 2021*, 12.

26. *Wallowa County: Economic Opportunity Analysis, 2021*, 42.

27. Interviews, August 30–31, 2022.

28. Memorandum of Agreement Between the Wallowa Lake Irrigation District, Confederated Tribes of the Umatilla Indian Reservation, Nez Perce Tribe, and the Oregon Department of Fish and Wildlife, June 22, 2020, https://www .dfw.state.or.us/fish/local_fisheries/wallowa/docs/20200622%20Wallowa%20 Lake%20Dam%20MOA_signed_CTUIR.NezPerce.ODFW.WLID.pdf.

29. Presentation at Western Collaboration Conservation Network Conference, September 20, 2022.

30. Kathie Durban, "A Small Town in Oregon Gets Ugly," *High Country News*, November 14, 1994, https://www.hcn.org/issues/23/672.

31. Interview, February 10, 2023.

32. Interview, February 13, 2023.

33. Interview, September 6, 2022.

34. Final Environmental Impact Statement for the Malheur, Umatilla, and Wallowa-Whitman National Forests Land Management Plans, Volume 3: Chapter 4, Glossary, and References, 54, https://www.fs.usda.gov/Internet/FSE_DO CUMENTS/fseprd584615.pdf.

35. Interview, September 1, 2022.

Epilogue

1. Amy Bridges, "Managing the Periphery in the Gilded Age: Writing Constitutions for the Western States," *Studies in American Political Development* 22, no. 1 (2008): 32–58.

2. John Locke, *Two Treaties of Government*, ed., Peter Laslett (New York: Mentor Books, 1965).

3. Thomas Jefferson to William Smith, November 13, 1787, Library of Congress, https://www.loc.gov/exhibits/jefferson/105.html.

4. Interview, August 31, 2022.

5. https://www.greateridaho.org.

6. Oregonian Live, "Greater Idaho Movement Wins Wallowa County by 7 Votes, Avoids Recount," June 7, 2023, https://www.oregonlive.com/news/2023/06/greater-idaho-movement-wins-wallowa-county-by-7-votes-avoids-recount.html.

7. Cari Scribner, "10 Largest Landowners in the State of Montana," *Farmland Riches*, April 20, 2023.

8. Dan Bigelow, "Foreign Ownership of Montana's Agricultural Land Has Increased, but Remains Low," *AgEconMt*, October 2, 2020.

9. Bridges, "Managing the Periphery," 1.

INDEX

Page numbers in italics refer to figures. Those followed by n refer to notes, with note number.

www.ingramcontent.com/pod-product-compliance
Lightning Source LLC
Chambersburg PA
CBHW020334100426
42812CB00029B/3119/J

* 9 7 8 0 7 0 0 6 3 7 0 4 1 *